D0983557

THE BATTLE
FOR BUENOS AIRES

The Battle
For Buenos Aires

SAX BRADFORD

HARCOURT, BRACE AND COMPANY, NEW YORK

CONTENTS

PART ONE

UNDER THE SOUTHERN CROSS A LAND LIES RICH

PART TWO

INVASION

PART THREE

"HE THAT REGARDETH THE CLOUDS SHALL NOT REAP"

PART ONE

UNDER THE SOUTHERN CROSS A LAND LIES RICH

CHAPTER I

THE CITY BY THE RIVER PLATA

BY EIGHT O'CLOCK the Calle San Martín was a narrow carnival of carretas, hucksters, housewives, wagons, and trucks down the center of which moved a thin line of early morning traffic, now dammed by flanking pressure from the curb, now breaking loose again to move in a cacophony of streetcar bells, motor horns, and a vocal pandemonium that seemed to be Turkish, Basque, and Castilian.

A motion-picture photographer's swinging overhead seat might have moved down this fantastic groove of stone and wrought iron from the massively forbidding convent of the cloistered sisters of Santa Catalina to the sunlit Plaza Mayo. If it had swung just under the continuous ledge of balconies and just over the sea of stiff Spanish caps, straw hats, and felt hats, berets and shawls, and bare heads that were brunette, blond, and red, the cameraman might have taken a sweeping panoramic record of the concourse beginning in heavy shadow and ending as the sun crept down the walls and onto the right-hand side of the street to close the morning shopping hour and drive indoors hundreds of women in dressing gowns and slippers, their arms laden with leeks and carrots and cabbages and pears and what not in the greengrocery line.

This was the street down which I beat my way each week-day morning for more than a year.

I began among the fishmongers pawing through their baskets full of slack-jawed, pop-eyed *pejerrey;* partridge-peddlers buried in pathetic dead birds hanging from yokes;

3

milkmen holding the ends of their black sashes out of the stuff as they poured it gingerly from battered tin cans into cloudy bottles; chimney sweeps riding their bicycles in black stovepipe hats; aproned baker boys picking up the loaves and buns they had dropped from tricycle delivery carts; scissors-grinders blowing shrill Panpipes; broom-and-duster sales-men bearing through the crowds like plumed monsters from a Guatemalan nightmare. There were brisk businessmen, German, English, Dutch, French, Syrian, Jewish; brown-robed Franciscans with ropes and beads; Dominicans in bowler hats, white robes, and black capes; small children playing among the big wheels of the carts, their nether world steeped in the acrid odor of horse urine; rag-collectors scat-tering from their wagons like scout planes from an aircraft-carrier, scouring the street and watching the upper windows as they cried their nasal query.

Gray-uniformed *porteros*, tall, thin-faced, and betraying their Ukrainian or Polish blood, stood majestically at the doors of apartment and office buildings watching in impres-sive silence as peons of a lesser caste polished the brass knobs and name plates sunk into the stone. A line of bucket-carriers bore wet concrete into the construction works behind a row of burlap screens built to block the walkways. A furniture-moving crew raised chairs and beds and dressers by block and tackle up the face of a building; men were scattered like monkeys up the façade on platforms and window ledges. (Windows are bigger than doors in Buenos Aires.) Tandem-hitched draft horses hauling tremendous wagons painted in gay colors snorted in dismay and disgust at the unseemly pounding of great trucks laden with rolls of white newsprint paper bound for the open ramp of *La Nación's* pressroom. The Italians and Basques sitting in shirt sleeves and sash high on the wagons looked content and masters of the world; truck-drivers were nervous and pinched of face. It was impossible to find a full square's length of unobstructed side-walk, and the short step from the miniature tiles of the walk to the cobbled street was a desperate gamble with sudden death.

Somehow, in the tradition of the *bailerina* and the toreador, pedestrians have survived the traffic here. As the shopping hour came to a close the carts began to thin out, giving way to Fords and Morris-Oxfords and Fiats and Opels and Citroëns and the *colectivos*, those bright microbusses that speed through the streets like lacquered June bugs. The horses lunged and minced and trotted to the hoarse shouts of their drivers. Men clung to the wheels of their machines and leaned breathlessly as they hurtled through narrowing gaps by inches. Tall, clear-eyed policemen stood in the heart of the confusion directing with subtle gestures, as a French-man conducts an auction of antiques or as a Chinese stevedore captain maneuvers men and winches with the flutter of a fan.

As the sun rose there could be heard faintly above the din a belated madrigal from the chorus of canaries where they hung in cages from the balconies. The smell of soapsuds was sharp where men and women on hands and knees scrubbed the checkerboard walks and the tileway entrances.

Just at this hour, when the curbside markets melted away and the trill of the scissors-grinder was lost in the distance, people of affairs began getting briskly to offices and shops. Scores of pretty girls in short skirts and silk stockings picked their way daintily along the street. They ran the gauntlet of ogling men out early to see the parade. Now and again a dark man slightly overdressed, his carefully trimmed hair glossy with brilliantine and his hips hard and trim from hours of dancing, took up the pursuit of a girl, as a barnyard cock bears grimly down upon a hen.

He followed his quarry and studied her movements while he appraised the possibilities of success. He hurried forward to a break in the sidewalk or a bottleneck of pedestrian traffic where he might close in on her. If the accidents of the chase permitted, he patted her thigh or rubbed his shoulder against hers, leaning a little to murmur words of soft endearment like *"Preciosa"* or *"Mi amor"*; or if she seemed the direct type, he whispered a provocative challenge. All this time the girl walked straight ahead with downcast eyes; if she had been at the game a long time, she might send just one sidelong glance. Her pursuer pranced and pirouetted and gave off a scent of shaving soap and toilet water. His eyes flashed, and he lost track of the world about him. At the door of the office building the chase stopped abruptly. If he were just out for the lark, he would turn and follow another one. If encouraged by a look or suddenly infatuated, he might wait until the girl came out at the noon hour, to take up the chase again.

As the buildings filled with clerks and business people, there was a continuous, nervous movement along the narrow sidewalks past the shop windows, the arcade entrances, and the doors. There were messenger boys with telegrams, waiters bearing trays, chauffeurs stretching their legs, army officers, lottery-ticket salesmen, laundrywomen. There were also a few bookstore-browsers. Bookstores are like housewives; they are attractive in the early morning only to those who love them. There are usually three or four men shopping the bookstore windows, frowning in at the front display and trying to talk themselves out of going inside.

El Relicario was selling out several hundred cheap paper volumes; they were all dumped in the window, where Genevieve of Brabant stood in the mouth of her cavern to receive the homage of a faithful knight. Genevieve was clad in a broad smile and a short frock of rushes, whereas the cavalier was fresh from the wars and stiff in chain mail and oaths of allegiance. Tolstoy peered with bearded dignity from underneath a volume, *The Truth about North America,* which flaunted on its cover a coterie of women in 1930 bathing costumes playing miniature golf on a Chicago roof. Just beyond Tolstoy some neighborhood puppy had chewed the corner of Jules Verne's *Around the World in Eighty Days.*

Next to the bookstore a lot of little men in black scarfs and baggy cotton pants were filing into an open doorway bearing baskets of hard red quebracho wood, like ants getting winter supplies in ahead of the wet season. The aromatic wood perfumed the street, joining the smell of parching coffee, of wine and olive oil, of soap, of gasoline exhaust.

Until early afternoon the Calle San Martín was shrill with racing, pinched traffic. Then it became silent, unnatural, in the hour of siesta. In the oppressively hot afternoons of early March, when it seems the humidity is visible in the air, this is an unchristian hour to be about. Where the street gave onto the Plaza Mayo at the end of the deep canyon of foreign bank buildings, the trimmed sycamores filtered the light into jungle dimness. The ice-cream man in white uniform standing beside his white cart drawn up to the walk looked as unreal as some incredible white moth hovering over the steaming midday earth deep in the shadows of the Chaco. The sounds that reached this bower drifted in tired and reluctant, and the sight of distant movement in the park was the vision of a dream.

When the heat wore itself out, life revived in the lengthening hours. The street was noisy and vibrating with movement again, but this time at a more leisurely pace, like that of a middle-aged man feeling his years for the first time. Twilight was deep, and the neon signs, small and concise against the dark faces of the buildings, came out of daytime hiding. The same chic girls of the morning scattered out of the big buildings and minced homeward hotly pursued by the same sidewalk cavaliers. Gesticulating men filled the side-

walk tables and the dim interiors of the *boliches,* sitting unaware of the passing hours, drinking syrupy black coffee from
tiny cups, swinging, rattling, and banging the *bidú* dice in
heavy leather cylinders, glancing up to mark the faces of
passing women only when their legs were trim, talking about
money and politics, politics and money. Curb attendants in
long smocks and motorman's caps directed the parking and
unparking of cars and collected the tips for their day's vigil.

The dark deepened all along the street toward the bleak
walls of the convent. There were dim lights in the almacén
windows, where cobwebs gathered on Mendoza wines, Spanish olives, Polish hams, Italian *grappa,* English tinned preserves, Bols gin, Norwegian sardines, and that exotic novelty,
Quaker Oats from North America. There was light, too, in
the cigarette kiosks and the flower shops. But the darkness
was good to the women of the night hurrying to the cheap
dance halls in cheap pastel evening gowns. It was good to the
young lovers standing holding hands in the doorways, reluctant to say good-by. The dinner hour was nine. By that time
the cafés had begun to fill with businessmen and their friends.
Married women ate at home mostly. At ten there was a general movement toward the theater district, and at one people
came drifting back along the street, some fishing out keys for
their street doors, some entering the *boîtes* from whose cozy
recesses came the melancholy voices of the oiled and perfumed men who roll their eyes and sing the interminable
complaint of the tango.

After two the street grew quiet again; gusts of wind lifted
the dust and scraps of paper from square to square down the
cobblestones. There was only the whine of a motor now and
then, or evidence of the ethereal journey of the owl car to
break the silence, or a faint scream from a window to an
inner court.

What is a street? In Latin cities it is a corridor from plaza to open plaza, a slice of solid gray stone gracefully concealing the rich, massive squares of living architecture turned within themselves. (And if you discount the gutted skeleton that once was Paris, Buenos Aires was in the autumn of 1942 the largest Latin city in the world.) Opening onto the Calle San Martín there were doorways that might have been mistaken for the front of dwellings. If you had looked into them you would have seen only the dimness of long tiled passageways. There were street-floor windows that seemed at first to be the front windows of homes, but they were mostly barred and shuttered and useless, like the windows of stage scenery.

Only toward the center of the city where commerce and business expediency have dictated does the street entrance become the front entrance. This side of the banks and the shops, the street doors lead inside to the central courtyards. Facing these patios people live and work within their own world, where the voice of the city is a distant rumor. The street is a necessity, a transportation system. The street entrance is the domain of the *portero;* he has kept this gate, father and son, for many generations. He alone understands the street and the people of the street, as his profession has understood these things since the days when it was a soldier's profession and the gate was held against assault. The patio is the domain of the women, and has been since earliest Moorish times, when the profane glance of the cruising male was to be shunned as conscientiously as the direct rays of the sun.

There are hundreds of streets like San Martín. They cut through this maze of cubicles in depth like a picture in an old-fashioned stereoscope. They form rank after rank up from the La Plata estuary into the sunset where the pampa swallows all life.

But there are other kinds of streets.

Avenida de Mayo, an esplanade of Madrid where miles of sidewalk cafés under awnings and shade trees spill with mag-

nificent aloofness across the grunting traffic, where modest
doorways open into luxurious Spanish hotels with marble fit-
tings and a quiet air of courtly living, where 2 pesos will buy
you the best seat at the Teatro de Mayo to hear gypsy Juan
Padilla sing the long plaint that is the song of Andalusia,
the *canto hondo* that begins with an opening minor chord of
the guitar and ends in the breathless passion of the South.

Calle Florida, a Hollywood dream of a shopping street
where pedestrians fill the pavement from curb to curb and
motorcars must keep off until after midnight, where the combination of flirtation and window-shopping has become a fine
art that seems to require a preliminary Cologne-water bath,
where lone-wolf males and girls in couples can begin at the
five-and-dime district next the Banco de Boston and wind up
an hour later where the trimly exclusive Parisian corset shops
debouch onto the Plaza San Martín.

Avenida Alem, the water-front boulevard chiefly famous
for its Sawdust Trail down whose archways must pass every
sailor who hits the port, where Cielo de California, the Chaco
Dancing, the Liverpool Bar, and a score more of honky-tonks
are jammed all night with men listening to the aphrodisiac
music, watching phony gaucho entertainers, flirting with the
painted barmaids, dancing with the hostesses who double in
brass later as prostitutes, drinking watered vodka, illegal
Pernod, or blended Scotch whisky, alternately sitting mor-
bidly disconsolate and beating each other on the back, declar-
ing they are having a hell of a time.

Calle Veinte-cinco de Mayo, the back door to Avenida
Alem, its flyspecked windows nauseous with intimate photographs of Spanish, Turkish, German, and Ukrainian girls
who entertain within, its dark Hotel zur Post where pimply-
faced boys who make up the shock troops of the German
Gestapo in Argentina meet to get instructions for the next
job.

Calle Pedro Mendoza that skirts the mouth of the Riachuelo in the Boca district whose restaurants are famous for fried
fish, spaghetti, and red wine, where at the Pescadito you can
drink Lachryma Cristi and hear a soprano shrill out *"Torno
a Sorriento"* above the accordions, where you can stroll along
the mole that might have been in Naples or Marseille and
watch a devout padre in rubber boots swab the deck of the
church ship *Cristo Rey* with its stained-glass windows, its
steeple and bell, getting readied for Sunday's cruise up the
Paraná to bring religion to its water-locked parish.

Calle Córdoba of the irregular façades, some out in mid-
street, some far in the back, a street soft and inviting in the
velvet nights like a setting for *Romeo and Juliet* with only
the bright Southern Cross overhead to betray it, a street that
somehow suggests love and tragedy.

Avenida Alvear, swank with its miles of magnificent parks
and fountains, but pitiful in the futility of its memories of
glory, humming with high-speed limousines until the early
morning hours, then starkly overtaken by reality, the avenue
onto which modern apartment houses intrude with an apol-
ogy that gives all their new families a sense of inferiority.

There is a house I know on Avenida Alvear. It is aloof
in its aristocracy. One can't come upon it directly from the
street, but must approach it by degrees, first through the iron
gate, then down the walk between the palms, then to the
corner of the terrace wild with jasmine and Virginia creeper,
on into the tiled passageway and up a staircase that leads to
the front door, well toward the center of the house. Here at
the barrier of leaded glass the visitor is welcome, and he
steps within. The austere interior is like an attractive maiden
lady who grows old gracefully with a few close and impec-
cable friends; from the ivory walls to the mirrored depths of
hall and salon, to the intricately bordered ceilings, the place
looks comfortable but proper. Everywhere the chairs stand

like mutely patient guests—the delicate Louis XIV chairs in the music room, the great squat chintz-covered chairs in the central parlor, the gilt, solid-looking chairs of the dining hall.

There is an air of dry rot in the gold brocade curtains, the tremendous carved sideboard, the faded paintings in crusted old frames. The cabinets full of hundreds of wineglasses wink in pale, amused welcome from their stations along the wall. There is a certain pleasant confusion, as in an elegantly careless attic. A vase of mummified orchids heavy with the dust of years and eloquent of treasured sentiment peers listlessly from a glass whatnot that is otherwise jammed with miniatures in silver frames, Dresden figures, a clock clambered upon by white cupids, yellowed tintypes, and a score of lesser souvenirs of two generations of travelers and lovers.

From an inner hall a hanging staircase like a white, airy flight to heaven skims the well that rises through the central parlor to the skylight. At the second floor a mezzanine railing rings the well. It has been polished by the forearms and elbows of many girls leaning down through the years to contemplate the brilliant scenes below. This house that is so solid and angular with stone and casement, so massive when seen from the avenue in front, is fragile and quick within. It carries its weight of melancholy with graceful unconcern.

In the elegant antiquity of this house lies the whole story of the blossoming and the dying of the landed aristocracy of the pampa. It is a simple story, one that has been a favorite with variations in name, setting, and other minor details since Biblical times. First the hidalgos and their retainers lived on the lavish land in grant from the King of Spain or the Viceroy, or later from the Republic. Then British capital built a network of railroads so that the numberless wild and far-ranging cattle suddenly became choice beef at fancy prices in the markets of Europe. A demand for grain completed the miracle, and the sons of the hidalgos were rolling in gold.

Most of them built magnificent homes in Buenos Aires, then stampeded to Paris to forget an austere tradition that had brought them strongly through the centuries in soft times and hard. They left their land in charge of Basque or British overseers. The young men stayed in gay, enchanting Paris as long as health and indulgent parents would permit. They came home laden with bric-a-brac for their homes on the Avenida Alvear, sometimes with wives or mistresses. Here was irony: a race born to endure hunger and cold and the collision of battle dying in the softness of wealth. Here whole families lost the feel and the meaning of the soil, many of the older women turning more deeply religious by way of solace. Here the seed of the conquistadors flowered boule-vardiers and literati, professional Army officers and academicians.

Stand on the top of the tallest building in South America and look out over the muddy tide of the estuary some early romantic named the River of Silver. Look down the estuary toward the open sea and you see that the Calle San Martín is one of many clefts running parallel to the docks on the rising ground above the water. Beyond the Plaza Mayo with its pink stone presidential palace the canyons of stone blend into a serrated gray bulk that spews itself into the smoky distance and dies where the green-bordered water laps at the pampa. That is southeast. Out there in the haze are the meat-packing plants and the breweries, and the dark, huddled dwellings of the factory workers.

Turn your back on this, as most do who live in this swank skyscraper apartment building, and look up the avenue where it follows the curve of the estuary, look across the Plaza San Martín to the ultrafashionable Parisian shopping district of Santa Fé, to the luxurious homes of the "first families," out across the sculpture-studded Elysian boulevards, the parkways, the palaces of fine arts, the dueling grounds, the bridle paths, the exclusive clubs and the garden cafés, and beyond to the boating paradise that is the lush delta of the Uruguay and the Paraná, where upon the polished teakwood decks of white yachts the mistresses of generals and admirals and politicians toast their delicate rose-petal skin during the summer season.

All along the water front, from the brawling, two-fisted Boca in the southeast to the effete suburbs of the northwest, the dockside of the city slowed to a halt during 1942, a pitiful scattering of deep-sea ships almost lost in the bewildering forest of cranes and winches and sheds built in the days of roaring prosperity when through this great world port poured the beef, the grain, and the wool that sustained in the manner of Croesus the families of the Avenue Alvear, and filled the bullion vaults of the Banco de la Nación to overflowing.

Between the exotic fringes of Buenos Aires, the meat and kernel of the city lying square and featureless back from the water front and the parks, was still a world essentially Spanish in its language, its way of living, and its appearance. Its Spanish blood had been thinned by Italian and German immigration, by Ukrainian, Yugoslav, Turkish, Hungarian, Syrian, Portuguese, Irish, Polish, Russian, and English immigration. But each of these alien races—if we except the German and the English—had after the first defiant generation bowed to the tremendous weight of Spain. The Negro blood that at one time in the colonial city's history was half of its blood had been absorbed long since, as the Spanish race itself absorbed its Negroid Berbers in the course of the centuries.

So the patios of Buenos Aires were Andalusian patios, and the tiles were Talavera tiles and the language of the narrow streets was Spanish with the influence of Italian and Quichúa Indian dialects. The *boliches* were the coffeeshops of Galicia transplanted. The almacéns were the provisions stores of

Toledo and Málaga. The early morning marketing, the toil
of the day, the siesta, the long hours of the evening over the
coffee cups, the Sunday stroll along the neighborhood alame-
das, the pooling of the family cash to buy the lottery ticket,
the absorption in newspapers and reviews, the reverence for
letters, music, artistry, title, and pomp—these things that are
the gristle of Buenos Aires were Spanish. What was not
Spanish was Italian, and as there seems little to choose between Catalonia and Liguria, so to the eye of the Northerner
it was hard to detect the fine line of demarcation between
Spain and Italy in the life of Buenos Aires. It might almost
have been said that there were several kinds of Spaniards in
Buenos Aires, the Gallego, the Basque, and the Italian—the
first contributing color and tradition, the second enterprise,
and the third solidity.

Of the world's great cities of character, this has been one
of the most disappointing to the snorting, guide-book tourist,
one of the most satisfying to the interested student. Its magnificent homes are closed to foreigners without social standing
—real social standing. Its roistering taverns occupy but a thin
flank of the water front, and their atmosphere is almost melancholy. The flatness of the land makes vistas like those of
Rio de Janeiro, Naples, and Hong Kong impossible. Its
trucks and automobiles give its business district an air of the
commonplace. Its tendency to cling to gray building stone
and low construction rob it of the eye-filling glamour of the
skyscraper cities.

In many respects Buenos Aires is more beautiful than
Madrid, but it lacks the homogeneity of Madrid. In many
respects its avenues and parkways are more lavish than Paris,
but they lack the living piquancy of Paris. Its Italian population is greater than that of any Italian city, but it has lost
the color of the homeland. Behind the forbidding walls, the

noncommittal street fronts, there are a people and a culture richly flavored, a way of life seasoned by the centuries. As each square block of dwelling places presents a solid wall to the outside world while guarding in its bosom the color and fragrance of its courtyard deep within, so the life of the city, in sharp contrast to the life as we know it in the flamboyant North, maintains an outer dignity that amounts to deception.

The first sight of the pampa is a shock; there is no stone or tree or hillock as far as the eye can make out across a land almost without horizon. The first sight of a Castilian hill town gives the traveler a sense of hardness, like the hard rock of which it has become a part. But in the course of years the senses sharpen on the pampa, and there comes a time when subtle changes in the direction of ripple on the grass, moods and tones of the sky and the earth, seasonal and impromptu scents in the air, roar in and out of the mind's perception centers like the crash of storm. And in the course of years the harsh Castilian town softens into the treasure house of tradition and manners that it is. Buenos Aires in 1942 was of Spain and the pampa, with reserve and dignity holding to itself languages, music, color, architecture, political passion, religion, poetry, and social grace.

There is a current of profound and unshakable sadness that shapes the life of the *porteño*—the dweller in the port, the man of Buenos Aires. His eyes are big as if with suffering; his clothes are elegantly somber; the music he loves is the tragic song of unrequited love; his horizon when he finds it beyond the screen of the city is the limitless sea and the limitless plain; his literature is the literature of nostalgia or despair; his outlook is fatalistic, and his religion is the solemn mass. In death as in life, he rides to his resting-place in a black funeral carriage behind matched black horses.

It is just here that the hand of Spain seems heaviest, the austere mother country finding itself renewed in the hearts of millions of its children halfway across the world. It is not by chance that the greatest Argentine novel, *La Gloria de Don Ramiro*, pictures with faithful understanding sympathy the religious severity of Avila, the sainted Gothic city. That this tradition should have survived the racial and cultural mixtures of the New World, the changing fortunes of commerce and politics, the dizzy expansion of population and wealth of this magic metropolis, speaks eloquently for the virility of Spain. Even now this tradition fights inch by inch and step by step motion pictures, birth control, political liberalism, Protestantism, women's "rights," and all kindred demoralizing influences, including Esperanto and Communism. If Don Quixote lives, he is here beating back the tide of modernism as valiantly as he attacked the windmills, and as proudly oblivious to the ultimate outcome.

It is still a matter of personal degradation for a girl to learn stenography and work in the offices of Buenos Aires, and some forced by family circumstances to augment the family income thus will never admit the shame except to intimate friends. It is still forbidden for a decent woman to go out on the streets alone in the evening, even to the movies. It is a loss of caste for a girl to appear hatless in a tearoom, to go to a dance unchaperoned, to stroll with her boy friend without little brother or sister along, to invite a young man to her home before Papa has appraised his family and perhaps his family's bank account.

The step onto the street seems to be a fatal move. A barrier is broken. Once a girl has stepped deliberately out of her own home, she begins to look at men as frankly as they look at her. Because Buenos Aires working girls are paid little, because they learn by going to the movies and reading magazine advertisements to want prettier clothes than they can afford, and because they feel they are already cheapened by the necessity of making a living, the prettiest of them are likely to fall early prey to the "madames" constantly on the lookout for new faces and figures. One Buenos Aires madame offers to let her wealthy male clients pick any girl out of any department store, promising to have her available in a few weeks. There is excitement, extra money (she is lucky if she makes the equivalent of $25 a month in the store), and the possibility of becoming a mistress. At the worst, the chances of happy marriage are no more remote than the first day she walked down the street unchaperoned. It is significant that the righteous use the same word to describe a loose woman and a revolutionary political thinker—"liberal."

This is the city in which children relieve themselves in plain sight on the sidewalk and families who haven't quite the money they pretend to have rent a vault overnight in the swank cemetery, the Recoleta, then in the early, deserted dawn cart the remains of Uncle Máximo away to a cheaper final resting-place.

This is the city where the name of the lady of the house is María Luisa Rosario Mercedes Eugenia Carrera Saavedra de Amaya and the last chambermaid's name is Ana Suárez, and the whole world lies between. It is the city that defies a continent and drives on the left. It is the city that holds carnival and strings up a loud-speaker system over which the morose populace is begged to be merry; that tips the ushers before it sits down to enjoy a movie; that burns corn on the cob in its furnaces when coal is scarce; that reads seventy-two daily newspapers and then stands in front of the bulletin boards to get the latest dope; that pours out to horse races and football games every Sunday, supports the biggest athletic clubs in the world, and is a stranger to sportsmanship in the Anglo-Saxon sense; that is the world's greatest exporter of fancy beef and hangs its own meat out in open-air markets where the flies swarm. It is the city where some of the world's most astute money operators manipulate the market in pengos, zlotys, reichsmarks, dollars, pounds, escudos, bolivianos, reis, and pesos fuertes, then go out and buy *The Old Monk of Mendoza's Guide to Numerals* before choosing a lottery ticket.

It is a city that requires the teaching of French in secondary schools; plays Viennese waltzes; uses English words exclusively (dancing, smoking, living, recital, week end, club, cocktails, hall, flirt, speaker, leader, standard, for instance) in speaking of those activities it has borrowed from English life; eats mostly Italian food; considers Hollywood movies immoral but patronizes them almost to the exclusion of all others; looks down on Brazilians and other Latin Americans as uncouth.

Buenos Aires is one of the most self-conscious cities in the world. It closed down its public brothels a decade ago because books were written about them by foreigners. It cringes whenever raucous North American journals, idly casting about for "local color," criticize the nude statues in its parks; when foreign pundits discuss its politics; when stupid journalists on hurry-up assignments confuse its suave, perfumed citizenry with the gauchos. It rioted and tomatoed the screen when a motion-picture theater made the mistake of showing *Argentine Nights,* with its technical errors about Buenos Aires life. From the exquisite, cathedral-quiet interior of its Alvear Palace Hotel to the stinking, noisy alleyways among the breweries and the slaughterhouses, Buenos Aires is proud, fanatically patriotic, and ready to resent aspersions.

Like the untraveled of every city and countryside, the *porteño* lacks a sense of proportion and the gift of objective thinking when he hears himself discussed. It is this characteristic above all others that must be kept in mind in any attempt to understand why Buenos Aires is a soft touch for traveling salesmen with waxed mustaches and words of flattery. He longs to believe that his *porteño* speech is pure Castilian;

that the tango, bastard of the slums of Buenos Aires and the cheap bistros of world-weary Paris, is a genuine musical expression of noble sentiments; that his culture is known and respected the world over.

When in 1570 a hard-bitten detachment of Paraguayan subjects of Carlos V, Upholder of the Faith, succeeded in landing on the shores of the La Plata estuary, throwing together a dozen mud huts and holding off the Indians, they may have had a vision. They may have seen ships and roads converging here at warehouses and docks. If they didn't, they had no sense of the correlation between geography and trade.

What they could not have seen was that this pitiful huddle of flea-infested cubicles would grow the hard Latin way for three hundred years, surviving as the race somehow survives through massacre and hunger and epidemic, then shoot like a frightened weed from a town of 40,000 to a world-influencing city of 3,000,000 in the one lifetime span between 1870 and 1942. It wasn't likely they could have seen the Spanish trader, the escaped Negro slave, and the captive Indian wear out the centuries ahead to be swamped at last by millions of laborers stampeding to the Promised Land from hungry Europe, thousands of technicians hustling from modest jobs in far-off cities to the fat bonuses of construction work in a new empire, hundreds of families of aristocrats from inland estancias crowding into the neo-French mansions suitable to landed gentry who have struck it rich. Nor could the first handful have foreseen the corollary of this dizzy expansion: the rise of an industrial civilization.

The funny thing about people who get rich accidentally, like the Argentine estancieros who happened to own the land when the land became wealth (as has happened in so many lands and in so many times), is that they don't realize that they got rich accidentally. They think they got rich (coy thought) through some individual virtue, through shrewd manipulation, or because they were just born to be rich. Only a few of the most profound of the accidental Argentine millionaires realize that the acquisition of too much wealth too fast was a shock which threw the hardy, dour race of hidalgos completely out of joint, and debauched it into largely giving up those racial virtues nurtured through generations of family life in tough Spain and colonial America. A select few realize now that the new wealth will be in industry and commercial management, and that of the happy, mistress-keeping, Paris-loving children of the hidalgos only those will survive who keep rigid pace in thought and action with world events. It is this unwillingness to face the fact of a world in change—and thus an Argentina in change—that must be kept in mind in any attempt to understand how the people who fear the growing political power of industrialists and labor have turned in desperation to the caudillo—the leader—idea, as in Spain.

The fact is that sometime during the last three decades the foundations were laid for a middle class in Buenos Aires. A middle class is something with which the Spanish colonial mind can't cope. Somehow the situation got out of hand, and the Basque, Italian, and German laborers began to accumulate enough money to go into small businesses, to send their children to school, and to wear store suits. The investment of foreign capital in factories for the manufacture of razor blades, textiles, soap, candy, furniture, shoes, and what not was a shrewd investment, and it has brought big returns. The estanciero-millionaire would have none of it. He believed the wealth was in the land—his land. Now the growth of industry has upset that happy arrangement by which the estanciero sold beef to England and bought English manufactured products. Not only that, but the simultaneous rise of a middle class and the organization of industrial labor have put a new face on things. Every important visiting journalist is entertained at the exclusive Jockey Club, taken out to the country for a beef barbecue, and told rapidly and with many gestures that Argentina is a land of rich cattlemen, that it cannot ever become anything else. Farther south, in Patagonia, they catch easily a certain large bird because it puts its head in the sand so as to blot out the pattern of coming events.

Even as the social leaders of Buenos Aires the landowners are beginning to lose ground, while the startling people who own the factories and finance the developments and don't care a hang for cloisonné and majolica have pushed in. The manners of Madrid and Paris are still to be seen in the ornate old Café España, where the practiced nostril can pick up the scent of Pamplona sausages, *paella Valenciana,* and *panqueque de manzana,* and a dowager duchess still gets a deep bow from the head waiter. But mostly the old aristocracy dines at home now, and the newer hotels are lush with the parties of Vienna, Berlin, London, and New York financiers who have an eye to business, sordid or not.

It is the middle class that is Buenos Aires. It is true that it has not yet made itself effectively heard in politics. It doesn't know its own strength nor its own destiny. It is true that the dazzle of the last soirees on the Avenida Alvear lingers in the eyes of observers. It is true that the "quaint" districts of the city where the protean struggle is endless among the dwellings of the poor give the impression that medievalism has only spread its squalor to conform with the flatness of the land. But in the decay of the rich and the emancipation of the destitute, a long and complex process, there is emerging a people. It is a middle-class people, like the people of the United States. It will produce scientists, poets, musicians, managers, technicians, and perhaps adequate political leadership. Its small, unit-type houses are beginning to change the face of Buenos Aires, eating into the private parks and the

miles of dark, narrow, dirty stone barracks that have de-
pressed the peoples of the Mediterranean for countless generations, throwing out suburbs along the river and back onto
the pampa almost to the basilica of the Virgin of Luján, out
there where an oxcart bearing an image got stuck in the mud
and the faithful did the handsome thing by building a magnificent church on the spot.

Great new apartment houses are going up like sleek white
monuments, stabbing into the skies, overlooking the tree-
packed plazas and the wilderness of flat rooftops. These are
the homes of the upper middle class; the native businessmen,
the imported factory managers, the General Motors and
Firestone Tire and General Electric district supervisors, the
Life photographer, the traveling man for the German dye
works, the chief accountant at the Italo-Argentine power
company, the university professor, the dentist, the correspondent for the United Press.

Lots of these are foreigners. But foreigners stay as a rule.
Homesick and irritable the first year, usually neglecting to
learn good Spanish because they are "going home next summer," most of them nevertheless pour themselves into this
tremendous mold, resigning themselves at last to the city.
Always the newest families take apartments in the newest
buildings, so that the transition back into the great stone
heart of the Latin city is gradual, as is the adoption of Spanish habits of life. Successive waves of apartment-house construction have given distinctive architectural characteristics to
the north or "fashionable" side, where the typical Spanish
structure hardly holds its own. But Spain triumphs again in
the heavy doors, the tiled walls and floors, the high ceilings,
the shuttered windows, the knobs and plates, the wrought
iron and the balconies.

It is hard to escape the conviction that what is of the past
belonged to Europe, despite the intense local patriotism of

the Criollo,[1] and the parallel conviction that what is of the future belongs to America. The colonial social system which maintained the "first families" forever in ownership of the land and of the bodies and souls of the peon workmen dominated this land by sword and by the Cross—so that not even a powerful and independent city growing up at its margin could escape it completely. And if the city was at the margin of the land, it was also at the margin of Europe itself by the sea routes that drew the mother continent closer than the trackless interior. It isn't strange that the old ways have endured here long past their allotted time—so that the breakup of the two traditional classes of society, the aristocrats and the serfs, into the new middle people who will swallow all that went before has brought trouble, anachronistic trouble with a comedy relief.

On Sunday morning I sat on the blue-tiled curb of a long dry and forgotten fountain in the heart of a deserted patio within sound of the awakening city. Pale autumn sunlight filtered through the young, chilled trees in hesitant transparent shafts filled with cobwebs and silver motes, with the broken husks of seeds, with stale breath and fugitive wisps of smoke like a current of discontent flowing forever upward toward infinity. A profound and unshakable sadness followed me out through the grillwork gate and onto the street. A broken ostrich plume, souvenir of last night's revelry, lay like an abandoned promise on the irregular squares of the walk. I boarded the electric at the great domed barn that is the Retiro station, clicking and rattling out into the suburbs north along the estuary. At the Belgrano station the sun was

---

[1] "Criollo" is not the same as "Creole" as we use it. A person born of parents who came from any European country is called a Criollo or Criolla. In Argentina the word is used chiefly to denote Spanish origin.

still low in the northeast, feeling its way into the square
green park beside the tracks.

There was a man standing on a portable pulpit just where
the gravel paths joined, reading from a Bible. The language
was Spanish, but he looked foreign. He was large and blond,
and his suit fitted him only in the shoulders; elsewhere it
was too tight. He kept reading in an aggressive voice. On
near-by benches a nursemaid with a child, two girls in their
teens, an old man with a tweed suit listened. There were two
or three men standing in front of the little raised pulpit.
When the blond stopped reading, they began to sing. The
child cried softly, and the maid jiggled her up and down on
her knees in time with the hymn. After the song, the blond
stepped down from the pulpit and a younger man stepped
up to take his place. The young man was dark, with a small,
soft mustache. He read in a little voice that hardly carried
to the nearest bench. His eyes were large and liquid. His
hands as they turned the page were small, with slender fingers. The older of the two girls sitting together began to pay
attention to the man's voice and to watch his face as he read.
The other turned to watch some boys on bicycles in the street.

The peanut-vender was very fat. He put down his sheet-
tin stove with a grunt, easing the strap from his great shoulder until the smoking thing rested on the gravel. There was
a black streak of smoke up his back from the tin chimney.
The smell of charcoal and roasted peanuts spread toward the
blond man who had released his pulpit, but he held his eyes
steadfastly on the reader. The peanut-vender looked slowly
at each face, then stooped to pick up his stove. As he turned,
he lifted the small brass horn from its sling across his chest,
blowing a melancholy blast, long, then short. Up the street
past the door of the restaurant Zum Goldenen Hirsch, a
boy came to the gate and looked with anticipation toward
the peanut-vender, now lumbering along the narrow walk.

A coachman stepped down from his cab, the second in the black line beside the station gate. His clothes were pinned, not buttoned. He stood beside his seedy-looking horse and began to whistle softly a Criollo tune. The other cabbies were asleep, their faces deep in their overcoats. The horn of the peanut-vender, one long and one short blast, came faint and melancholy from far down the street. . . .

The placid waters and the green banks of the delta moved closer to the tracks, the train came to a halt, and I climbed into a small boat, paddling about until the regatta started. Oarsmen from the rowing clubs were competing in the final races of the season. Moving up close to the line marking the course, I was soon hemmed in by more spectator craft. The banks and the water were jammed under brilliant pennants whipping against the sky. Eight youngsters in a rowboat next to mine were playing a portable phonograph, trying to repeat some of the English words of the songs. They were playing "I Wanta Make Whoopee." To the vast delight of the boy who manipulated the machine, the record caught at the word "whoopee," repeating "whoopee, whoopee, whoopee" until the spring ran down.

When the ice-cream boat came past, one of the boys called out in English, "Hey, you! Commere!" The harbor police launch moved in close and the same boy yipped, "Cheez, de copes!" All the boys laughed and looked at me self-consciously. On the other side of my boat an Italian family was fishing, looking up occasionally in mild surprise when a close race brought a wave of cheering down the bank. They had a fish on the line when the eight-oared crews finished and so missed the best of it. Promptly at four o'clock the owner of the launch to which we were all tied came out on deck and brewed himself a gourdful of yerba maté, which he sucked

through a silver bombilla, thoughtfully watching the race
course as he drank. . . .

It was damp dusk going home. Among the willows the
red, yellow, and green beams of the *recreos* flaunted faded
bits of end-of-season bunting. Toward the city the dying
light fell softly on suburban houses calcimined apricot and
pink, all blending into the color of stone in the twilight as
the train flew toward Retiro.

Who can say how much of the old life was bad and how
much was good? Who can say whether this energetic city
has gained or lost because the world is getting to be a jitter-
bug world, because youngsters are picking up English from
the gangster films, because modern newspapers and automobiles and radios are opening horizons that have nothing to
do with religion, race, or tradition? Who can say that the
gradual emergence of women from the gloom of Moorish
harems, to the semilight of Spanish salons, to the bright day
of Yankee "freedom" is a good thing or a bad thing? Who
can say that the inevitable breakup of the large, wealthy
Criollo families and their disappearance in the inevitable
advance of industrialization is a thing for lamentation or
rejoicing? Are we to be happy or disconsolate because the
immigrant has come out of her shawl or his boots, losing the
piety, the discipline, and the solidity of peasant life and finding independence and aspirin and automobiles?

These narrow, darkly cobbled streets, green tunnels in the
summer under the overhanging locusts, sycamores, and aca-
cias, these streets lined with the continuous stone façades
broken by shutters and iron grillwork and massive doors,
these streets that look by day like water-color paintings and
by night like stage scenery—they are still Latin streets, but
fewer families sit outside along their walks of a Sunday
afternoon talking interminably; fewer lovers stand all night

together in the doorways; fewer children make their circles chanting *"Lo estás, lo estás?"* In their places are the new *porteños* preparing to drive into the country for an "English Saturday," the fashionable new week-end picnic; or listening to North American swing on their radios; or dressing for an excursion down to the Bijou Theater to see James Cagney and Bette Davis in *The Bride Came C.O.D.*

All this worries the old conservatives. They see their wonderfully gracious but wonderfully selfish and secluded civilization breaking up and tumbling about their ears; they watch it with the same unregenerate hatred that embittered the lives of the old Southern families of the United States who gave ground to mills and factories, losing year by year and acre by acre the land and the life they loved.

They see the children of serving women and *porteros* dressing in cheap but stylish English suits and California frocks swaggering along the walks whistling tunes from the new Yankee shows—along the same walks whereon their parents had stood in humility a generation ago, opening the black and brass doors of carriages to the quality folks. They see diamonds flashing on unkempt fingers where the men of affairs watch the fluctuating commodity and currency prices on the bolsa. They see the lovely daughters of fine families kept as mistresses by the shoddy new industrial capitalists. This does not sit well.

In their tremendous confusion of mind they identify all that is disturbing and new and cheap with the coming of the motion pictures, with liberal politics, with the factories and the merchant class, with foreign capital and foreign ideas. To them, Europe is not foreign; it is the homeland. North America is foreign. North America is responsible. The life and the tradition they love must be preserved at all costs. "Too bad no strong champion has appeared to rally what is left of the best people and the best way of life. Too bad there is no Cid Campeador whose bugle echoing through the streets of Buenos Aires as once through the Valencian hills might call the true men to the colors." And so on and so on.

While all this is running through the minds of the disinherited, the new middle class briskly, grimly tends to business and watches its slowly growing bank balance. It is noisy, active, self-assured, quick to take advantage, absorbed in making money and winning social position, not too careful about ethics and civic honesty, materialistic, impatient.

In the late autumn of 1942, the city of Buenos Aires lay voluptuous and undefended across verdant margins of the salty brown estuary—without apparent will or purpose. It was confused by the essential conflict of tradition and reality and by an economic and social evolution too big to stop, too complex to understand. It was without real leadership at the moment of crisis. Its most aggressive sons were busy making money so fast that they had no time for reflection, for evaluation. Its decadent families were shut up in their French boudoirs and drawing rooms as rose petals from a lovers' tryst are pressed in a favorite book of poems. Its intellectuals were paralyzed by the rapidity of world events about it, its soldiers were seduced by meaningless slogans fed them by foreign propagandists. Its springs of thought and action were deliberately paralyzed from without and within, so that it lay like some civic Lucrece waiting in vague, unconscious disarray for the footsteps of Tarquin.

The history of a woman is the history of her race, her family, and her trained habit of thought and action confronting the accidents of life. It is the same with a city. Given the facts of its Iberian heritage, its recent racial mixtures, and the characteristics of its growth at the crossing of the sea lanes from cultured, tired Europe and the river lanes into the humid jungle and the trackless pampa, given the inexorable movement of the war rocking the continents about it and always closer to its very water and soil, the story of Buenos Aires is now ready to unfold. The dramatic clash of men and materials propelled by ideas, the conflict in which its existence was unwillingly at stake, seemed distant and almost casual to its people—as a beautiful queen might lie with half-closed eyelids hardly aware of the approach of the barbaric ravisher.

CHAPTER II

THE PONCHO AND THE FRAC

ARGENTINA was settled by conquistadors who dribbled through the Andean passes southeasterly from Peru. Stung by the mountain winds, brain-weary from the search for golden cities and the slaughter of Indians, they came at last out into the lush valleys of Jujuy and Catamarca and Tucumán, where the very air sang with a promise of eternal spring. They built homes and presidios and churches, venturing year by year down the great river courses into the jungles of the Chaco, setting up new towns where the waterways met. In the first century after the Incas were destroyed, Spanish captains and viceroys were disputing among themselves possession of an inland empire reaching from the fabulous silver mines of cloud-cradled La Paz down to the mouth of all the sluggish rivers draining southeasterly through the heart of the continent, an empire bigger and richer than Spain itself.

In the inevitable push eastward from the Peruvian and Chilean highlands to the sea, the twice-essayed founding of the village of Good Airs—Santa María de los Buenos Aires— down where the brown water merged with the salt was hardly a matter of notice or concern. Reports of the richness of the pasture down on the flats drifted in time back to the already flourishing and conservative upland towns. Then as now, nearly four hundred years later, rumors of the wild, free life of the port were a disturbing element in the orderly progress of culture and industry among the Andean hidalgos and their

31

retainers. Then as now the upland people handed down from mother to son the troubadour songs of Roland and Oliver, of Charlemagne, of Aucassin and Nicolette, of Richard of Normandy. In this tradition-steeped pastoral paradise the llama and the alpaca were tamed, corn was cultivated and milled, orchards were planted, textiles woven. The language and the faith spread across the face of the new land, moving always eastward and southward, to be halted at the edge of the great pampa. Religion and government, commerce and transportation, tradition and the arts—all the treasures of Spanish colonial culture flourished solidly, as the oak flourishes in firm soil.

The pampa is an immense plain almost without feature or variation, sweeping the west bank of the La Plata estuary, skirting the cold Atlantic to the south, and lapping against the Andean foothills to the west. It is divided now into two Argentine provinces, Buenos Aires and La Pampa, but it steals the corners off three or four others. Across the estuary is the sister territory once called the East Bank on the Spanish maps, now by a series of political happenstances the Eastern Republic of Uruguay, playing the role of buffer state between ambitious modern Brazil and ambitious modern Argentina. The pampa is of startling richness, its alluvial clay soil more than two hundred feet in depth for hundreds of miles. It is an almost inexhaustible agricultural treasure, one that some day may influence the history of the world.

For two centuries after the founding of Buenos Aires the pampa belonged to bands of savages. The white man held only a ridiculously thin strip of land close to the sea and the river, where he pastured his cattle at great peril. The savages were mountain Indians attracted down onto the ocean of grass because of the cattle that strayed into it from the other side. The smell of free beef and the prospect of abducting an occasional white woman were irresistible. The lure of plunder ended in their extermination, but only after long and relentless campaigns that steeled both races through attack and endurance and attack. Here there was no quarter asked and none given.

Type creates type, and the beast of prey is in turn preyed upon. The gaucho became the scourge of the pampa. In its mysterious fumbling for a traditional hero to personify all that is romantic south of the border, North America has pounced upon the remnants of the gaucho and hugged him like a rag doll to its collective bosom. In the North American mind the gaucho still lives. He is, in fact, a sort of Cossack with a black mustache, certain Robin Hood tendencies, and a taste for garlic and red wine. The greatest fear of the Argentine citizen who comes in contact with the United States is that he will be mistaken for a gaucho, as many Americans in London and Paris have been asked to bring their cowboy clothes and show off their yodeling and rope tricks.

The gaucho flourished in the nineteenth century; a few preceded and a few survived that compass of time. He was the product of a very narrow strip of prairie land that might be considered the suburbs of Buenos Aires. As often as he was Spanish he was British, French, Negro, or Basque. He had nothing to do with interior Argentina, and everything he represented was alien to the austere Andean towns. He never left the pampa except as he was impressed into armies by contending leaders in the civil wars and precipitated in martial fury onto his neighbors. His place was in the deep solitude of the measureless earth. He began life because cattle must have men to tend them. The wars disillusioned him and taught him to shun all society. He was forced farther and farther out of the fringes of civilization. Fighting Indians and eluding conscription made him tough, as if a life in the saddle weren't tough enough.

If he ever saw a house it was only a smoke-filled mud-

walled room. His chair was a bleached ox skull. He hardly
knew the word "woman." Most of those who tried to bring
wives into the pampa lived to see greater tragedy than their
brothers. He seldom tasted vegetable or fruit, but cut his
roasted meat steaming from the hide as he ate, washing it
down with bitter-brewed yerba maté. On the rare occasions when he could find a drink it was *caña*, white distilled
cane juice. The pampa, so broad and still and deep that he
had to dismount and put his head to the ground at night to
make out the horizon, put the iron of tranquillity into his
quick temperament. Once in a while when he drank too much
caña he used his knife on his fellow man, but as a rule the
gaucho was easy-going. Like most countrymen, he was a
sucker for a slick-talking businessman or politician.

In a savage land he represented civilization. He won inland against all odds mile by mile, until it was safe to run
cattle where sudden death once lurked. Sometimes he went
wild and joined the Indians. When this happened he became
the most cunning and implacable of foes. When he had killed
in anger or cupidity he was branded a *gaucho matrero*, and
his name became the terror of the comarca. But he was more
often a musician than an outlaw, wandering from estancia
to estancia with his guitar slung by a cord over his shoulder.
He wore a blanket he called a poncho, baggy trousers he
called *bombachas*, slippers he called alpargatas, usually a
wide belt or sash and a long butcher knife. He carried the
usual accouterments of a horseman, and his hat tended to
turn up at the front brim.

Some gauchos marked by destiny, or perhaps just more
alert and aggressive than their fellows, became local Daniel
Boones, leaving behind them a wealth of legend that in the
course of the years has been richly exploited. Santos Vega
and Martín Fierro are tradition in the pampa. The paper-
bound history of Martín Fierro is so popular that country

merchants stock it along with salt, flour, and sugar. The
gaucho lives again in the Wild West motion pictures, in the
dime novels, and on candy wrappers. Elsewhere he is ex-
tinct. It is true that some young blades still dress the part,
as the dude-ranch cowboys in Wyoming still feel it their
duty to wear hair pants and tote six guns for the benefit of
the summer visitors from the East.

As the city grew out across the flats and the Andean cities
became centers of archaic and self-sufficient provinces, there
was a no man's land of impenetrable wilderness between the
one and the other. They never fused and they never influenced each other in a cultural sense. The pampa has always
been the outer fringe of Buenos Aires; the gaucho belonged
to Buenos Aires as the goatherd belonged to Athens. Agriculture and husbandry as they were carefully developed in
the provincial towns were unknown to Buenos Aires. In the
last half of the eighteenth century there were only fifty
farmers out of 12,000 inhabitants—and that was two hundred years after the city was founded. In all the tremendous
expanse of pampa there were only thirty-eight estancias.

These were all metropolitans who began to spread slowly
and stubbornly up and down the shore and out onto the flats.
The men who moved onto the soil were not country people,
they were *porteños* who scattered outposts across the limitless
horizons. Thus fanwise from Buenos Aires across the land
that was like a world-filling mirror after the rains and like
a carpet in the spring the gaucho moved out and multiplied
until the city was presented with its own back country and
its own peculiar peasantry. While in Tucumán and Salta and
Córdoba the Spaniard and his vassal Indian danced the classic dances and said the classic verses and brought down generation after generation the wonderful mixture of arrogance
and humility that is the gift of Iberia, the port and the

pampa grew wild with racial mixtures and loud with new languages and new songs.

In the disasters and recoveries and changes of fortune and direction of its early life, Buenos Aires has been in turn almost entirely Criollo, almost entirely Portuguese, then Criollo and Negro, and so on until in 1830 it numbered 60,000 native-born, 8,000 English, 6,000 Italians, 5,000 French, 4,000 Spanish and Portuguese, 3,000 Germans. This was the restless mélange that gave the city and the pampa their cosmopolitan character in definite and final form, separating them once and forever from traditional Argentina sleeping against the hills.

This was the beginning of the political and economic schizophrenia that in 1942 still held a nation in its grip, making public life a struggle for survival rather than a co-operative effort toward a common goal.

This was the uncompromising split between the imaginative, volatile, rich lowland—with its unbelievable contrasts of poverty and luxury, of barbarity and sophistication, of tin-pan-alley tango and imported grand opera—and the hard, enduring, changeless Andean provinces. This city and its fantastic flat arc of land steeped in the cheap literary lore of Martín Fierro, yeasty with the theory of Karl Marx, suave and elegant beyond the perfumed dreams of Madame Pompadour, fierce with hunger for liberty, equality, and fraternity yet despising simplicity and inner rectitude, worshiping money and success as they have never been worshiped before —this baffling, confused city has been and is putty in the hands of the men who know how to handle it. And as often as not the men who have worked it and shaped it to their will have been the shrewd, patient men of the hills, certain of themselves and of destiny but alien to all the impulses and the prodigious, unformed ideals of the city. Thus a country of great resources and great promise has been drugged and atrophied against the normal progress of its time and its place—as in so many epochs so many new nations have been held and hindered from destiny.

The character of the inevitable internal struggle for Argentina shaped itself during the first three decades of the nineteenth century when Buenos Aires fought for and won its independence from Spain while the provinces, in complete chaos, bred war lords and armies of freebooters. The very pampa of the city in this hour of agony fell into the hands of local political bandits, who gradually assumed the character of personal leadership that has always seduced the Spaniard. During the confusion most of the cattle had been slaughtered for their hides, driven off by bands of Indians, or commandeered for the wars, leaving the gaucho naked on the pampa, a great hunger gnawing at his intestines and a rising hatred of mankind darkening his soul. He formed mounted companies the better to pillage his neighbor's pasture and keep himself alive. These companies fell naturally into the hands of those leaders who seemed most desperate and likely to afford action, into the hands of the caudillos who promised regular meals and a sense of common security.

Buenos Aires was an island in a sea of violence, eventually falling prey to a young, arrogant dictator, Dr. Marcelo T. de Alvear. Then as now the easiest way out seemed the easiest. The town council (the electorate of Buenos Aires was as impractically idealistic, as politically inept, then as it is now) invited the East Bank gaucho chief, José G. Artigas, to come and take the city and rid it of Alvear. It was inviting in the same breath a century and a quarter of disaster. The cupidity and the blood lust of the caudillos have never been sated after that first glimpse into the helpless, glittering metropolis. Artigas organized that magnificent fraud called Federalism, a continuous conspiracy to keep the people of Argentina from having anything to say about how their country should be run, a political sleight-of-hand trick by which somehow the handful of "best families" has managed to hold feudal sway over increasing millions. In the six years between the revolt of the vice-regency of La Plata and the fact of an independent Argentine nation were sown the seeds of the perennial conflict that has been simplified into the classic phrase "the poncho versus the *frac.*"

In 1820 a wealthy, aristocratic young estanciero who in another time and place might have ridden out of Avila to meet the Moorish knights, provided 25,000 cattle with which Buenos Aires bribed off another brace of attacking caudillos. Don Juan Manuel Rosas, handsome, daring legendary horseman, friend of Indian chiefs and supreme gaucho among the gauchos, became Argentina's greatest Criollo figure—and later its bloodiest tyrant. He led his own scarlet-clad Rosista cavalry in the civil wars. He bided his time. While his countrymen were engaged in a life-and-death struggle with Brazil to the north he waited on the southern pampa, recruiting and drilling until his private army grew big and tough.

Buenos Aires, exhausted by its own patriotism and unable to deal deftly with force, finally called on Rosas to govern the city and the province. A strong man with his own troops ended in a few hours twenty years of anarchy and military chaos. *Porteños* went to bed that night to sleep peacefully, their responsibilities—and their liberties—securely in the hands of the popular hero of the moment. Rosas knew exactly what he wanted. He held a plebiscite and had his powers as supreme dictator confirmed. The city at last came to pay the full price for its license, its indecision, and its internal confusion. Rosas immediately ordered into existence an Argentine Confederation. He treated with the Andean provinces, promised them there would be no Argentine Republic. In return they recognized his right to rule the city and the pampa, making him at the same time by joint consent national Executive and Conductor of Foreign Affairs.

There was no internal Argentine government, only a common policy toward the outside world. This was exactly what the caudillos wanted: the chance to rule and exploit without both the interference of outside Powers and the danger of political challenge from within. Those who came to realize that somehow the people had been cheated were shot or driven into exile. Rosas filled the jails and the morgues within his jurisdiction. Those who could escape evacuated to Montevideo across the estuary. Those who could not were forced to wear scarlet shirts, dresses, sashes, at the whim of a dictator now drunk with power. Portraits of Rosas were painted on everything from handkerchiefs to church altars, and nobody dared crack a smile. Rosas and his caudillo confederates encouraged their own gaucho horsemen to slaughter and rape. They made Quantrell's boys look like a squad of Western Union messengers delivering birthday greetings.

There was born the Sociedad Popular Restauradora, an inspiration to violence for the next hundred years. This society of sinister importance was commonly called La Mazorca, after the head of maize that was Rosas's most popular cryptic symbol. This lighthearted club was bent on assassination. It put spies in every home, inspiring children to report their own parents. It was an official Maffia, wiping out without fear of legal process all the citizens it could find who dared question the Leader or grumble about conditions. So many wanted to flee that emigration was officially forbidden. Many who tried to escape were found with their throats cut. Those who even intimated they would like to escape were slapped into the Santos Lugares concentration camp, where political prisoners were often stretched and staked face-up for hours in the blazing sun before they were mutilated and shot. Rosas eventually got sick of it himself, and he thought

of retiring in 1849. Some English *porteños* who had found
business good "now that law and order had been restored"
signed a petition asking him to stay.

This nightmare, but certainly not its consequences, ended
with the defeat of Rosas by a rival cutthroat, General Justo
José de Urquiza, on the battlefield of Monte Casero. Rosas
was spirited away to England, where he farmed and medi-
tated for twenty-five years near Southampton.

Adversity breeds character and strength. Buenos Aires survived as a community in exile in Montevideo, and in doing
so developed its most powerful intellectual, political, and
literary figures. Among them was Domingo Faustino Sarmiento. To him modern Argentina owes its constitution and
its yet unfulfilled democratic ideals. He became the first
strong spokesman for the city's deep liberal aspirations. With
one great book, *Facundo,* he dissected Rosas's most blood-
thirsty lieutenant and dispelled with the cold light of reason
the romantic haze that clung about the head of the tyrant
himself. Since *Facundo,* Rosas has been despised.

The provinces took fright when Buenos Aires recovered
some semblance of self-mastery. They threw a gaucho army
at the city in 1852, besieging it with savage cruelty. When
ten years later the inherent strength of the city had at last
triumphed over all aggression, the provincials came quickly
in to dicker and to compromise. The Argentine Republic was
born, with Sarmiento as its President. By the terms of the
compromise the federal Government was established as a
guest within the city, so that the governments of Argentina
and Buenos Aires grew up as unhappy twins in the same
cradle. They were often at war with each other. In 1880
there were 3,000 casualties in a battle in the suburb of Belgrano. Eventually the provincial government of Buenos Aires
was moved away to the town of La Plata, so that now the
manipulators of Argentine "politics" find it easy to remain

in control, away from the suspicious surveillance of the liberal electorate of the port.

Out of the growing pains and the skirmishes attendant on the consolidation of national power in the hands of the "first families" there rose another popular leader, tall, melancholy, prophetic Leandro Alem, the Abe Lincoln of Argentina. Alem's father was a Rosista. Father and son represented the yearning for expression inherent in the landless masses—betrayed, rising in hope, and betrayed again, following first the call of violence and then the call of radical politics.

Rosas deceived the people who trusted him. He inspired reaction as a strong dose of poison acts as its own emetic. The reaction to Rosas became civic consciousness. Out of civic awakening grew the Socialist and Radical parties that were still sweeping the Buenos Aires elections in 1942, still fighting to put into the hands of the electorate the power to master its own destiny. Sarmiento called it the war of the poncho versus the *frac* because he visualized the struggle as of frock-coated intellectuals of the city girding themselves to fight off the poncho-clad hordes of the caudillos.

It is ironic that the gauchos, scattered far and wide by interminable district wars, became at last incorporated in the armies that attacked the city of their origin—and so came to personify tyranny backed by armed might. It is tragic that the history of this land tends by oversimplification to identify the gaucho with the war lords of the interior who used them —as Adolf Hitler later learned to use the desperate and the destitute by dressing them in Storm Troop uniforms and turning them loose against the liberal resistance of their middle-class neighbors in Germany. Actually the armies of the city and the armies of the provinces were both made up of gaucho cavalry; for the one they fought because of an instinctive desire for freedom, and for the others they fought as mercenaries or as retainers following in blind loyalty their hereditary chieftain.

As soon as the city found leadership and loosened at least the military grip of its oppressors, the modern Argentine Republic began to grow inland from the busy port. British capital was called in to build a network of railroads that cut across the fabulously rich flatlands, pouring a golden stream of beef and wheat through Buenos Aires. The gaucho, already scattered and changed in character, disappeared completely. His place on the pampa was gradually usurped by the industrious Italian and the Basque. The solitary horseman gave way to the men of seasonal wages, small businesses, and big families.

It is here that the history of Argentina changes from the pastoral to the preindustrial. The pampa becomes the center of wealth and Buenos Aires becomes its market place and vault. Criollo wealth is in land and cash. The Spanish colonial mind does not grasp the complexities of industrial economics. The hill provinces, still the repository of tradition, still the cradle of political mastery, fade into insignificance as the pampa expands. Modern Argentina is the product of British and to a lesser extent of Continental capital. Railroad lines brought beef and wheat to the port; refrigerator and grain ships carried them to ready markets across the Atlantic. By 1890 London banks controlled Argentina so extensively that the failure of one of them, Baring's, plunged the country into a ten-year depression.

We shall see later how the Axis-manipulated nationalist propaganda screamed into the befuddled ears of millions the story that the nation was being strangled by British economic imperialism—blandly ignoring the decades in which Argentina begged for working capital on which to grow. We shall see how millions dispossessed by the political machinations of the traditional ruling families were taught by newspaper, magazine, and radio, even from the pulpit, that not their own people but the Anglo-Saxon bankers had condemned them to misery.

Argentina in the late nineteenth century, armed with a liberal constitution, its bloody internal conflicts stifled, its virgin prairie opened by railroad, its promise for the future as rosy as the hopes of the New World, drew immigrants from southern Europe in a mad stampede. The first were the Italians, who came to hire out as harvest hands, returning home at the end of the season to spend the money. They were called *golondrinas*, for like the swallows of that other Spanish colony, Capistrano, they arrived and departed with the almanac. As things got worse at home more Italians stayed this side of the Atlantic. They were joined by the Welsh, who settled central Patagonia, by the Germans, who poured into the subtropical jungles of the northern waterways, by the Basques and the Galicians, by Poles, Turks, Ukrainians, Irish, French, Dalmatians, Greeks, Syrians, Hebrews, Scandinavians, the men of the Danube, the Dneiper, and the Don.

They swelled the port and burst across the new land. Their comic-strip travesty of the language of Castile has become the standard of the lowlands. Their accordions chased the violins and guitars into the hills forever. They brought with them a superficial, first-generation love of the homeland and an expansive love of freedom and independent expression. They brought with them all the political ideas festering in Europe; the very suggestion of some of them frightens on still nights not only the feudal conservative families of the back country but the Socialists of Buenos Aires as well. They brought the germs of Bolshevism, Menshevism, Nazism, Falangism, and Fascism, as any migration of millions of normal, healthy human beings must carry with it the unsuspected latent toxin of future epidemics.

The mere fact of 13,000,000 energetic, pioneering individuals swarming across this quiet, unhurried pastoral community demanding razor blades, motion pictures, automobiles, radios, airplane service, advertising, and women's clubs just scares the pants off the older folks. A generation behind North America, Argentina is hell-bent on the same road to industrialization. The consequences are bound to be cataclysmic. By meeting enthusiasm and idealism with craft and election fraud, the smart political manipulators have been able so far to nullify the tremendous majority against them. They have managed to keep a hand-picked conservative federal Government within the very gates of overwhelmingly liberal Buenos Aires. They have wooed the city and threatened it, bribed it and robbed it. They are realists, and they know that if Argentina preserves any democratic processes at all they will be swamped soon by the rise of industrialism and its corollary middle class.

But conservative politics is a long way from beaten. The ruling families are capable and well informed. Like people of means and restless energy the world over, they travel, study, and mix. The provincial families run the city themselves, as the Scotch are supposed to run London. They are represented in the intellectual and art circles of the capital, in the Army and the Navy, in big business and big pleasure. Their names monopolize the society pages of the newspapers, the picture sections of the smart reviews. Some of them moved bag and baggage to the city during the great cattle boom, burning themselves out in Paris and among the stone mansions of the Avenida Alvear. Some of them have formed alliances with the industrial millionaires, with the utilities magnates, smugglers, tradesmen, and financiers who keep on top by their wits and their imaginations. They are determined that if they have to share the wealth of Argentina they will share it with the few, not with the many. They

have made up their minds that power, like tradition, must
be the responsibility of a class—else it will be squandered
away in spineless acceptance of the plausible but dangerous
theory that men were created to be free and equal.

Buenos Aires has not in recent years produced liberal leadership capable of meeting the conservatives on their own
ground; the strategy of the liberals has been the strategy of
retreat. As Buenos Aires was besieged by force of arms ninety
years ago, it is besieged now by political wiliness. Liberal
leaders of the great capital have succumbed with discourag-
ing regularity to government contracts, appointments, conces-
sions, preferments, and all those pretties designed to distract
the attention of dangerous liberals from their fell purpose.
Many of them have their mistresses, just like the quality
folks. Some of them are getting so rich they can now afford
to quit posing as liberals and join the aristocrats in seeing
that strong government stays in the hands of the strong. Or
if the aristocrats let the reins slip into the hands of the industrialists, these trusted leaders of the people are prepared to
rationalize themselves into believing that political power is
best lodged in the hands of capable business managers—as
we used to think fondly before we got Coolidge and Hoover.
This is the old tragedy of ineptness and betrayal. Like most
tragedies, it must run its course once the protagonists have
put it in motion.

At the La Plata racetrack they dope the horses to make
them run faster. The dope is made in the municipal hospital
of Avellaneda, a suburb between Buenos Aires and La Plata
with something of the reputation of Cicero, Illinois, in the
days of Capone prosperity. At a recent banquet at the La
Plata Jockey Club the speaker praised the impartiality of the
track, so different, he said, from the swank Buenos Aires
tracks of Palermo and San Isidro. The speaker, who was

president of the club, pointed out that all entries at his track are doped without prejudice or favor, whereas at the other tracks an occasional clandestine doping of horses tends to give an advantage to the unethical. Avellaneda is the center of the numbers racket, called *quiniela* for short.

The *quiniela* bosses make millions of pesos a year, all illegally, of course. They own the town, and most of the province about. I know a municipal employee in Avellaneda who makes 800 pesos a month. He does not really do the work; he farms it out to a second man to whom he gives 600 a month. His clear profit for not working is 200 pesos a month. The second man does not work either. He farms the job to a third man, to whom he gives 400 pesos a month. A fourth man does the work. He gets 200 pesos. The first man has several municipal and provincial jobs. There is a young clerk in Avellaneda who earns 150 pesos a month. He never collects his salary, but raffles the pay check at 1.50 a ticket to the 300 employees of his department. He makes 450 pesos a month this way.

The police of Buenos Aires and surrounding municipalities were chosen for many years by the conservative party in power from Andean communities where the great stature and fearlessness of the Indians is proverbial. The city coppers break up popular demonstrations with a will. After all, *their* families are far away in the mountains; there is no danger of clubbing an uncle or a sister. A recent radical political rally at Avellaneda reached the stage of heated denunciation of the grafters. The local boss had the big Indians called out, then took up a station in an archway across the street from the plaza to see the fun. At an unexpected moment the battle surged in his direction and he got a terrific beating at the hands of his own cops, who took him, in their stolid fashion, for one of the enemy. Decorum prevents a faintly suppressed cheer at this point.

The elections of Buenos Aires Province are fixed, as are most elections except within the city itself. The conservative Government has restored open voting, so there is none of this secret monkey-business at the polls. It takes a lot of nerve to vote openly against the Government in Argentina. Some ballots are printed and marked beforehand, so that when the voter reaches the polls he finds he has already voted. If he is smart, he turns quietly away and goes home. Just before the elections of March, 1942, when the acting President was trying very hard to get a congressional majority to back his isolationist policy, thousands of these phony ballots were found in the process of being printed. The print shop was an appendage of one of the two English-language newspapers of Buenos Aires.

All these things make for a certain amount of civic discouragement in and around Buenos Aires.

Argentina, with its hot head in the Chaco jungle, its feet white in the eternal snows of Patagonia, its right side the towering Andes and its left the shores of the south Atlantic, is in area one of the great nations of the world. Its treasures have hardly been tapped. Nearly half the population lives in Buenos Aires and suburban communities. Nearly a fourth of the population is foreign-born. Like North America, Argentina is hardly acquainted with itself yet. While its university presidents, its religious hierarchy, its landowners, and its hereditary official families babble about preserving the Hispanic tradition, the country is boiling toward a destiny linked willy-nilly to the New World. Its granaries and pastures could feed all of Europe. Its upland slopes are purple with vineyards, and the quality of its wine is growing with each harvest festival. Only Australia competes with its wool shipments. Its northern forests are rich in hardwoods, and some day its low black delta country will be a perpetual vegetable

garden. Its cotton fields are becoming important. Argentina
raises good tobacco, linseed, table fruits. It is an important
source of tannic acid and dressed hides. In the south, men on
horseback still chase a lamb or a calf with lasso or *boleadores*,
dismount and cut its throat, disembowel it, throw it across
the saddle, and gallop to the ranch, where it is spitted still
hot and in its hide, roasted, and eaten in great reeking
chunks.

In the north, Indians still wander into town and work six
or seven months in slaughterhouses or lumber mills, collect
their wages, buy themselves a pair of pants and a jacket, a
dress for the woman, a sack of flour, and some tobacco, and
head back into the jungle as broke as when they came. In
the slums of the city, men in pyjamas still labor from dawn
to dark carrying stones on their backs or mortar in buckets
for the equivalent of 30 cents a day; their wives take in
washing and their daughters turn to prostitution. There are
rich territories beyond the railroad lines, unprospected ore
fields and oil deposits, wilderness valleys that some day will
be pregnant with crops. Argentina is in length the distance
from the Caribbean to Hudson Bay. It has provinces with
the climate of California; the biggest American city south of
Chicago; the highest mountains in the hemisphere; and
rivers next in size to the Amazon and the Mississippi.

This is a tremendous land almost untouched. It is filling
with people of vision and backbone who will some day make
it great—if it is not sold out from under them before they
get the feel of it.

In the heart of the pampa not far from Nueve de Julio
is a *boliche* standing four-square to the world where a dark
clump of ombú trees offers surcease from the glare of the
sun. Cart tracks mark the sod in all directions, losing themselves in the limitless distance. Over the yawning doorway a

neatly painted, faded sign reads "La Guernika," a sentiment that stirs nostalgia and fierce pride in the heart of every Basque who remembers the sacred city. Inside, the gloom is cut by white labels of bottles back of the bar that occupies the depths of the room. Stacks of heavy country clothes, balls of twine, saddle blankets, boxes of hardware, and sacks of flour stand on the floor behind a heavy wire screen. Near the small barred window there are four or five heavy tables, half a dozen crude straight chairs, and some long benches.

Joaquín Apestegui leaned against the recently calcimined mud wall and thrust his hands into the front of his black sash. He looked out across the featureless earth and squinted to measure the distance between the sun and the horizon. He turned and listened to the click of the *bochas* from the alley on the other side of the *boliche*. He listened to the cries of the players as they tossed the wooden spheres.

"They are all Basque, but they are talking Castilian," he said. "Some of them came over with me; the younger ones were born here. The young men started speaking Castilian, and now we are forgetting Euzkadi. Imagine the sons of Vasconia speaking to each other in the tongue of Castile. We are from Guipúzcoa and Pirineo and Vizcaya where the roof of one house touches the doorstep of the next above and where the wind in the pines high on the mountain is the same wind that chases sparkling light across the sea below. Now there is only the flat earth like a dinner plate, solitude by day and eternity at night. Only the stars and the earth.

"The children won't dance the aurescu and the jota. They dance the tango. They won't play the *txistu* and the *tamboril*. They play the accordion. Without the shrill of the *txistu*—ah, how it carried from glen and crag and across the orchards and the fields!—we are no longer Basques. For a longer time than any written history will tell you we have danced the *ariñ-ariñ* and the aurescu across the courtyards and the ancient stony meadows of our homeland. I have been back twenty-six times—nearly every year until Franco. I have never come up the river to Bilbao without tears starting from my eyes. I can stand here now and call: 'Urrizaba, Larralde, Arestegui, Lezarra!' and they will come from the *cancha de bochas*. They were the names of my neighbors when I was a little boy. Like me, they knew every path through the mountains. They knew how to jump the *kale-jira* and to send their voices across the valleys like the sound of trumpets. And now their boys are wearing hats instead of boinas, and dancing the tango to the accordion."

Joaquín Apestegui spread his hands palms down in a gesture of weariness and regret. In his face was the look of a mountain man who seems to see just beyond. His wrists and his neck were like the branches of the oaks above San Sebastian. He stood with the ease of a man who has conquered. He and his people have made this land, and his regret was a passing sentiment for his homeland without peer.

It was a Basque who founded Buenos Aires. Basques have been Presidents of Argentina. Many have become millionaires. Basques own the sheep business, with some competition from the English and the Scotch. Three little provinces of the Pyrenees have peopled and influenced Argentina—as they have Chile—out of all proportion to their importance on the Continent. Among the conquistadors were great Basque captains, as at sea in the golden days of the Spanish Empire they were Spain's greatest navigators. These are of colonial Argentina, and the families like that of Anchorena are numbered in the estancia aristocracy. But the Basque flood that followed the railroads inland provided the modern pampa with its most aggressive and stable population. In the long course of the years, where essential honesty, industry, and enterprise come into their own, the Basque is supreme. Like his partner in peopling the wilderness, the

North Italian, he forgoes the brilliance of the Spaniard in favor of his own tradition of steadiness and responsibility.

I walked through the Plaza Santa Rosa and down one of the town's shaded side streets between the low flat-roofed houses that have not changed their appearance nor their appointments since colonial days. The Casals family was sitting in a group on the sidewalk, watching other townsfolk out for the Sunday afternoon promenade. Across the street was another family, father, mother, and assorted sons and daughters of all sizes, out getting the shade and the air.

As I came up the walk, Old Man Casals sang out politely: "Ring the bell and ask the maid for a chair."

I rang, and when Rosa came out with a chair I took my place with them. We exchanged pleasantries with the family across the street, and spoke from time to time to friends as they strolled past.

Casals was a Catalonian. He was telling about how his father used to sit with his *sac de gemecs*, the Catalonian bagpipes, playing in a rustic orchestra of three or four pieces. Usually they picked a shade tree by the dusty wayside where the country people came down into Barcelona. Sometimes they sat on a bench near the entrance to the church and played. Usually the other pieces were the *flabiol* and the *gralla*, enough wood winds to make the countryside ring. But Casals was no musician; he was a businessman and a good one. Here he sold farming machinery, and such were his powers of persuasion that he had some of the hardest-headed old-timers using gasoline contraptions.

Casals was laughing with his wife about the time last winter when the priest called and they had to keep him talking at the door until the maid could get the covers off the furniture. In the wintertime everybody lives in the kitchen in this country. Family life spreads out around the kitchen stove as it has done in Spain for these many centuries. When the young man comes to court the eldest Casals daughter, she brings a little charcoal stove to the cold entrance, where custom demands they must both stand. In the summertime, there is the open air, the patio, the tiled walk on the street. Casals was glad he came away from Barcelona in his youth. He was not sorry he knew nothing about the scale of notes of the *caramillo* nor much about the classic written Catalan of the troubadours. Nor was he sorry the other youngsters called his girl Isabella instead of Isabel.

"These days there is not much room for sentiment," Casals said.

Down the river Paraná and into the jungle-bordered bayous of the delta float green islands from Mato Grosso and the Gran Chaco in the heart of the continent. Some of these islands are no bigger than a dime, microcosms trailing their delicate threadlike roots into the life-giving brown stream like the tresses of the Lorelei. They are glossy emerald-green above, so that from a few inches in the air where hover the hummingbirds and the bumblebees they seem to be drifting patches of moss; from below they are a deep red against the opaque light of the stream's surface. Some islands are hundreds of yards across, literally acres of cane and bulbous roots and jungle grass bearing swiftly and silently down the lower reaches of the river, carrying the nests and dead bodies of ducks and otters and other waterside creatures drowned in the storm that broke this land loose from its moorings far in the northwestern wilderness. After the cataclysm in the interior the river is laden with these islands and with cows and horses and the trunks of trees and sometimes the bodies of Indians. In the Paraguayan war a band of López' soldiers drifted down the river among this debris, capturing a part of the Brazilian Navy anchored in the stream. That was farther up, where they talk in whispers about Jane of Noontime (Juana de Mediodía).

In the Chaco they frighten children into taking their mid-day siestas with the story of Jane of Noontime. She flies just over the treetops, silent, sinister. Nobody can hear her as she passes in that panting, luminous heat. Swift as the wind she crosses mountains, rivers, and forests. She changes into a dragon, a horse, a tree, a great clutching hand, or a tiger as rapidly as she wishes. Sometimes she stops, becomes a fantastic bird, and disappears over the roof of the hut in an instant. She is terrible and silent. Only a few have ever seen her, surely none who lived. No one has heard her voice.

Jane of Noontime is more swift than Pombero, king of the night and friend of the bats and the fireflies. She is much more swift, because Pombero is nearer the ground, where he must move among the plants that hug the earth. Pombero is heavy and sluggish, crawling sometimes between the walls and the thatched roof. But Jane of Noontime is swift. She is more terrible than Yasi-Yatere, who slips out of the sky at the siesta hour, as she does, in search of little children who do not go to sleep. Sometimes they quarrel over the children they find. Yasi-Yatere is a friend of the birds, the butterflies, and the streams that run under the trees. He knows their voices and can imitate them. Sometimes he sounds just like the running of a brook in the distance. He is an enchanting blond boy, handsome and happy. He has large clear eyes, long curls, and cheeks like the lapacho flower. He carries a light golden wand and with this often makes himself invisible. It is said that if this wand is ever stolen from him he will lose all his powers. He will immediately become a poor child in rags.

At the siesta hour Yasi-Yatere hides close to the huts, spying about and calling with a sweet voice to children who are not yet asleep. He knows many pleasant games; he calls children out to run with him and bathe in the streams and pick the flowers and chase the small birds and sample the sweetest fruits. But when night comes he disappears, leaving his victim lost and alone in the jungle.

Jane of Noontime does not laugh and play with children. She never leaves them alone at night. She whisks them away, and they are never seen again. Nobody knows whence she comes nor whither she goes. The wind brings her and carries her away. She is the shadow of fleeing clouds. And when it is time for her to speed across the land, little children run into their huts and go to sleep while her form darkens the panting midday, darkens the fields, the waters, and the forests.

Hour after hour into the night I stood in the corner of the principal sound-stage of the film studio San Miguel, an hour's ride from town. The director, a solemn counterpart of the genus *Hollywoodiensis*, was yelping: "*Luz, acción, cámara . . . corte!*" It was a church scene. The dainty little heroine was taking the vows because her lover had left her for a foreign hussy. As she knelt at the bright altar the bishop cut off her dark tresses and blessed her for life in the nunnery. Miguel Machinandiarena, producer, roamed through the sets with the quick steps of a panther. He was a short, volatile Basque with the face of an ascetic who had just finished an unaccustomed bottle of wine. This motion-picture lot—complete with trimmings—was his own, his very own. He owned the casino at Argentina's Atlantic City—Mar del Plata. After taxes, bribes, and incidental expenses were deducted he had cleaned up $1,000,000 during the summer season just closed. He might lose only half that operating the studio this year.

His bright eyes were on the altar where Señora Machinandiarena, a legitimate Italian countess gaudy with diamonds,

fussed over the heroine's costume. The Señora is wardrobe
chief of the studio, and good at it. There was an argument
about demure Santa Teresita in her little shrine at the back
of the church. It seems that the picture represented Buenos
Aires in 1870, long before Santa Teresita was born. The
Señora stopped the show, and with a yard of tulle, a pair of
shears, and some pins she transformed Santa Teresita into
Santa Rosa de Lima. The pews were filled with extra girls
patiently sitting in modest dresses and the fantastic headgear
of the Sisters of Mercy.

I talked with large, pleasant, smooth-faced Señor Obli-
gado, coauthor, about the music for the picture, and was surprised to learn it would be the work of Manuel de Falla,
great Spanish composer now an exile in the Córdoba hills.
To make conversation I remarked that the name of my com-
panion was that of Argentina's foremost poet, Rafael Obli-
gado. He bowed. "My uncle," he said. Then we found ourselves a quiet corner off the baptistry, where we were deep
in argument over Gustavo Adolfo Bécquer and Rubén Darío
and Calderón de la Barca and others who have made the
language of Castile the language of lyric expression—when
they closed up the studio and hustled us out into the cool air
of early morning.

CHAPTER III

NARROW IS THE SEA

ARGENTINA is the living bridge that brings Southern Europe into America. The city and the pampa are Mediterranean in race, culture, language, spirit, and sentiment, because for nearly four hundred years the sea routes in and out of Argentina have been the routes to Mediterranean ports. That of Argentina which is British has been made British—against the grain—by the enterprise of English men and ships. That of Argentina which is German—and is still alien—has been forced in by solid, homogeneous immigration. Argentina has absorbed a great deal of the British and the German already, as North America makes baseball players out of the Di Maggios. Among the most militantly nationalistic of all Argentine families are the Rawsons and the Von der Beckes.

The strong warp and woof of Argentine life was grown and carded and spun on the shores of Mare Nostrum. Even that part of Argentina which is Parisian is of the Latin side of the Seine—the side of Renoir and Zola, and Laval. The very names on the shop fronts of Buenos Aires read like a register of commercial life from the Levant, from Anatolia, from Thrace and the Aegean Islands, from Dalmatia, Sicily, Liguria, the Camargue, around the peninsula to Biscay. These are all peoples of careful bargaining and direct thought. Despite the romantic implications of the tango and the rich animal passions of the gaucho, despite the aura of musty sentiment hovering over the leather-bound copies of

Villon and Baudelaire in the decaying drawing rooms of the
Avenida Alvear, the common thought of Argentina is practical thought. Just as there was never a more practical business proposition than Fisherman's Wharf, San Francisco,
with its studied background of concertina music—or Los Angeles' Olvera Street, where quaint Mexican shops are laid
out by blueprint. This statement is no shock to an American
traveler in Italy who has stopped to contemplate the departed glory of Pompeii and had to ward off half a dozen
salesmen of obscene postcards.

Liberal politics in Argentina has had to fight not only the
great strength of the conservative tradition among the literate population, but also the strongest surviving relic of
Mediterranean political thought: personalism. That which
has been inherent in Latin politics from Belisarius to Franco,
the yearning of men for a strong leader who combines in his
personality the virtues and vices of the race, has found repeated explosive expression in the rake-hell days of independent Argentina. In the bewildering procession of militant
Argentine chiefs of state the occasional political philosopher
like Sarmiento or Alem stands out in startling contrast.

Argentina is unique among Spanish American countries in
its continuous intercourse with the mother soil across the sea.
Whereas Peru and Colombia, for instance, have solidified in
the seventeenth-century Spanish tradition, forging and weld-
ing a nation out of the steel of Gothic Spain and the softer
Indian alloys, Argentina through the geographical accident
of the port of Buenos Aires has been molded with contemporary Europe. Argentina rocked with the ideals of Mazzini,
recoiled in terror against both the Kaiser and Lenin, gossiped
over the abdication of Edward, and took sides in the divorce
of Fritz Mandel and Hedy Lamarr. With European news
agencies feeding Continental current events into Argentina's
newspapers, with hundreds of thousands of Argentines ac-

tually commuting back and forth to France, Spain, and Italy, with trade across the Atlantic increasing in geometrical progression, it's no wonder Argentina was thrown into the controversy between democracy and Nazism-Falangism-Fascism from its inception in the minds of the desperate of Europe.

The world-rocking isms which were at first inconceivable to North Americans (and therefore underestimated) were instantly recognized as logical in Argentina. Thus the Southern republic with its realistic attitude, its eye on cause and effect and its practical mind on survival, was already weighing the strength of both sides and talking about its future course when most of us in the United States thought Japan was just clearing up a local police impasse in Manchuria, Italy was avenging a border raid in Ethiopia, and the conservatives were fighting for political rights against the irresponsible rabble of Spain. Argentina has never been handicapped by the vague idealism that keeps us from seeing a spade as a spade. Argentina can no more understand the pachyderm floundering of the Colossus of the North than we can understand its incisive materialism. It believes our motion pictures must be accurate reflections of our civilization, and we believe Argentine men must be wonderful lovers. Argentina believes we got into the war to get some trade and territory for ourselves, and we believe Argentina has stayed out because it doesn't understand that all the world must fight for the survival of the best way of life. The inertia of mutual ignorance is so great as to make slow and tedious the process of North American penetration into the daily life of Argentina, in sharp contrast to the progress we have made in imposing chunks of our civilization on the other Southern republics. Most of the things we understand Latin America to be, Argentina is not. Most of the things we always understood Europe to be, Argentina is—and Europe is no longer. We persist in treating Argentina as

American with a South European accent and Argentina con-
ceives of us as North European with touches of Hollywood
and Al Capone. No two people could be more mistaken about
each other.

A look at a map seems to show that the boundaries of the
South American continent are well defined where the sea
meets the land. That is the primary mistake. Argentina is an
extension of the Iberian Peninsula by virtue of the steamer
lanes. Two days out of Buenos Aires by the narrow-gauge,
wood-burning railroad that smokes and showers sparks across
the southern Chaco—or two days out of the same city by the
Scottish-built river boat bound for Asunción up the Paraná—
you begin to come into America. It is a Spanish-speaking
America, of course, but the set of the land, the color of the
people, their free walk, and the uninhibited sprawl of the
towns, proclaim it as a province of the New World. The
Chaco Indians drinking maté beside red stacks of quebracho
wood, the Jujueños in gypsy jackets riding their Moorish
saddles, are only a little more tropical and bizarre than the
New Mexicans and Californians of a generation back. But
this is the picturesque back country of Argentina; it has little
to do with the great landed families and their metropolis,
nothing to do with modern Argentina playing a part in modern power politics.

The best way, then, for an American to understand Argentina is to draw on a map of the world a group of radiating
lines fanning out from Buenos Aires to the French, Italian,
and Spanish ports. These have been the routes of intercourse
for generations—quick, easy, cheap routes. Only in recent
years has Buenos Aires been in touch by rail with its nearest
neighbors on its own continent. Because Argentina grew eastward from the Andean passes to the Atlantic coast, its restless
aristocrats never had the incentive that brought New Eng-
landers, New Yorkers, and Virginians "out West" in our own

country. That may explain why Britons built the Argentina railroad system into the pampa and why Germans peopled the Argentine Mesopotamia of the Paraná and the Uruguay rivers while the best blood of the conquistadors commuted between the estancia, the town house, and the Folies-Bergère.

It may explain, too, why the same propaganda that confused Vienna, Prague, Warsaw, Oslo, Rotterdam, and Paris into paralysis can be pumped into Buenos Aires. The ground has been prepared not only by the qualities of mind that make the Latin amenable to discipline and strong leadership but by the habit of Argentinians of bringing Europe home with them. The same arguments the board of directors fails to beat into the head of the president of the company can be insinuated into his ear by a gentle mistress. It should be of tremendous import to North American statesmen that the mistress of Buenos Aires is Latin Europe—particularly Paris.

Only by understanding the facts of the case do we arrive at last at an appreciation of Argentina's stand against involvement in the war on the side of the United States and Great Britain. Only by looking dispassionately at these facts do we begin to make a pattern of the isolationist statements of Argentina's President Ramón S. Castillo and the antisolidarity moves of the Argentine Foreign Minister, Dr. Enrique Ruiz-Guiñazú in 1942, at the Rio de Janeiro conference of "American" nations.

PART TWO

INVASION

CHAPTER IV

THE NAZIS MOVE IN

"WE ARE the delegation to promote travel to the Leipzig Industrial Fair," said Georg Bein and his happy group of Germans as they presented themselves in the late 1930's to the Argentine immigration inspectors. They were admitted with solemn courtesy.

The Leipzig boys were one group. There were lots more. There was even the Bureau of German Railroads, with clerks as busy as beavers. All of them were engaged in the business of stimulating trade and travel at a time when there wasn't a German ship crossing the Atlantic and the German-Italian airline was so full of espionage agents and contraband that it couldn't carry a passenger if it wanted to.

What were the travel-promoters doing?

A special committee of the Argentina Chamber of Deputies reported to *La Nación*, September 17, 1941:

"All these commercial agencies or industrial representatives are institutions of nominal functions; their real character is that of organizations in the exclusive service of Nazi propaganda directed by the Reich Government itself, or through the intermediary of its diplomatic agents in the Argentine Republic."

This report was signed by Raúl Damonte Taborda, the thirty-three-year-old National Deputy who in May, 1941, engineered the parliamentary move that uncovered the structure of the Nazi propaganda network strangling Argentina with misinformation. For two days Damonte Taborda and his fellow Radicals cross-questioned the Minister of the Interior, Dr. Miguel J. Culaciati, on the fifth column operating in the republic. Although the subject was within the province of his Ministry, Dr. Culaciati's replies were so alarmingly vague that they stirred the Chamber to vote a special investigation. (The only dissenting voice was that of Deputy Amadeo Videla Dorna, who distinguished himself six months later by casting the only vote against the expulsion of Baron Edmund von Thermann, the Nazi Ambassador.) Damonte Taborda was named chairman of the investigating committee.

The executive branch of the Government, in the hands of that shrewd conservative Acting President Castillo, blocked every move made by the investigating committee. Damonte Taborda was advised he couldn't raid premises or arrest individuals without court order. He found a judge, Ramón F. Vásquez, willing to co-operate to the extent of providing the court orders, and the committee went ahead digging the rotten apples out of the barrel politic.

It was the Damonte Taborda committee that proved what most intelligent Argentines had already suspected: The German Embassy under its diplomatic cloak was financing and managing the entire organization devoted to selling totalitarianism to the susceptible, and confusion to the rest. It proved that Berlin was directing a propaganda invasion of Argentina to be compared in thoroughness and efficiency only with the German military operations in Europe.

It wasn't only the commercial agencies, the travel-promoters. When the Damonte Taborda committee got into the heart of the propaganda invasion it found that the Leipzig boys were small fry. The big organization included news agencies, newspapers, radio stations, newsreel distributors.

Every method learned from North American advertising and publicity experts was being employed by the Nazis to destroy the old Argentina from within and to build a new Argentina with ideological tendencies capable of being molded into the Nazi pattern. The printed page, the air, the motion-picture screen, were busy identifying totalitarianism with family security, religion, public order—everything in fact that appealed to the man of goodwill and common sense —while democracy was being identified with the breakdown of moral standards, the abuses of capitalism, political degeneration, and individual despair. Every have-not was being told to join up and wait for the revolutionary stroke that would bring him a share of the wealth. Every property-owner was told that liberal democracy led eventually to social revolution and social revolution would rob the wisely provident of their substance. Youngsters were told that their future and salvation lay in militant action, and old folks were warned to insist on discipline within the state in order to preserve sound institutions.

The complete cynicism of this program is apparent only when the observer stands off and looks at it with a critical eye. In operation, it seemed to be diverse, spontaneous, genuine, some of it the work of inspired pamphleteers genuinely concerned with the future of the common people, some of it springing from the foreheads of patriotic editorial writers, intelligent radio commentators.

"Only by ideologically destroying it from within can Germany conquer Europe," Hitler said. The fact has never escaped the German Government that Argentina is a part of Europe.

The Nazi technique has never been effective against intelligent people; it isn't supposed to be.

In the Axis-financed campaign to support Dr. Castillo's "neutrality" policy as outlined at the Rio de Janeiro conference, and made a congressional campaign issue in February, 1942, we have the amazing spectacle of the Nazis—traditional advocates of action, war, "the virile, beautifully dangerous life" and so on, as opposed to pacifist and somnolent democracy—mouthing such soft terms as "the Socialist and Radical parties are in favor of a belligerent policy, but no Argentine who is a lover of happiness, and has the well-being of his country at heart, can have any doubts regarding the decision he should make . . . as regards keeping aloof from the conflict. The Government is responsible for keeping the country from war, therefore it is your duty to support the Government." This quotation is from the newspaper *El Pampero*, financed secretly by the German Government until exposed by the Damonte Taborda committee.

There is nothing new or ingenious about this technique. It has been used over and over again cold-bloodedly and effectively against every active or potential enemy of the Axis. It is the technique of saying repeatedly and with emphasis anything that seems suited to the situation at hand, regardless of truth or even consistency. The theory is that the unintelligent public will be so impressed with the vigor and the volume of the words that it will neglect to analyze them or relate them with what has gone before. On the face of it, it seems inconceivable that the Nazis can sell war to themselves and pacifism to their enemies, can sell revolution to the poor and discipline to the propertied, can sell paganism to Nordics and the Church to Latins. But that is exactly what they have done—and simultaneously in every part of the world where they can raise a voice or get a pen to paper.

Nazi propaganda in Argentina comes from so many sources and goes to so many points of ultimate consumption that even the Damonte Taborda committee hasn't been able to catch up with it. News channels controlled from Berlin, Rome, and Madrid pour exaggerated stories of Axis military successes and exaggerated stories of Allied losses into the Argentine ear, frightening potential enemies and exciting potential friends. Spanish ships of the Ybarra and Aznar lines dump tons of printed matter on the Buenos Aires docks every month. Until the Condor-Lati airline was stopped by a fuel shortage, planes carried great loads of propaganda into Argentina. Short-wave radio broadcasts from Axis capitals are the most powerful received in Argentina. But the most effective Nazi propaganda has been manufactured in Buenos Aires itself, manufactured in the Spanish language and thinly disguised as of Argentine origin. Its theme is "Save Argentina." It demands that Argentina be saved from the North American monster, from the Jews, from politicians (meaning democratic politicians), from the capitalists (meaning democratic capitalists), from liberalism and attendant immoralities, from participation in the war, from almost anything Germany doesn't like at the moment. It cries for the establishment of a strong state (meaning a totalitarian state) and whimpers mightily about the suffering of the Germans, paladins of Christianity, in their struggle against the Soviet Beast.

No organization or individual is spared. Propagandists are in the Church, in politics, in industry, in labor organizations, in homes, on park benches, in universities, in hospitals, in the Army and the Navy, everywhere. Anybody who reads a newspaper, listens to a radio, or opens his mail is in for a barrage of Nazi propaganda.

Argentina not only poisons itself thus with Nazi help but Buenos Aires also serves as a clearinghouse for propaganda destined for other Spanish American republics. The Argentine post office, queried by the Damonte Taborda committee, admitted that it dispatched for the German Embassy in forty-four days in mid-1941 two and a half tons of propaganda parcels to Chile, nearly a ton to Colombia, half a ton each to Mexico and Paraguay, and a lesser amount to other near-by countries. These were parcels only. The figures don't include letters and other light mail. Nor can they include the 20,000 covers a month mailed out by the Bureau of German Railroads, nor the fat output of a dozen other agencies not publicly associated with the German Embassy. Early in 1942 the Colombian Minister to Argentina protested officially to the Foreign Office, asking Argentina to put a stop to the flood of Nazi propaganda going from Buenos Aires to Colombia. He said Colombian authorities were seizing and destroying tons of the stuff, but couldn't get it all. Some of it was printed in Germany, some in Spain, and some in Buenos Aires itself.

After the Rio de Janeiro conference of the American republics early in 1942 Uruguay adopted energetic methods against the invasion by propaganda. The Nazi organizations, little used to dealing with energy in Latin America, were caught by surprise. But they recovered themselves in time to do the following:

1. Open a secret print shop in Montevideo. 2. Form an Argentine firm to edit a small periodical which was sent by mail to Uruguay in ordinary envelopes. 3. Establish a special German radio hour across the river in Buenos Aires for Uruguayan listeners. 4. Put into effect a special telephone code between Buenos Aires and Montevideo so as to disguise instructions to Nazi agents as harmless social or business conversation.

As long as the Nazis can hold Argentina there will be no lack of propaganda pipelines into the other Spanish-speaking countries of the continent.

If ever there was a propaganda success story, it is the story of the Nazi invasion of the Argentine "news" field. In order to understand why the Berlin radio could inform Argentina and the world on May 12, 1941, that Dr. Castillo would declare Argentina's complete neutrality as the cornerstone of his speech opening the Argentine Congress on May 21, you must understand the organization called Transocean. The Transocean news agency is an offshoot of the Deutsche Nachrichten Büro, the official Nazi propaganda agency operating from Berlin. Its ace Buenos Aires reporter is Mario Rocha Demaría, one of the ablest journalists in a city noted for journalistic excellence. The director of Transocean for South America is Walther von Simons, able, aggressive, with twenty years' experience among the Latin Americans. Transocean is not a legitimate news agency, but an arm of the Nazi Government at war. It has been expelled from most of the American republics it served, but in mid-1942 it was still flourishing in Argentina. In addition to its propaganda activity (mostly the transmission of news favorable to the Axis, news calculated to stir dissension among the American nations, editorial matter designed to bolster the prestige of Germany and convince the world of the inevitable defeat of the Allies) Transocean has been in Argentina a center of German espionage. It has specialized in the maintenance of communication between Nazi agents and in the corruption of local officials. In its character as a news agency it has bribed forty daily newspapers in Argentina through the simple expedient of offering them a complete news and picture service free as long as they agree to uphold the cause of the Axis Powers. Newspaper business managers who understand the cost of news coverage will understand what a temptation this offer is in a country not particularly interested in the merits of the two contending sides in the present war.

Although Transocean has carried the ball for the Nazis in the field of doctored and propagandized news, it is not to be assumed that Germany will be left flat-footed if an unexpected move eliminates this agency in Argentina, as has happened in some of the other American republics.

There are still Havas, the French agency; Stefani and Andi, the Italian agencies; and of course the Japanese Domei. There is a fifth, the dark-horse Franco-Spanish agency, EFE. Of these the only organization with the prestige and enterprise necessary for the occasion is Havas. It seems that Havas is now called Havas-Telemundial for purposes of its Argentine operation. As a result of an agreement between Vichy and the Argentine Government the latter is paying some of the Havas expenses in Argentina; in return the Argentine Embassy in Vichy is receiving some money to finance certain Argentine activities in France. Havas also had an arrangement with the United States Government whereby it received small amounts of money from French funds blocked in the United States. The Buenos Aires Havas office, manned by Argentine nationals, gets 10,000 words a day from neutral points, particularly Clermont-Ferrand and Berne, Switzerland. Havas serves some of the most notoriously Fascist newspapers in Argentina, including *La Fronda*, whose reporters were declared by the Chamber of Deputies committee to be paid salaries "from the Transocean agency maintained by the German Government." The Andi agency had a close working agreement with Havas.

In this dark picture there is a bright spot. The great metropolitan dailies of Buenos Aires are anti-Nazi to the core. These dailies, particularly *La Prensa*, *La Nación*, and *Critica*, are served by the United Press, the Associated Press, and the British Reuters.

As a matter of fact, if it weren't for *El Pampero* (the accent is on the next to last syllable) the average *porteño* would find hard scratching to get the official German propaganda version of the progress of the war.

"Pampero" is the name of a cold, dry, killing wind from the wastes of Patagonia; it is a wind that paralyzes the pampa and numbs the will of living creatures. It disputes with the zonda, the Andean chinook, the mastery of the changeable Argentine weather. *El Pampero* the newspaper is not like any other newspaper ever published in the Western Hemisphere. Nobody knows who owns it; nobody knows at

a given moment who is its editor; it carries advertising for
firms who don't know they are advertising in it.

El Pampero was organized at the outbreak of the war by
Enrique Osés and friends who had already made themselves
notorious with a vicious little sheet called *Crisol*. The new
enterprise was designed to bear aloft the torch of Nazi propaganda and light up therewith the little minds capable of
being warped by broad, bold lies often repeated. Señora Es-
tela Bernasconi de Santucci and her son, Adelqui, seem to
have some part in the ownership. At least Señora Santucci put
up either 97,000 pesos, 210,000 pesos, or 245,000 pesos (to
get dollars, divide by $4\frac{1}{4}$), according to varying testimony
of the Santuccis and the Oséses before the Chamber of Deputies committee. Further questioning of Señora Santucci revealed that it wasn't exactly her money, but the money of
"various friends" whose names she was not at liberty to
divulge.

Whenever *El Pampero* was cited by the Argentine courts
for libel or contempt, the newspaper produced a dummy editor, the jailhouse editor, whose duty it was to march off in
the custody of the police. The paper appeared as usual. Señor
Osés told the investigating committee that the paper had
five editors in addition to himself, Adelqui Santucci, Eduardo
S. Castilla, Armando Cascella, Olegario V. Andrade, and a
mysterious individual named Fausto E. de Tezanos Pinto.
Questioned closely, he admitted the terms of office of the five
extra editors were indeterminate, "from twelve days to six
months depending on circumstances." *El Pampero* was thus
the despair of the process-servers. When it served the purpose of the German Embassy, the paper was subsidized
through advertising printed for various German firms with
or without their knowledge and consent. Usually, however,
the representative of the Nazi Government made direct payment by sight draft on the Deutsche Ueberseeische Bank

(called in Buenos Aires the Banco Alemán Transatlantico) or the Deutsche-Südamerikanische Bank (called in Buenos Aires the Banco Germánico de la America del Sud).

In the same building with and part and parcel of *El Pampero* is the publishing house of La Mazorca, named after the bodyguard of the tyrant Rosas. Osés controls *La Mazorca* as he controls *El Pampero*. One of the comrades of La Mazorca is Manuel Roberto Espinosa. On June 26, 1941, Espinosa and some other comrades killed José Fiore, a money-lender. Espinosa and some of the others are still serving prison sentences.

Osés himself is known throughout the Argentine Nazi propaganda organization as the First Comrade. A moody, mystic, ambitious Latin with aspirations of becoming the Quisling of totalitarian Argentina, Osés is ordinarily at swords' points with other equally ambitious nationalist leaders all bent on the same distinction. Because he controls the propaganda, Osés has constantly the inside track.

Almost as thoroughly organized and as effective as the Nazi printed propaganda, Nazi newsreels have been a tremendous influence in influencing Argentina. Before the Condor-Lati planes stopped flying, Berlin shot its best war pictures direct to Buenos Aires. They were complete with effective Spanish subtitles. The most successful of these was the notorious screening of the panzer march on France—*Blitzkrieg in the West*. Since air transport is no longer feasible, Spanish ships bring Berlin's celluloid salesmen.

Well into 1942 American motion-picture representatives were dealing with Nazi newsreel houses. A flagrant example was the Cineac newsreel theater on Corrientes Street, where UFA and LUCE newsreels of German and Italian (!) military successes were shown for a time along with standard North American newsreels. While these houses were showing North American films to keep their patronage, they were slipping in enough Nazi propaganda to poison their patrons. At the same time the North American newsreels, which might at the time have been vital documents justifying the course of the United States in the light of world events, were showing such items as the following three gleaned from a reel I saw in March in Buenos Aires:

"Strange case of Friendship between Dog and Bear."

"Aqua-skiing in the Florida Everglades."

"Pepito the Monkey Trying on His New Pyjama Suit Presented Him by the St. Louis Zoological Society, and Drinking Beer from Bottle."

It is not to be supposed that the entire German propaganda effort has been centered on news and editorial comment through the various standard communication channels. A tremendous load has been carried by German, German-American, and German-Spanish societies, mostly manipulated from Berlin and all of them existing for the one purpose of selling totalitarianism. It is impossible to say how many foreign propaganda organizations exist in Germany, but here is a list of the *official* societies of this nature as compiled by National Deputy Juan Antonio Solari early in 1942:

Teuto-Japanese Society; China Club; Institute for the Study of the Problems of Eastern Asia; Nordic Society; Teuton Academic Club of the Exterior; Society of Foreign Friends; Ukrainian Institute; Movement for the Liberation of Russian Nationalists; Baltic Legion; Sudeten Legion; Austrian Legion; Deutsche-Amerikanische Bund; League of the Adherents to Nazi Oaths; World League against the Communist International; International Anti-Marxist Institute; World Anti-Jewish League; World Anti-Semite League; Aryan Alliance; Institute for Racial Investigation; Institute for the Study of German Problems; German Colonial Association; Colonial Academic League; Colonial Feminine League; Colonial League of the Reich; Institute of the Exterior; General German Academy; Union of German Associations; German League of Culture, Languages, and Libraries in the Exterior; Reconstruction of the Exterior; German Society of Students in the Exterior; Exterior Department of German Gymnastics; Institute for the Germans of the Exterior; Ibero-American Institute; League of Professors and Teachers of German Extraction in the Exterior; German Schools of the Exterior; Associations of War Veterans; NSDAP (Nazi party) in the Exterior; German Labor Front in the Exterior; Germanic Union; German Singing Associations; Association of German Engineers in the Exterior; German Hispanic Institute; Bureau of German Railroads; Humboldt Club; German-Ibero-American Medical Academy; Commercial Union for South America; German-Argentine Commercial Union; Fichte League.

Of these perhaps half are active in Argentina at the moment. One of the most sinister is the Ibero-American Institute operated from Berlin by General Wilhelm Faupel and his wife Edith, known to her intimate friends as "Peter." This is the outfit that puts the *Schmalz* in Germany's cultural relations with its Spanish-American neighbors. It is a racket that begins where Nelson Rockefeller leaves off. For years the General has paid the expenses of Spanish-American scholars, professors, and writers who yearned to go to Germany. The Institute controls as far as possible everything these people say about Germany after returning to their homelands. This institute subscribes to all Spanish-American magazines of importance. It maintains a close watch on all Spanish-American nationalist movements, insinuating as much pro-Nazi feeling into them as possible through its card-index control of writers and speakers.

The General himself edits *Ensayos y Estudios,* a Spanish-language review of culture and philosophy. When he is not at his intellectual labor, he and Peter wine and dine the visiting South American intellectuals. German espionage agents destined for service in Spanish-speaking countries very often go through General Faupel's Spanish classes to get the proper intellectual training. The institute has its own espionage service, dealing with commercial and economic subjects. It publishes a magazine, *Army, Navy and Air Force*, through which it keeps close contact with military establishments in Latin America.

The entire organization is a masterful example of German thoroughness, and of German understanding of the problem in hand. Years ago it understood, for instance, that ideological penetration should be guided first by cultural penetration. It understood, too, that cultural penetration is achieved by a steady flow of writers and teachers between countries.

When you multiply the effective work of the Ibero-American Institute by the number of similar societies on Deputy Solari's list, you get an idea of how it is possible for Germany to smother a comparatively small country like Argentina and control its thought and action even though it is thousands of miles away from the Reich.

It is typical of Nazi methods that no foreign government has ever discovered how much of the propaganda let loose within the boundaries of any country is financed from Berlin, how much by Nazi Germans within the country itself, and how much by silly people like Señora Santucci, who seemed so vague about the bookkeeping system of *El Pampero*. It is quite likely that Austria, Czechoslovakia, Norway, Denmark, the Low Countries, and France—like Argentina—footed the greater part of the bill themselves. It is certain that in Argentina every German and every Argentine of German descent is assessed unmercifully for this purpose.

However financed, Nazi propaganda has been so successful in Argentina that after three years of virtual isolation by sea, after the United States and Great Britain have exhausted every effort to choke off air communication, radio programs, news services, and other intercourse between the two nations,

Argentina has held firmly against pressure to bring it into line with other American nations in a declaration against the Axis. The body will not do what the spirit refuses. Nazi Germany has shown itself diabolically shrewd in manipulating the spirit of its victims.

CHAPTER V

MARKED FOR CONQUEST

GERMANY has shipped the machinery of conquest to the New World in much the way that De Lesseps shipped his canal-digging apparatus from Suez to Panama. Results obtained by the Nazi fifth column in such countries as Poland, Norway, and France have offered no inducement to the German High Command to revise that machinery.

In Norway, the entire defense system of an intelligent, heroic, and stubborn people was wrecked from within. This was a systematic wrecking engineered by German propagandists, saboteurs, and spies working under high organization and tremendous pressure. The day German troops landed in Norway all of the German diplomatic and consular corps, all attachés and business advisers, including cultural relations missions and travel-bureau managers, appeared in the uniforms of officers of the German Army or Navy. That's exactly what they had been all the time. Nazi squads appeared on the streets and immediately took over all communications systems, sending out their own orders by telephone, telegraph, cable, and radio. In Norwegian, they ordered entire Army divisions to lay down their arms, entire fleet units to cease operations, forts to refrain from firing at the enemy.

When the German Army advanced, they used maps superior to Norwegian maps, the work of years of labor by experts sent to Norway for that specific purpose. Most of the German officers in the invading army had spent many months "vacationing" on the ground they marched across. Most of the naval officers who took Oslo and the west coast had spent their summers yachting in those areas until every landmark was familiar. In some cases the German knowledge of the terrain was so good that Norwegian troops were outmaneuvered in their own hills and valleys. German landing parties at many coast towns found the place already in the hands of Nazi troops who had posed as consular and commercial representatives, even as tourists. Sea and air squadrons found landing-fields and ammunition dumps marked by ground signals by day, fires and rockets by night.

The same story can be told with sickening regularity throughout conquered Europe. The penetration of France is a classic example of conquest through propaganda. Pacifism was encouraged in France by German agents. Political antagonisms were deliberately fostered and kept alive. The entire French defense program was sabotaged through strikes engineered among the Communists and other excitable labor groups. Individual German travelers poured across France talking to French people and sowing doubt in their minds. Newspapers were bought and turned into organs of confusion. Gradually French morale was lowered as Frenchmen were taught to mistrust their only powerful ally, Britain. As most modern people see ethics, this program can be compared to bribing the doctor of a boxing opponent to send him into the ring anemic. Of course German pilots knew France like a book, having flown constantly across it in commercial planes. Of course German officers disguised as students had hiked and motored through every square mile of the country into which they later advanced at the head of their columns. As they say on the Jersey docks, "It was moider."

Not only has the same system of attack been used in Argentina, but a great many of the individuals utilized by Germany in subduing Europe have been sent there. Because of their superior technical skill, Germans are in control of Ar-

gentine communications. For many years they have dominated commercial flying. They know the Paraná and the
Uruguay waterways as few natives know them. Through
their sports clubs they have penetrated into the labyrinthine
delta country. Organized hiking has taken them through the
Andes. They have climbed peaks no Argentine would attempt. In the hill country and the lake district back against
the mountains they dominate the hotel business, and thus
control travel across the Chilean border.

Germans know the coast of Patagonia, and they have magnificent charts (as have the Japanese) of the Strait of Magellan. They comprise something like 80 per cent of the white
population of the rich territory of Misiones, and are so autonomous there that they operate their own post-office department and police the thousands of Polish and Ukrainian colonists with their own Gestapo. They smuggle arms and
agents in and out of the river provinces without hindrance,
forming with the Germans of Paraguay and southern Brazil
a Nazi unit of hundreds of thousands of members extending
in a wide arc from São Paulo inland to Asunción and south
to Buenos Aires.

German technicians swarm over the state-owned oil fields,
the YPF. They are in the British- and American-owned oil
fields, too, and all over the petroleum deposits along the
Patagonian coast. One Scotch oil-field laborer told me he
watched a Nazi bring out and study a complete chart of the
pipes and valves of the Shell field at Comodoro Rivadavia.
Nazis are in the trucking system, the highway department,
the docks. They control airports south of Buenos Aires. They
hold key positions in the electric light and power systems.
They are in the police department, the lawcourts, the custom
and immigration services, according to National Deputy Juan
Antonio Solari, who made a special study of this type of infiltration into the Argentine civil services.

When the investigating committee of the Chamber of Deputies asked the Foreign Office for particulars about the nationality and antecedents of its personnel, it was coldly refused. The request came after Senator Alfredo Lorenzo Palacios discovered that documents on Argentina's relations with Germany in 1914-18 had disappeared from the Foreign Office after passing through the hands of some employees who were not Argentine citizens. The same committee discovered that a woman employee of the municipality of Buenos Aires belonged to the Nazi party and had given an oath of loyalty to Adolf Hitler.

It is common knowledge that the German banks in Buenos Aires extend unlimited credit to certain local officials. The story persists that Argentine Army and Navy officers can go to certain German clubs and play poker with the expectation of winning regularly.

To say that Nazi Germany seems to be ready at any moment to spring across the South Atlantic and seize Argentina with the help of an organized fifth column may seem a hysterical interpretation of the facts. Yet every move Germany has made in Argentina in the past five years parallels its pre-attack penetration of a now enslaved Europe.

From March 1, 1941, to October 31, 1941, a total of 1,295 Germans arrived in Argentina. They weren't just out for the air at a time when Germany was massing every available man for the assault on Russia. During the same period hundreds of German agents arrived with fake Spanish, Portuguese, and assorted Latin American passports. Sometimes the Argentine immigration officers find blonds who don't know a word of Spanish presenting passports from Barcelona, Madrid, and Valencia. They laugh and let them through.

Leon Hirsch made the mistake of leaving a bit of scribbled waste paper when he rose from his table at the Restaurant Larue, Place de la Madeleine, Paris, one May evening in

1939. He got a fourteen-year sentence at hard labor. Hirsch was an Austrian spy, agent of the bloody Otto Abetz and the Geheime Staatspolizei, at the moment engaged in getting their hands on the plans of the Maginot Line defenses. Abetz and Hirsch are credited with the collapse of the French defense wall. Later Abetz got Hirsch out of prison when he took over Paris. Hirsch was one of eight Nazi agents arrested by the British and taken off the Spanish liner *Cabo de Hornos* in October, 1941. The *Cabo de Hornos,* with Hirsch and some friends, was bound for Buenos Aires. He called himself Leopold Hirsch. The British say he was living the life of Riley aboard, drinking champagne, smoking pure Havanas, and entertaining hordes of guests at every port of call. The story was current in Buenos Aires that Hirsch had $50,000 in traveler's checks on him when arrested, and that he carried orders from Hitler to direct Gestapo activities in Argentina. Whatever his mission, Hirsch was one of many men and women poured into Argentina by the Nazi authorities in an effort to hold South America in line.

Most Nazi agents entered Argentina by the Condor-Lati airline, which operated from Rome to Buenos Aires through Rio de Janeiro. Condor was German-owned, Lati Italian-owned. The line operated on gasoline sold it by a North American oil company over the protest of the State Department. The gasoline supply was finally stopped in December, 1941, when the company's subsidiaries in Brazil were black-listed by the United States. While operating on United States gasoline, Condor-Lati carried tons of propaganda from Berlin to Buenos Aires. It carried a great many spies, including General Faupel, Paul von Bauer, General Hans Kundt, Edgar von Speigel, Prince Stephan zu Schaumburg-Lippe, alias Fritz Held. It carried to Germany strategic war materials from South American mines and chemical plants. There was almost no attempt to disguise this operation as commercial.

Nor was secrecy necessary. The prodemocratic newspapers of Buenos Aires have been full of the arrival and departure of crack German agents. They have printed column after column of the revelations of the Damonte Taborda committee. Yet little official action has been taken to keep agents of Germany out of the country or to deport those known to be active. In late 1942 the Chamber of Deputies was calling for action in vain.

CHAPTER VI

HOW HIVE THE TERMITES

ACTIVE Nazi penetration of Argentina began in 1938 after the German Ausland Organization went into partnership with the German Foreign Office to control the political activities of Germans overseas. Until that date the AO was merely an intermediary between the Nazi Government and Germany abroad (*Auslandsdeutschtum*). In 1937, Hitler made the capable AO chief, Ernst Wilhelm Bohle, a member of the Foreign Office. This move and the appointment of Von Ribbentrop as Foreign Minister brought a powerful new instrument into play—a combination of German diplomatic establishments and German private-citizens organizations abroad. What actually happened is that the Foreign Office became an instrument of the AO.

The effect on the German Embassy in Buenos Aires was electric. In the fiscal year 1938, the Embassy spent only 850,-000 Argentine pesos. In 1939, it spent 3,150,000, and in 1940, 5,900,000 pesos. The Embassy's activities as measured by the yardstick of expenses advanced wildly after the AO took over.

The true character of these activities was uncovered in Argentina when the Damonte Taborda committee called Gottfried Sandstede, ostensibly an employee of a Buenos Aires shipping firm, to testify. Sandstede immediately claimed diplomatic immunity. He was in fact a "press attaché" of the German Embassy at the time he was presumed to be engaged in the shipping business. After this discovery was made on

August 26, 1941, Sandstede eluded the investigating committee's process-servers, slipped through a cordon of Argentine
police, and got aboard a plane bound for Germany. Not only
was his usefulness at an end, but had he been closely interro-
gated about his duties as a press attaché, his Government
would have been embarrassed. It is generally supposed that
Sandstede was engaged in the direction of the Nazi political
organization in Argentina under the AO. His flight tended to
confirm this supposition. He was actually the third to flee
Argentina in a few months. He was preceded by Karl Arnold
and Alfredo Mueller, both Nazi organizers whose identities
and functions became known at an awkward time.

The advantage to the AO in utilizing diplomatic immunity
in its questionable activities extended to correspondence.
Through the medium of diplomatic mailbags, a courtesy extended by custom to foreign Legations, Nazi instructions,
propaganda, even secret radio transmission sets for contact
with Germany, slip in and out of South American countries.
Oddly enough, it was Argentina that blocked the Rio de
Janeiro conference designed to stop this practice by closing
all German diplomatic establishments in this hemisphere.
Oddly enough, because Argentina's diplomatic courtesy has
been the most flagrantly abused in this respect. One of the
radio sets was discovered when the Damonte Taborda committee seized three "diplomatic mailbags" addressed to the
German Embassy, Buenos Aires. The bags were taken from
a Pan-American Airways plane at the Argentine city of Córdoba July 25, 1941. Immediately they became the subject of
a three-way debate, mostly on the bitter side, between the
German Embassy (which hollered it had been robbed), the
Argentine Foreign Office (which said the bags should be returned to the German Ambassador), and the Chamber of
Deputies (which said unprintable things about the other
two).

Thus the German diplomatic establishment has been forced to act as liaison between the Nazi AO and the hundreds of thousands of German residents—many of them peace-loving and law-abiding—living in Spanish America. The time-honored intent of diplomatic representation has been shoved aside while the AO goes to town in the fertile field of *Auslandsdeutschtum*. Hitler said: "I want to make it quite clear that I make no distinction between German nationals and Germans by birth"—whether the German nationals like it or not. The AO organizes and controls them with thoroughness and purpose.

The AO works in two fields in Argentina: among the nationals (the *Volksdeutsche*), of whom there are about 50,000, and among the 200,000 Argentines of German parentage.

Until the AO got to work there weren't enough South American Nazis to form a color guard for a small swastika; and in the early days of Hitler there was not much time to spend on organizing Germans abroad. Once the home front was thoroughly in hand and functioning along Nazi lines, say in 1933, many thoughts were turned to the remote places on the maps in the Wilhelmstrasse. Already in 1884, Dr. Carlos M. V. Calvo, Argentine Minister in Berlin, had reported to his Government a German plan to colonize and control southern Brazil, Patagonia, Paraguay, and the Argentine provinces between the great rivers.

The Nazis had conceived the plan of dividing South America so that Argentina would include Uruguay, Paraguay, southern Bolivia, and the Falkland Islands; Brazil would include the Argentine river province of Misiones, French Guiana, Dutch Guiana, and northern Bolivia; Venezuela would include British Guiana, Trinidad, Barbados, Aruba, and Curaçao; Peru would include the southern and eastern sections of Ecuador. Since then there have been other methods of division proposed, but the kernel of the matter is that

Germany is to control all of the redivided states as it controls the states of Europe since their redivision. The guiding principle of the New Order is apparent in the Nazi attitude toward Latin America's boundaries.

The important thing about all this planning is that a complicated machinery was drafted and built. This machinery was to bring about the Nazi dream for South America. Individuals were trained for service, then sent across the Atlantic with blueprints. This machinery went into action with the wedding of the AO and the Foreign Office. Its cardinal principles of operation included personal terrorism along approved Nazi lines, and the complete domination of German commercial firms already doing business in South America. Those who lived abroad and had relatives or friends at home could be reached easily by the simple threat of the Gestapo. Those business houses which were foreign branches of German establishments could be reached the same way, plus the additional pressure governments know how to put on business to get what they want. The foreign branches became *Stützpunkte*, Nazi nuclei, numerous and strongly placed. Prominent in the Nazi commercial ganglion were the chemical houses of Bayer and Schering, the two German South American banks, the Hamburg-American steamship line, the metal firms of Thyssen and Siemens-Schuckert, heavy industries like Krupp, Lahusen, Pfaff. The lesser houses were kicked into line in short order.

Nazi firms in South America became the spearhead of the attack. Their managers and employees were strong Nazi-party men, picked for their aggressiveness. They went to work closely with the commercial attachés of the German Legations to secure and exercise the tightest control over German business in the area. The organization grew in efficiency and size, distributing propaganda, spying on individuals and businesses, bringing in a constant flow of new "em-

ployees" from Germany, keeping records, acting as covers for
Nazi funds being poured into the country for the work at
hand. Firms unwilling or unable to fit themselves into this
network were sent efficiency experts and commercial advisers
from Germany, who soon reorganized them along the proper
lines. The German diplomatic establishments provided lever-
age where needed. By 1940 the AO controlled all German
commercial activity in South America and used it extensively
as a Nazi-party weapon—and by now by virtue of the war it
was considered a weapon for the triumphant Fatherland.

The art of persuasion through the pocketbook, an art perfected already at home, was thus exercised for patriotic purposes among the hundreds of thousands of reluctant Germans
most of whom had fled their own country looking for surcease from Prussianism. Professional men who failed to see
the light lost their clients. Laborers lost their jobs. The German Legations can refuse passports, refuse birth certificates
to new children, refuse marriage licenses to young German
couples who have been stubborn or whose parents have been
reluctant to come into the program. They can withdraw trading privileges.

All German nationals in South America must report regularly to their Legations or consulates, where there is a record
of all their relatives living in Germany. Unco-operative Germans are reminded that they have an obligation to keep their
people at home from harm—a broad hint that works like
magic. For those few with no close ties at home, the haunting fear, fostered by smart propaganda, that Nazism is going
to triumph everywhere in the world, including South America, works as a powerful persuasive. Children in German
schools are taught to report disloyal parents. German societies
and clubs boycott non-Nazis and drive them from the German community. Young Germans and older ones too emotionalized by the war to differentiate between fact and fiction

are kept at fever heat by the constant flow of propaganda from the homeland distributed not only through German newspapers, periodicals, and radio programs, but through the schools and clubs to which the Teuton clings when away from home.

Politically, Germans in Argentina are under the strictest control. They owe allegiance to the *Landesgruppenleiter* appointed by Adolf Hitler and advised by the Auslands commission for South America, whose chief in 1941 was believed to be Willie Koehn, who enjoyed diplomatic immunity through official attachment to the German Embassies in both Buenos Aires and Montevideo. Actual organization of the German population has been effected through (1) the NSDAP (the Argentine Nazi party); (2) the Hitler Jugend (Hitler Youth); (3) the Nazi Frauenschaft (Women's Organizations); (4) the Deutsche Arbeitsfront (Labor Front); and (5) the Kraft durch Freude (Strength through Joy). There are specialty corps such as the SA (Storm Troopers), the SS (Security Troopers), the Deutsche-Argentinische Pfadfinder Korps (Boy Scouts), and the Bund Deutscher Mädchen (German Maidens).

Subsidiary to these, but all grimly Nazi, are singing associations, theater groups, professional clubs, sports clubs, and social clubs. Membership and discipline are maintained at a peak that is a constant source of astonishment to members of the other foreign colonies in Argentina.

Before Acting President Castillo came into office in Argentina, the Argentine Nazi party (NSDAP) and the Nazi Labor Front (DAF) were outlawed by decree of President Roberto M. Ortiz. That was May 15, 1939. In June, 1939, the Nazi party was dissolved. Two days later there appeared in the same offices, using the same records, equipment, personnel, telephones, and methods, the Federation of German Benevolent and Cultural Societies. The Nazi Labor Front was dissolved. Two days later there appeared, again using the same materials, files, and persons, the German Trade-Union. It is possible the Nazis may have believed the Argentine Government incapable of connecting the Nazi party with the Federation of Benevolent and Cultural Societies. But the German Trade-Union has been since 1934 an affiliate of the German Labor Front, with headquarters in Berlin. The airy manner with which these two new organizations set up shop to carry on the work illustrates as nothing else can the contempt in which Germany holds official Argentina.

Most of the official Nazi organizations maintain headquarters in the tremendous dark building known to Buenos Aires as Number 145 Calle Veinte-cinco de Mayo. Over the Banco Germánico extend floor after floor of offices all dedicated to the same purpose, from the German Chamber of Commerce to the Association of German War Veterans. There are twenty-eight central groups operating from this pile of stone with its maze of elevator and staircase systems, its public and private doorways, and its dim corridors. Here, too, is housed the German Embassy, presided over until his recent "vacation trip" home by Ambassador Baron von Thermann, who represented the liberal Weimar Republic, then turned pro-Nazi at the advent of Hitler.

The dark house here in the heart of Buenos Aires' old financial district overlooks the lower traffic artery of Avenida Alem and beyond the avenue to the broad docks and the muddy river. Its back doors open onto the narrow chasm of Calle Veinte-cinco de Mayo, where it begins to form with Calle Reconquista the honky-tonk district paralleling the water front. Not a block away is the dark doorway of the Hotel zur Post, where German is spoken in low voices over steins of Quilmes and Bieckert beer. Toward the north a few hundred yards is the Jousten Hotel, with its banquet halls like a vision of Valhalla where the Nazi great are feasted as never were visiting firemen. Beyond that is the Hotel Vienna, which holds the overflow of the Nazi hierarchy, the lesser fry for whom the Jousten clerks simply can't make room tonight, so sorry. Within five minutes' walking distance is the entire nerve center of Nazi Germany in Argentina. Here the traffic is heavy with long, sleek Mercédes-Benzes carrying silk-hatted diplomats and Nazi overseers just in from Berlin— and the little American-made station wagons loading up with propaganda pamphlets to be distributed to students at Cór-doba or cane-field laborers at Jujuy.

There was a lot of speculation about what went on at Number 145 Calle Veinte-cinco de Mayo until the Damonte Taborda committee, armed with a court order issued by Judge Vásquez, raided the party headquarters up on the fifth floor. As a result of files seized in the raid, the committee was able to prove to the Chamber of Deputies (and the Chamber pointed out to the Government, to no avail) that the Benev-olent and Cultural boys and the Trade-Union were just a blind. The committee also found out the mechanics of the party system that furnished the local backlog of men and funds so necessary in Nazifying Argentine Germans and keeping them active and ready. Collections of money were disguised in many cases as voluntary charity. The Winter Help Fund and the Ring of Sacrifice dunned Germans regu-larly, but no accounting was made to contributors. The money actually went to finance organization and propaganda, as it had done frankly under the NSDAP before it was outlawed.

The Trade-Union was discovered to be actively collecting cash contributions from employees of industrial and commer-cial establishments controlled by Germans. This also is in vio-lation of the Argentine law. It was found that even the per-sonnel of the German Embassy belonged to the Trade-Union and contributed to its treasury. Records were found of the remittance of large sums of money from the German Embassy and the German Labor Bank to the Trade-Union. So flagrant were the violations and evasions that the Damonte Taborda committee recommended:

That in view of the repeated falsehoods in which the authorities of the German Trade-Union have been guilty in supplying the Government with information, it would be advisable for the National Labor Department to investigate carefully in order to establish the exact facts and apply the proper punishment for this offense and for the violation of the laws applying to labor. The Government should intervene and dissolve the German Trade-Union and apply to its leaders the legal measurements the case demands.

The Government did nothing.

General Manuel Calderón, until recently chief of the National Gendarmerie, reported about the operations of the German Trade-Union in the Misiones territory:

There also exist organizations and associations which formerly functioned under the name German Labor Front. Admittance to these organizations has to be approved by the home office of the German Trade-Union, 1250 Calle Alsina, Buenos Aires, which directs all the activities of the affiliated groups throughout the country. Members are obliged to pay a monthly subscription, which is collected and remitted to Germany, and have to prove their membership by a carnet signed by Dr. Ley, Labor Minister of the German Government.

A great many German technicians hired by Argentina were found to belong to the Nazi Labor Front. At the same time, a large number of Germans were expelled from membership as punishment for taking out Argentine citizenship papers. Heinz Lowenthal was expelled January 21, 1941, when it was discovered he had "native" blood in his family. All members were required to be pure Aryan.

Members of the Labor Front carry international passes

similar to passports. Wherever there is a German colony in South America these passes are good for employment. In return, the employee is under careful observation, and his membership in the Labor Front is controlled wherever he may be working. A complete list of movements of members is kept at headquarters.

Actually the Labor Front is a part of the Nazi party itself, operating in this instance among wage-earners. The Director of Party Organizations of the Reich is chief of the Labor Front Nazi Affiliates. These are the Storm Troops for labor, an elite corps selected for physical fitness, political aptness, purity of race.

The Damonte Taborda committee reported itself "amazed" that these intensely organized groups in possession of maps dividing Buenos Aires, for example, into cells and blocks and strong points, should be tolerated by the nation. The committee concluded:

It is also evident that the German Labor Front or German Trade-Union forms part of the National Socialist party, designed to work for its expansion in Argentina against the laws and institutions of the country, and to grow strong so that should the occasion arise the affiliated groups could act as one.

It is useless to speculate how many well-trained, equipped, able-bodied men of military age Germany could count on in Argentina in case the changing tides of war made a landing in the Western Hemisphere feasible. If there is a "German minority" of 280,000, as the *Berliner Tageblatt* claimed on January 10, 1939, it is not hard to believe the usual estimate of from 50,000 to 80,000 men ready to bear arms. This is probably a great deal more potential German soldiers than the Nazis actually had inside Norway, Denmark, France, and the Low Countries at the time of the invasions.

Before the Damonte Taborda committee became active in

exposing Nazi activities, Germans held regular drill meetings
which they attended in uniform with all the pomp and ceremony so dear to the Prussian heart. Buenos Aires newspapers
have printed photographs of some of these affairs at which
the oath of allegiance to Hitler and the salute to the swastika
were foremost on the program. April 10, 1938, 10,000 Nazis
jammed Buenos Aires' Luna Park in brown uniforms—both
men and women. They maneuvered and shouted at the command of excited Nazi leaders. Across the front of the temporary platform a tremendous banner bore the legend *"Ein
Volk, Ein Reich, Ein Führer."* Flags and banners bearing the
swastika fluttered in the quick breeze from the estuary. An
orchestra struck up *"Deutschland über Alles"* and the thousands sang with right arms proudly upraised. Prominent German diplomats and Austrian Nazis spoke, praising the recently consummated *Anschluss,* first step toward Gross
Deutschland.

Argentine democrats who were barred later from holding
demonstrations in the same stadium in favor of the Allied
cause will long remember with bitterness the noise and the
pride of this great Nazi conclave. Such demonstrations are
now impossible, prohibited by decree. Nevertheless, physical
fitness among the German population is still one of the cardinal points of Nazi policy under the rule of the AO. I have
watched the big blond oarsmen of the Ruderverein Teutonia
sweep the international shell races along the Paraná River
in front of the Tigre boating clubs. The Reiter Sturm, the
Brown Shirt cavalry, still exercises at the German Riding
Club. The Fleiger Sturm, the Nazi Air Corps in Argentina,
calls itself a Glider Club and maneuvers regularly under the
notorious Erich Hoerhammer. The Nazi infantry marches
without uniform at its "sports camps" at Villa Ballester,
Munro, and Quilmes. Gymnastic activity is kept at a peak.
Nazis have boasted that the crack invasion troops of the Reich

are the products of the Turnvereins and the hiking paths. The German instinct for choral singing, mass gymnastics, military drill, and other forms of disciplined action has been exploited to the limit to keep Argentine Nazis in tiptop condition for common action—if and when the occasion arises.

In Argentina in 1939, there was turned up a document supposed to be a facsimile of a report on the factors bearing on a German occupation of Patagonia. The report was addressed to the Colonial Policy department of the NSDAP; one copy was destined for the AO. Included were military and communications maps, photographs of strategic points, plans of Argentine defenses and oil reserves, and other pertinent data. The German Embassy denied its authenticity. Yet the very existence of such a report, detailed and thorough in every way, indicates that someone was interested enough to mobilize all the facts bearing on a possible invasion. The signatures on the document apparently were those of Counselor von Schubert of the Embassy and Alfredo Mueller, chief of the Nazi Labor Front in Argentina. In June, 1940, there was discovered across the estuary in Uruguay what is called the Fuhrmann Plan for the seizure of the territory contiguous to the Uruguay River. The plan was drafted by Arnulf Fuhrmann, Julio Dalldorf, and seven other Nazis. Eight were arrested, but Dalldorf enjoyed diplomatic immunity as press attaché of the German Legation. Otto Langmann, the German Minister, denied the whole affair, and threatened with libel proceedings the Uruguayan National Deputy who discovered the plot. Langmann also threatened to break off diplomatic relations, and all eight Germans were released. Public outcry was so vociferous they were all rearrested and brought to trial.

The man on the street will never know how authentic are all these reported "putsches" throughout South America, but at least they have been in the public eye frequently enough to arouse a bitter resentment against Germany in the minds of ordinary citizens. Paraguay, Chile, Bolivia, and Argentina forestalled military uprisings in 1941; in most cases these were traced to Nazis. The existence of heavy deposits of arms and ammunition in the river district of Argentina points to a continuous contraband traffic. Some of the stuff is smuggled in from the German provinces of Brazil; some of it has been bought from soldiers returning from the Chaco War. The notorious lack of border vigilance on the Argentine frontiers makes this trade easy and profitable.

It must be remembered that at a time when the United States badly needs hemispheric unity in order to defend itself and keep raw materials coming in from the south, distractions and disorders among the Latin republics are a serious form of sabotage. Even discounting the possibilities of setting up one or two pro-Axis states in South America, these disturbances greatly help Germany. Whether or not the Peru-Ecuador War was instigated by German agents, there is evidence that they encouraged it and helped prolong it. At least at the present moment, it is likely the German High Command is interested in fostering internal and international disorder among the American nations rather than preparing a frontal attack. But there is no reason to forget that in Europe Hitler used both these methods and was prepared for both, from Narvik to Bucharest and from Riga to Bordeaux.

It became more and more apparent in Buenos Aires in 1942 that unless Germany were defeated quickly and thoroughly at home, its foothold in Argentina was a solid threat to the continent. Germany was thoroughly organized there, as it was in the Sudetenland when it issued its ultimatum to Czechoslovakia. Careful groundwork had given Germany a highly unified micronation within the boundaries of Argentina, in many ways better prepared and better organized than the Argentine nation itself. Through its schools (more than two hundred Nazi schools in Argentina teach children Hitlerism) it was recruiting the next generation. Through its sports, music, social, and study clubs it was keeping bodies and spirits alert. With the economic pressure of its thoroughly organized business and industries it was holding merchants and tradesmen in line. Through its outlawed but still functioning party and labor fronts it was assessing, propagandizing, and watching every adult German and most adults of German descent. With the Gestapo it was terrorizing and controlling every potential backslider.

In these activities Germany was successfully defying a nation's public opinion and imposing its will in many subtle ways upon a republic at an incredible distance from Berlin. It was doing even more; it was manipulating a wedge into the political affairs of that nation which gave every promise of making it over into its own Nazi pattern.

CHAPTER VII

THE FALANGE: THE RISING SUN

WITH usurious interest, Franco is paying his debt to Hitler in South America. He has provided Nazi Germany with a shipping service that passes the British blockade. Every two weeks his combined freight and passenger liners clear Buenos Aires for the Spanish ports laden with correspondence, drugs, strategic minerals, food, en route to Germany, in the end. Many of these ships were confiscated by Franco from the Basque shipping family of De la Sota, which was driven into exile for daring to fight for the Spanish Republic.

Falangist Spain has provided more than an easy communication and freight system for Nazi Germany. It has provided a supplementary commercial and political espionage system through the Spanish diplomatic and consular establishments. The German Co-ordinating Officer in the Spanish Ministry of Foreign Affairs seems to be the real power behind the Spanish Foreign Ministry, as he must be in Italy, Rumania, Bulgaria, Hungary, Finland, and the dozen lesser puppets. Uruguayans say a Spaniard in the Legation at Montevideo was transferred to Santo Domingo on orders of the German Co-ordinator because he resisted co-operation between the German and Spanish Legations in Montevideo.

The Spanish Ambassador in Buenos Aires, the Marquis de Magaz, was for several years Spanish Ambassador in Berlin. There is no question about his friendly collaboration in Argentina with the German and Italian Embassies. His closest friends are Nazis and Fascists. This situation goes a long way

toward nullifying the ejection of the German diplomatic network from the South American republics following the Rio
de Janeiro conference. What it means is that the Nazis have
Spanish stand-ins everywhere they are needed.

Argentina is close to pure colonial Spanish in language,
culture, and institutions; it must be more than half Spanish
by blood. Perhaps one-tenth of the people of Argentina are
Spaniards of recent immigration or the children of Spanish
parents. They are called Gallegos by the natives. Galicia happens to be the maritime province of Spain that of recent years
has furnished the bulk of peasant stock for the great estancias,
the small farms, the small businesses, and all the humble labors of Argentina. The Spanish stock is looked at in Argentina in much the same way North Americans looked at the
poor Irish immigrant of the nineteenth century, or would
have looked at Cockney English immigrants had there been
many of them. To be called a Gallego in Buenos Aires is like
being called a mick or a wop in the United States. This is in
spite of the fact that in sentiment the Argentine dreams himself back to the Golden Age of Spain for the inspiration of
all he finds good and enduring in life.

The Spanish immigration into Argentina is divided politically about as Spain was: three-quarters vaguely republican,
one-quarter fiercely totalitarian. Spanish totalitarianism is
called Falangism. Spanish republicanism isn't called anything
(except by a few professional agitators); it's only a state of
mind. Falangism is the lifework of Franco, the Caudillo.
Through it he and his backers and close collaborators control
the bodies and minds of all Spaniards within reach as Hitler
controls all Germans through the organized emotion called
Nazism. Franco created on November 2, 1940, El Consejo
de Hispanidad in an effort to control as well as his own
people the people of Spanish America.

As the essence of the Nazi system in the Western Hemi-

sphere is energy, the essence of the Falange in this hemisphere is finesse. Spain toys with Argentina. Whereas Germany shouted and threatened when the Argentine Chamber
of Deputies seized its "diplomatic baggage" and censured its
Ambassador, Spain quietly and smoothly closed its center of
propaganda, the Casa de España, at the first hint of political
embarrassment. What Germany is unable to get directly from
Argentina by blunt demand, Spain can get for it in the Spanish way. Three-quarters of Argentina boils with wrath at
each Nazi affront; yet Spanish agents slip in and out of the
country almost unnoticed. In the frequent arrival of former
administrative officers of the various defeated and forgotten
Spanish republican governments there is a certain reserve, an
absence of bitterness and recrimination, that illustrates the
attitude of Argentina toward the civil war.

The confused elements making up both contending factions
in the Spanish struggle—the apparent lack of clear issues, of
popular heroes and popular villains—reflect strongly in the
minds of all Americans, North and South. As it is difficult to
get an intelligent argument about the Spanish Civil War in
New York or San Francisco, so is it difficult in Buenos Aires.
There is the dull feeling that follows any sort of tragedy
whose necessity and meaning are not quite clear. Falangism
insinuates itself into Spanish America by avoiding open battle,
by taking advantage of the lethargy of thought that has overtaken the partisans of the republic. In this way it overcomes
a real numerical disadvantage, growing stronger in the
stronghold of the enemy. This is a job that requires tact and
perseverance.

El Consejo de Hispanidad, the Hispanic Council, was conceived in this spirit. It is an agency designed to tighten cultural ties between Spain and its former colonies within the
Falangist conception. This council includes Spanish soldiers,
priests, artisans, artists, capitalists, students, professional men

—who form the intellectual hierarchy the Falange counts on to command respect abroad. Among these are such men as Manuel de Falla, the great composer now resting in Argentina; the Rev. Fr. Silvestre Sancho, rector of the University of Santo Tomás in Manila (if the Japanese have left him undisturbed); José Ortega y Gasset, author of *The Revolt of the Masses*. A great many of them allow their names to be used as members of the council in the interests of extending Spanish culture and keeping it alive throughout the world. They would hotly deny a part in the propaganda of Falangism. For example, De Falla is convinced he is helping to hold the tradition of Spanish music in the hearts of Spanish-speaking people. Others believe they are working to maintain intact in the minds of men the golden words of Calderón and Cervantes, or the rich brush strokes of Goya and Velásquez, or the tradition of the Cid Campeador or the overblown beauty of the Andalusian *romería*.

In the new battle for the world there is no weapon so subtle or so effective as culture. In the alliance of English-speaking nations against Germany, who can judge how much of the persuasive force for the common cause is enlightened selfishness and how much an instinctive gathering about an old familiar standard? New Yorkers meeting casually in Montana will become fast friends in a matter of minutes. An American and a Canadian will make common cause if attacked in Tibet. "He talks my language" is the clearest reason for sympathy and friendship. If Spanish America can be brought back to Spain by the appeal of common culture, the labors of Cortès and Pizarro will be paralleled in modern times by an office full of smart clerks.

One of these smart clerks is José María Pemán, a handsome gentleman in the Latin manner and distinguished in a mild way through authorship of a half-dozen books full of mysticism. José María arrived in Argentina in June, 1941, and proceeded from cocktail room to lecture platform in a flutter of local literary excitement. At first his talks were without much point, but full of nicely expressed longing for the return of Argentina to the Spanish fold. José María concealed well his inner disdain for the crudities of Argentine speech, only skirting the subject in a lecture in which he traced the "current variations" in the language of Old Castile as practiced in the new, rough countries. Almost holding his nose, José María made the grand tour, winding up in one of the largest auditoriums in Buenos Aires under the auspices of the Argentine Academy of Letters and selling Falangism. On his return to Spain he was showered with honors, as they used to pass out plaques and silver cups to the winning sales team at a national convention of automobile salesmen in Cleveland or Chicago.

Another smart clerk is Benito Perojo, Spanish motion-picture director, who sailed from Lisbon February 19, 1942, bound for Buenos Aires and a Spanish Argentine movie rapprochement. He told the Associated Press at Lisbon that he was going to "intensify cultural ties between Spain and Argentina through the film industry." He was invited to the New World by the Argentine Ministry of Public Instruction.

All of these enterprises are legitimate. Their danger to America lies in the fact that Spain is at the moment in the hands of a man who is in the hands of Hitler, or dangerously close to it. General Faupel's Ibero-American Institute shines through every move of the Falange on the American continent. The very methods of penetration used by Falangist Spain are Nazi methods, down to the system of utilizing blocks of Spaniards as focal points for organization and propaganda. The idea of forcing Spanish immigrants into Falangist groups by the threat of withholding notarial and other consular services is another Nazi inspiration translated.

Two Buenos Aires newspapers carry the burden of Falangist propaganda in Argentina: The *Diario Español* and the weekly *Correo de Galicia*. The daily is openly pro-German; it receives a cash subsidy from the Banco Germánico. It is aided by the Transocean, Stefani, Domei, and Havas news agencies. Nevertheless its circulation is small; it exists by the publication of Falangist propaganda booklets circulated among families of the Spanish colony. The *Correo*, or *Galician Mail*, is the work of Señor Lence, a personal friend of General Franco and a journalist of high quality. The *Correo* prints about 25,000 copies, and is the official Franco organ in South America. The Falange in Argentina also produces a monthly magazine, *Orientación Española*, which goes to all party members and wherever else it may "do some good." It is similar in appearance and contents to the magazine *Spain* distributed in 1940 throughout the United States to newspaper editors and others who might conceivably influence public opinion.

Wherever Falangist propaganda in Argentina follows the cultural channel it finds easy going. Where it loses its head and tries to bludgeon Spaniards and Argentines into accepting Franco and Company at face value it falls flat. The Falangist chiefs have accordingly learned to confine the direct appeal to party members trained to accept it. That may explain the comparatively small circulation of the frankly propagandistic *Correo* and the tremendous audience reached by Pemán and Perojo and the other traveling salesmen for the Golden Age of Spain.

When Spain emerged in 1939 as a fascist state policed by Italian divisions and German tanks and planes, the Nazi mind was not long in grasping the possibilities of using the mother country in America. While Germany was busy creating and holding together "Aryan minorities" throughout Brazil, Argentina, and Chile, it was prodding Spain to keep alive the Hispanic sentiment in the hearts of Spaniards in the same area. Germany reasoned that a Spanish America linked closely to Franco might serve Nazi purposes better than a Spanish America dabbling in Roosevelt democracy.

The Falangist influence throughout the Latin American republics now emerges as the most serious obstacle to what we call Pan-Americanism. In Buenos Aires, Rio de Janeiro, Montevideo, Lima, and Havana, where Franco was able to open Embassies following his triumph in Spain, his agents have subtly and effectively fought the idea of a United America. A representative of Franco at a meeting in Cuba had the courage to make the statement that "Cuba must place itself again under Spanish dominion." There can be little doubt about the Nazi sponsorship of the Hispanic America campaign in opposition to the idea of an America bound to protect itself from whatever external aggression. In one of his many speeches, General Faupel said:

The Pan-American idea is a perfidious invention, and it is necessary to oppose it with the idea of a Hispanic America. The countries of South America and Central America are close to Spain, not to the United States.

Again, in the *Lokal Anzeiger* he made the statement:

The United States spreads its poison gas insidiously over South America. The Ibero-American states must reject any idea of collaboration with the United States, which has nothing in common with South America and which bears the name "America" only by accident. The roots of the Ibero-American states reach toward Europe, because the Spanish and the Portuguese first arrived on their shores as conquerors and then the Italians and Germans as bringers of the arts of peace.

General Faupel learned enough about the Latin mind as professor in the Argentine War College, as inspector general of the Peruvian Army, and as Ambassador to Francoist Spain, to know that pride of race is a weapon that never fails where

Spanish is spoken. From the Nazi point of view a great deal of credit is due the General and his Institute for the Argentine blockade of the Lima and Rio de Janeiro conferences.

It is inconceivable that Spaniards in their right mind should expect to re-create the American empire of Charles V, yet the publicly announced program of the Falange reads:

We have the will of Empire. We affirm that the historic destiny of Spain is the Empire. We claim for Spain a pre-eminent place in Europe. We do not support international isolation or foreign interference. With respect to the Hispanic American countries we favor a unification of culture, of economic interests, and of power. Spain points to its place as the spiritual axis of the Hispanic world in support of its claim to pre-eminence in the great universal enterprises.

Farther along, the program says:

Our armed forces—on land, on sea, and in the air—will be big and powerful enough to assure Spain at all times complete independence and the rightful place that belongs to it in the world.

Later it says:

Spain will again find its glory and wealth by the routes of the sea. Spain must aspire again to become a great naval Power, for battle and for trade.

Serrano Suñer, chief of the Falange and formerly Franco's Prime Minister, presided at the founding of the Fascist-American Federation in Barcelona and shortly afterward of the Consejo de Hispanidad. At the first ceremony he called on all Americans of fascist thought to join the cause. At the second, he said:

Spain knows from experience what it costs to discover a world. In order to rediscover it the Hispanic Council will be no less generous in expense. We will put everything we have into this enterprise; but let it be well understood that this time Spain is not disposed to allow other countries to take advantage of the discovery for the benefit of ideals other than those that by divine gift belong to Spain and to Hispanicism. The Hispanic Council will restore the unity of conscience of all those peoples who make up the Hispanic community.

Serrano Suñer has thus conjured up the Council of the Indies that ruled the greater part of the New World for centuries until it drove its victims to desperation and revolt.

Although people laugh at these bombastic speeches in Latin America and blame them on the political necessities of Franco in Spain, nevertheless they have been followed by ample action. Falangist penetration into the key states of Spanish America is no laughing matter. The propaganda of Falangism appeals to two types of Spaniard: the wealthy and the bureaucratic. It offers discipline for the masses; security of property or the equivalent for the natural leaders; protection against atheism, liberalism, and kindred foreign devils; a sense of the glory and the destiny of the race; preservation of rigid marriage customs that keep the family intact and women in their place; a place in the New Order when it triumphs throughout the world. This appeal when properly sugar-coated is as valid for Spanish Americans as for Spaniards—perhaps more so as pure propaganda, because the Spanish American lacks the experience of its operation.

With true Spanish tact, the Empire idea has been soft-pedaled in the Falangist propaganda used abroad. The over-bubbling of the Spanish diplomat in Cuba is an exception. The smart Falangist agent in Argentina does his best to foster the ideals of his organization under the guise of preserving Spanish culture, without ruffling patriotic feelings. He does what the Nazi agent does: He whips his own nationals into line and tries to encourage the organization among Argentines of nationalist groups inspired by the Falangist idea. Falangism is like Nazism and Fascism; it is a purely opportunist program employing the slogans that sell best. It works with any other outfit that offers it something. It worked with the Communists when the Berlin-Moscow pact was in effect. It works with the Japanese now that the Berlin-Madrid-Tokyo agreement is operative. If the Seventh Day Adventists seize a part of the world and offer it a working agreement next week, the Falange will be hand in glove with Adventism before you can say "Santiago de Campostela."

You can call Falangism inconsistent, an anachronism, juvenile, and broke. But backed by official Spain it is the greatest single threat to the unity of the American nations.

CHAPTER VIII

THE FASCISTS: THE LITTLE BROTHERS

ITALIAN Fascism is like a big growling yard dog that bars the way to the postman, then wags his tail and licks his hand when he reaches the steps. In Italy in 1939 I watched the fierce legions of Mussolini swinging past the Palazzo Venezia on their way to conquer the world—or that's what it said in the script. It has become the fashion since to make jokes about the Italian armies. I watched that same month hundreds of columns of white-smocked youngsters marching away to summer-school camps shouting in unison: *"Duce! Duce! Duce!"* and singing their inspiring songs about the beauty of being in step, the beauty of being alive, the beauty of breathing the state-owned fresh air. Since those days when golden autumn hung over Tuscany and Liguria, the Romagna and the Valley of the Po, while Rome and Naples slept through almost unbearable heat—the last great autumn of Fascism with a capital F—something has happened to the Italian people. The newsreel look I see on the faces of Italian prisoners in Libya is not the look on the faces of the wine-soaked youngsters bound by third-class railroad carriage for the passes of Savoy the night of August 30, 1939.

Italian Fascism in Argentina has begun to wag its tail at the closer approach of the postman.

It is a mistake to read Fascism into the daily lives of the Italian settlers of the Western Hemisphere. Fascism is an exotic flower, outgrowth of a special condition brought about by the poverty and disappointment that followed the First

107

World War. It has never flourished in America. It is only when you speak of fascism with the small "f" and dissociate it from Italy that you begin to talk about something serious and universal—and then the chances are your neighbor doesn't know what you mean.

There are more Italians in Argentina than any other foreigners. About half have become naturalized Argentine citizens. Nearly half a million are still Italian citizens. Since they outnumber the Spaniards, the Basques, the Germans, the Central Europeans, and the rest, they might be expected to exercise a heavy influence in the country of their choice. They do—and mostly for the good. They give the Argentine stock a stability it never had before. They give Argentine politics men of talent and democratic aspirations. They till Argentine soil that otherwise would still be open range. They operate small businesses, get fat and marry off their daughters to the best young men in the block, or in the village. They like spaghetti, ravioli, the soups of Milan, red wine, and garlic, and they have taught all Argentina to like them. They have softened and corrupted the Castilian tongue until with a parallel infusion of Indian dialect it is the despair of the Spanish Academy. They have made the accordion the national instrument and music a national vice. Of summer evenings they fill the Avenida Costanera with lilting song that echoes out across the turgid river as once across the Bay of Naples from the Via Caracciola.

The largest part of Argentine Italians are not, however, from the Bay of Naples, but from the rugged north. They are taller, better-educated than the average Italian immigrant in the United States. Sicilians are few in Buenos Aires, Piedmontese many. They give the *porteño* his characteristic height and good looks. Thus northern Italian blood is 35 per cent of the blood of Argentina. The comparative prosperity of Italians in the new land, their broad outlook, the natural love of liberty that drove them from the homeland in search of better opportunities in a free land—all these things have made the Argentine Italians difficult ground for the sowing of Fascist seed.

Nevertheless some of them have succumbed to the constant bombardment of propaganda from Rome. Since most of them are literate and most of them own or have access to radio sets, the Axis provides them with printed matter and with radio programs from powerful European stations. As water wears away rock, these words wear away resistance. Particularly, young Italians are susceptible after a number of years of intense propaganda. There is no democratic radio program interesting enough or powerful enough to break into the totalitarian monopoly of the air. The Axis says slyly that the democracies use radio to make money but "we use it to make more totalitarians so that democratic money will be no good."

Centers of Fascist propaganda within Argentina are the Consociazione Italiana (formerly the Fascist party and the Dopolavoro); the Associazione Argentina Pro-Italia; the Italian World War Veterans' Association; the Dante Alighieri Society; Italian hospitals; Italian schools; the publications *Il Mattino d'Italia, La Patria degli Italiani* and *Terra d'Oltramare* in Italian, and *Oiga!* in Spanish. These are watched over by the Federazione Generale delle Società Italiane. Official Fascism is bound up, too, in *El Pampero,* which counts many Italian Fascists on its editorial staff, although it purported at first to be an Argentine newspaper. Members of the executive committee of the Consociazione are the recognized leaders of Italian Fascist society in Argentina. Among them are a millionaire highway contractor who is Knight of the Order of Malta and Commandatore of the Italian Crown; the manager of the vermouth company which does its biggest business with the United States; the richest Italian in Argentina, worth 100,000,000 pesos and director of so many industrial and banking concerns that he has lost track of them; the editor of *Il Mattino d'Italia*, former violent Fascist Storm Trooper from Turin; a San Francisco newspaperman of Italian name who delivers lectures on "The Decadent United States." The propaganda waxes and wanes with Italian enthusiasm for the war—which in turn depends on how things are going on the battle fronts.

The Fascist party itself was dissolved but, acting on Nazi inspiration, reappeared in other forms, chief of which is the Consociazione. There are in addition cultural groups, sports clubs, and target-shooting clubs busy with the work of Fascism.

The Italian secret police, OVRA, is attached to the Italian Embassy, thus escaping interference from Argentine officials. Its chief is a minor employee of the Italian consulate in Buenos Aires—another trick learned from the Nazis. In the palmy days of Fascism there was nothing the Gestapo could teach the OVRA, but times have changed.

In December, 1940, when it appeared to Italy that the war would soon be over if America could be kept out, there was organized in Rome the CAO, designed to use Italian Americans for sabotage, propaganda, and every possible kind of confusion. It was reorganized six months later to operate in North America and South America in independent units. The idea had been tried out in Paris, where the Italians worked effectively for the general internal breakdown of France. Of course the entire program was Nazi-conceived and Nazi-directed. In the United States it was supposed to scuttle the armament program through labor strikes, to spread isolationist sentiment, and to lower morale in the armed forces. In South America its program included shipping sabotage and the encouragement of local resentment against the United States.

It is clear that in spite of the best of intentions, the Italian ideological penetration into America has followed the course of the Italian military penetration of North Africa and the Greek Peninsula. Italian Fascism in Argentina has been reduced to third place. The Nazis and the Falangists are more active and more effective. Only in one field do the agents of Fascism hit pay dirt: the military, naval, and civil diplomats of Italy in Argentina are socially successful and, being socially successful, they plant the word-of-mouth propaganda of the Axis where it will do the most good—or harm. Nothing succeeds in Argentina like charm, and Italian diplomacy has been blessed with more than its share.

Gradually as the grim game has worked itself along through the years from 1938, Germany has learned what it must do for itself in Argentina and what it can depend on from its companions in the New Order. It has itself provided the trained man power, the initiative, the technical and philosophical brains, necessary for penetration. It has called on Spain to make the racial and cultural appeal needed to disarm the victim. It has had to be content with a lot of promises and not much action from Fascist Italy. But that doesn't exhaust the roster of Germany's allies. There are the Ukrainians, the Hungarians, the Baltic people.

There are 220,000 Ukrainians settled in Argentina, Paraguay, Uruguay, and Brazil—all densely placed in the same geographical arc that represents the axis of German settlement in South America. They are the immigrant type, slow-speaking, slow-thinking, slow-acting, but good solid agriculturists. Because of the simplicity of their mental processes they are easily led by the priesthood and a few intellectuals. Following closely the differences in ritual, in liturgy, and in language that mark life in the Ukraine, each South American settlement, however small, has its own national Church and its own priest or priests. The Ukrainian priests are fanatic nationalists, and their devotion to the Church comes second. The Ukrainian schools in Argentina are taught by priests and nuns for the most part, although sometimes by lay scholars.

Since the hopes of nationalists for an independent Ukraine lie entirely with a German victory in Europe, a powerful and solidly knit community is at the command of the Nazis. Only the Communist Ukrainians, who believe in the political status quo of the homeland, stand in the way of unanimity. Intrigue, espionage, and military action are bread and butter to the men of Central and Eastern Europe. It should be expected, then, that the Ukrainians of South America would be up to their ears in the Nazi program. The three organizations that embody all this fierce ferment (so strange in a great land of peacefully flowing rivers from the tired jungle to the sleeping sea) are: Proswita; Widrozdenie; Sojuz Hetmanskich.

The first, Proswita, is a cultural and social society. Its influence is tremendous. Its motto is "Before Everything an Independent Ukraine." It publishes a weekly paper, *Ukrainskie Slowo*. Its principal task is to keep alive the language and the customs of the Ukraine in the new land. It had on January 1, 1941, a total of 18,000 paid-up members.

Widrozdenie means *"Resurrection."* It unites in a mystic, terroristic society the flower of fanatical nationalism. It is militant and military. It reveres the national heroes of the Ukraine, the Konowalec. It worships terrorists like Maciejko of Eastern Galicia. Members of this society are under strictest discipline; they are prepared for any orders. What they want is an independent Greater Ukraine under the protectorate of Nazi Germany. They were outlawed along with the Nazi party and the Nazi Labor Front in 1939. But like those two Nazi organizations they function still. At present they act through the Proswita; from this cover they direct the Ukrainian espionage and sabotage system. Despite being proscribed, they have never abandoned their fundamental organization, which is strikingly similar to the Ausland Section of the NSDAP. Their official paper is *Nasz Klycz* (*Our Cry*).

The third organization is Sojuz Hetmanskich Dierzawnikiw, a group of about 1,000 members subsidized by and answerable to Germany. It has its own organ, *Plug i Miecz* (*The Plow and the Sword*).

There are 40,000 Hungarians in Argentina. Within their colony the same forces are at work that make the Ukrainians a menace to the security of democracy in the Western Hemisphere—the forces of Nazi persuasion. The center of Nazi propaganda is the Hungarian press in Buenos Aires. Guillermo Magyari, editor of *Magyar Szo*, once worked for the rabidly Nazi German daily, *Deutsche La Plata Zeitung*. The German Embassy helps finance both. The second Nazi Hungarian newspaper is the *Magyar Elit*, influential enough to bring about the removal of the former Hungarian Minister in Buenos Aires, De Bobrik. The Minister failed to embrace the Nazi cause with sufficient enthusiasm.

There are 30,000 Lithuanians, who are among the poorest of all Argentine immigrants. Among them there is a great deal of Nazi activity, particularly since the occupation of their homeland by Russia. The Lithuanian weekly, *Zinius*, probably subsidized by the Nazis, constantly reminds its people that the occupation of Lithuania by Germany delivered the Lithuanians from Soviet bondage. Nevertheless, a great many intelligent Lithuanians in Argentina are far from sure that certain matters have been improved at home by a change of masters. Among them is Dr. Casimir Grausinis, Lithuanian Minister in Buenos Aires, who was considered pro-German and very likely was so until German promises of a free and independent Lithuania dried and scattered in the winds.

The Nazis do some work, too, among the Poles, and any other Central Europeans they can get their hands on.

Within the arc of the heaviest Nazi influence in the Argentine province of Entre Rios (Between Rivers), there are 60,000 or more Russians of German descent. The thoroughness with which Nazi Germany has dominated this hybrid group may be called typical of the Reich's methods and a warning to any who may underestimate the Ausland Organization. According to the Committee against Fascism in Argentina, there are only 700 German nationals in this territory, yet in two or three years the entire German-speaking population has been forged into blocks and cells by which they are held under Nazi discipline. These German Russians have been sixty years in Argentina. Most of them are Argentine citizens. Yet they belong to the Opferring (the Nazi collection agency which operates as a charity), the Nazi party (with thirty-five locals), Hitler Youth groups, and all the other Nazi organizations specifically or in spirit outlawed by the Argentine Government. They send their youngsters to eighty-five Nazi schools. They distribute among themselves all the Nazi propaganda current, hold Nazi rallies, and attend courses of instruction along party lines. They celebrate Nazi Labor Day, Adolf Hitler's Birthday, and all the other holidays in the Nazi calendar.

Ironically, these are the same people the Nazis used to call *Russenschweine* before they got orders from the Ausland Organization to bring them as quickly as possible within the fold. Now they are fed a special propaganda pap which honors them as of German blood and as Aryan conquerors fit to rule the debased and mixed peoples among whom they have settled. None of these Russians have ever seen Germany, yet they have been on the receiving end of so much effective propaganda that they have shed their natural reticence and become enthusiastic German Nazis. At the town of Lucas González they have their own magazine, *Der Russlanddeutsche*, printed in German by Jacob Rieffel. Herr Rieffel arrived in the colony in 1938, after fruitless wandering through the territories of heavy German population. He set up a small printing plant and left for Germany. He returned a sort of district Nazi chief, imported a staff of propagandists, and set up a modern print shop with the best equipment.

Villa Crespo and Concordia in the same province are Nazi headquarters. From them spreads a network of physical organization and a constant flow of propaganda of all kinds. In Villa Crespo the Cooperativa Agricola (Farm Co-operative) is credited with being the blind for Nazi activity. In Concordia, Arnold Fuhrmann has been the supreme chief since the district was organized by a supposed traveling salesman for a German commercial firm. So Nazified is Concordia that the traveler frequently stands astonished before store fronts smeared "Death to the Jews!" Concordia, situated on the Uruguay River, is the center of communications, the smuggling of arms and ammunition, and the movement of propaganda and agents between Argentina, Uruguay, and southern Brazil. So powerful is Fuhrmann here that Nazi agents wishing to cross the border and operate in Argentina can buy through him an Argentine police identification for the equivalent of $2 or $3. The Congressional Investigating Committee of Uruguay established this fact. In all this area of which Villa Crespo and Concordia are the center Nazis are so bold as to boycott those of their own kind who marry into Argentine families "to the everlasting shame of the race."

The Germans have brought the heaviest influence to bear on the German-descended Russians of this district, as they have upon the Ukrainians who also suffer the misfortune of having settled just where German colonization is heaviest. It is among those who ordinarily do not speak German that the propaganda of the Reich has had the hardest sledding.

It is easy to overestimate the Nazi influence among all the so-called allies of Germany at war, even among the peoples whose governments are the closest military collaborators at home. The same numerical majority of democrats and "indifferents" that plague the Nazi Germans in organizing the Argentine Italians and the Argentine Spanish is a handicap in dealing with the Rumanians and the Poles and the Lithuanians. Of the Ukrainians it must be said that they seem willing to follow nationalist leadership wherever it may lead them; at the moment it has led them Naziward. The Nazis have succeeded in buying newspapers and organizations, but it is another thing to buy the minds and souls of thousands of independent individuals who fled Poland and Hungary and the Baltic States and the Balkan countries to escape the heavy hand of militarism. Given a German victory in Europe and a few years of intensive propaganda through the channels already controlled by Germany, and these people will succumb, but it is too early to call them Nazi. The very fact that there are Nazi elements among them operates tremendously to the advantage of the Axis in Argentina. Not only does it add to Argentina's poorly concealed fear of Germany and German methods, but it is another element of confusion. There is nothing Germany wants in South America so badly as fear and confusion.

Willing or unwilling, Vichy France has been among the Nazi collaborators. Immediately he had Paris in his grasp, Hitler had also his heavy hands on the "first families" of Argentina. It has been said that never a sparrow chirps along the Bois de Boulogne without being heard on the Avenida Alvear. You could blindfold a Frenchman and set him down,

say, on Santa Fé at about the cross street Carlos Pellegrini
and he would look for the Eiffel Tower first off. With the
power of life and death over every human being in Paris,
the Gestapo did not find it hard to persuade its way into
Buenos Aires through the French colony. Officially, the
French diplomatic and consular representatives refrained
from political activity. They dared not oppose the Nazification of South America by word or action. Many of them quit
their posts and endured poverty rather than continue at their
jobs and peddle the pro-Axis propaganda funneled to them
through the home office. But many of them, with that practical sense that makes them akin to the Argentines, stuck to
their meal tickets and did what was expected of them. When
the world finally passes judgment on the role of France in
the present war, its position in Argentina will be viewed in
that light.

Abel Gance, the French film-producer, left Vichy with a
staff of assistants and technicians in February, 1942. It is
hardly coincidence that the Spaniard Perojo sailed from Lisbon the same month. Both were bound for Buenos Aires for
the same purpose: to reorganize the Argentine film industry
along European lines. The artistic superiority of French motion pictures makes them universally acceptable. The tremendous racial and cultural propaganda inherent in Spanish motion pictures exhibited in Spanish America appeals to the
propaganda offices of Madrid, Berlin, and Rome. Hollywood
pictures are full of liberal ideas; they are anathema to the
Axis. Besides that, they extol the virtues of the United States
in the most effective manner. It is obvious why every effort
must be made to squeeze North American films out of South
America.

Count Jean de Bravoura spent a year in Argentina and
Brazil as advance man, preparing the ground for Gance and
Perojo. The French film star Daren organized a French film

company in Buenos Aires. French business houses in Argentina were supposed to finance this project, but Gance was heralded as on the pay roll of the French Ministry of Information. There is no reason to suppose that just at this moment in the history of France it had become important to establish a French motion-picture industry in Argentina. It was too much like the Japanese Government's sending a staff of Shinto missionaries to spread the culture of the East among the Alaskan Eskimos. The whole project was directed from Berlin, and it smelled remarkably like something from General Faupel's Ibero-American Institute. It not only included the production of native films tending to reveal delicately the advantages of social discipline but it also provided a better outlet in Argentina for the pictures produced in Germany, Italy, and Spain for propaganda purposes. Spanish pictures pointing at the heroic sacrifice of Falange heroes in "the defense of the sacred Motherland against the Soviet Beast" would lead Argentine movie audiences to believe that Franco and his boys were out looking for the Holy Grail.

But if France has been used for Hitler's purposes in the Western Hemisphere, it is not because Frenchmen want to be so used. As in the case of the Spanish and the Italian population, the Argentine French will resist the pressure of the Axis as long as the course of the war gives them any hope of a victory for the democratic peoples.

With the outbreak of war in the Pacific, Germany acquired a new, capable, fanatical ally—Japan. Although there are less than 5,000 Japanese in Argentina, there are nearly 250,000 in near-by Brazil. Like the Germans, they discipline themselves and maintain their national character. Like the Germans, they despise the people among whom they settle, but flatter them when it seems politic. Like the Germans, they spread cultural propaganda. Kokusai Bunka Shinkokai scatters lectures and prints and cloying little bits of poetry all over Buenos Aires. As the official Japanese culture bureau it decorates windows with Samurai dolls and with railroad posters picturing the beauties of Kyoto of the Thousand Temples, Nara the Chaste, Mt. Fuji from the harbor at Yokohama, and so on and so on. Nothing is said about the detailed military maps, the plans of highways and bridges and airports, the off-coast soundings and other nautical charts that Japanese tourists, fishermen, farmers, pants-pressers, and chauffeurs have been carrying back to Nippon for lo, these many years.

Under the careful eye of Dr. Alberto Pugnalin, former Argentine Minister to Tokyo, the pocket magazine *Oriente y Occidente* publishes the most rapturous accounts of Japanese civilization, the most brittle fragments of Japanese art and literature, alongside learned articles on naval warfare written by Japan's most illustrious admirals. Throughout the magazine there is the implication that the United States is a doomed nation, while the Rising Sun has just begun to make its warmth felt among the happy people of the Coming Dispensation. This theme is repeated at lectures on Japanese subjects given to local study groups. It is repeated in Domei news dispatches channeled through the newspapers under the domination of Transocean.

The Japanese point of view is: With the development of transportation and communication the world has shrunk until it can now support only two or three dominant nations or groups of nations. One of these will be the Greater Asia Co-prosperity Sphere, which will include the Indians of North and South America (originally Asians). Japan is now fighting to control Greater Asia and help it realize its destiny under capable leadership. During or at the end of the war Japan will emerge as one of the World Powers. The leaderless people of the world (now mostly democratic) will be directed by the emergent nations whose compact racial, cultural, and religious antecedents make them homogeneous and effective. The vassal industrial states without unified purpose, mixed of race and background, are bound to lose out in the remaking of the world.

This creed explains the amazing contempt in which Japan holds China, Russia, Great Britain, and the United States, and the audacity with which Japanese agents have surveyed and sized up Latin America for future operations should they become necessary. Brazil rounded up some Japanese "farmers" in the state of São Paulo in March, 1942, and found among them General Yoshii Tonogawa. Two weeks later they arrested a dentist, Ichiro Lhimuzu, with complete maps and aerial photographs of Rio de Janeiro. These are only two of hundreds of Japanese agents seized by the Brazilian authorities in the past months.

In Buenos Aires the Japanese organized the CACIP, a trust which in short order froze Argentine fishing companies out of business. This company now controls the Argentine fishing industry. Its Japanese crews worked for so little that it was supposed the company was subsidized from Japan. Since the Argentine Government ordered aliens off ships operating offshore, the company has been able to recruit Argentine crews. Two of the CACIP ships are modern 800-ton trawlers capable of 12 knots and seventy days' cruising. They put to sea February 27, 1942, in defiance of the Argentine demand to place observers aboard. They cruise the coast of Patagonia, where the Argentine naval bases are located. They fish close to the British-owned Falkland Islands and the Strait of Magellan, where they could be of service to Axis Naval Intelligence. From these ships, the *Presidente Mitre* and the *Presidente Roca,* it has been possible for Japanese naval men to obtain charts of the Argentine coast better than any in possession of the Argentine authorities. The Brazilian newspaper *O Globo* learned that the populous Japanese colony near Santos was operating a fleet of launches, three of them new and powerful. These not only charted the Brazilian coast, but also unloaded contraband from Japanese ships.

Most of the Japanese espionage activities have been common knowledge in South America, as were their similar activities off the Pacific coast of North America, in the Philippines, and in the Netherlands East Indies. But the Japanese have the valuable asset of a humility which is often mistaken for stupidity or lack of enterprise. In Buenos Aires the Japanese own two-by-four cleaning and dyeing shops. In Peru and farther north they are mostly barbers. In Brazil they farm. It is difficult to associate these timid little brown men with military prowess. Years ago it was difficult to associate them with commercial prowess, and as a result they flooded South America with cheap bright made-in-Japan goods and thus gathered in the money and the materials with which they are now fighting.

With the Japanese, as with the Germans, there is no question of the duty of the individual. Every male is a soldier, every woman a producer of soldiers. In Argentine and in other Latin American republics the Germans and the Japanese make up the nearest thing to an army of occupation that diplomatic relations will permit. With the connivance of those elements of the European-born population attached to the cause of the Axis—the Ukrainians, the converted Poles, the converted or managed French, the Italian Fascists, the Spanish Falangists, the terrorized Rumanians, Hungarians, and Lithuanians—they have set up within Argentina a totalitarian state ready to function the moment world events make it practical. Counted with their allies within the native population, they make up a large enough proportion of the total to give pause to every intelligent Argentine.

CHAPTER IX

THE ROMAN CATHOLIC CHURCH

IN A CITY that speaks five or six languages to the square block, that prints its menus, its theater programs, and its notices in two to four languages; in a city whose men wear bloomers, skirts, trousers, sashes, slippers, boots, shoes, bowlers, Homburgs, panamas, black straw sailors, Saratogas, beanies, and fedoras; in a city that drinks Scotch whisky, Bols gin, vodka, anisette, Pernod, cane juice, vermouth, Cuban rum, Liebfraumilch, Tokay, champagne, sherry, Chianti briollo, grappa, and domestic wines; in a city where you can open your apartment window of a Sunday morning and hear a tango, a mazurka, a Viennese waltz, a polka, a jota, Benny Goodman's swing, or a piper's band; in a city whose bookstores display Turgenev, Upton Sinclair, Aldous Huxley, Enrique Larreta, Marcel Proust, Elinor Glyn, Gustavo Adolfo Bécquer, Daphne Du Maurier, Ernest Hemingway, Oswald Spengler, and Zane Grey; in a city whose theater crowds have their choice the same night of the *Ballet Russe, Pepe le Moko, Captain Blood, Maria de la O,* the Yale Glee Club, *The Parson of Panamint, The Return of the Spider,* or a Communist vs. Nationalist street riot—in such a city it is hard to say where Nazi propaganda leaves off and the Argentine social revolution begins. It's even hard to tell where revolution leaves off and counterrevolution begins.

The world changes. Some of us think it changes for the better; some of us think things are going to pot. Among those of us who think things are going to pot are a good, solid proportion of the body politic who think they can stop evolution in its tracks. Professional radicals call these people reactionaries. Most of the rest of us call them sentimentalists. They are like the eccentric old millionaire with nostalgic memories of childhood in Indiana who has an outhouse built on the back of his estate. Sentiment for bygone days when the world was young and green takes many forms in many earthly pastures. In Spain it becomes the spiritual heart of Falangism. There it is the conviction that the good way of life was the way of Roderick the Goth kneeling in nightlong vigil in a chapel in the mountains of the north. In Spain the longing was for return to discipline and hardihood and to the passionate flame of young, militant Christianity, to the early Church and the hazards of the life of sword and Cross. This is not to assume that there were no economic, personal, international, or purely casual forces at work to engineer the Franco revolt in Spain.

The social revolution in Argentina is even more complex. It visions not only a return to the primary virtues of Gothic and Catholic Spain but to the colonial life of the Vice-Royalty of La Plata. Only this time, most Argentine nationalists think, the ties with the motherland will be spiritual rather than political. The Argentine nationalists want to have their cake and eat it. They want the discipline that has been lost, but they want to be independent of outside discipline. They want another tyrant like Rosas, and they want the kind of free, virile, dangerous life Charles Darwin saw when he visited the camp of the gaucho chief—or the kind of life W. H. Hudson wrote about so prettily. These are the nationalists who have property, or whose families once had property, and who expect to find themselves again the spiritual, military, and political leaders of a pastoral people. They forget that time marches on, that the pastoral life must disappear, that the make-up of the peon class has changed—

they forget a lot of things. Or if they remember them, they believe somehow that the new social discipline Hitler, Franco, and Mussolini have devised will replace the old and serve just as well.

Because Argentina is one of the most intensely Catholic countries in the world, it is customary to blame the Church for the spread of the Falangist idea through the Argentine aristocracy.

The Catholic Church in Argentina consists of the dioceses of Tucumán, Córdoba, Buenos Aires, Salta, San Juan de Cuyo, Paraná, La Plata, Santa Fé, Catamarca, Corrientes, Bahía Blanca, Azul, Jujuy, La Rioja, Mendoza, Mercedes, Rio Cuarto, Rosario, San Luis, Viedma, and Resistencia. Of these only two or three are metropolitan; the rest are of the pampa, the jungle, and the Andean foothills, where the genius of colonial Spain has left an ineradicable print on the minds of men. In the clean air of the open country the Church is as serene as on the crags of Montserrat, untouched by the tainted breath of liberalism stealing through the city's streets and alleys. Among the cloistered orders far from the distraction of yeasting populations there lives in its purest state that wonderful mélange of mysticism, piety, business sagacity, administrative genius, and showmanship that like mankind itself survives miraculously, triumphant throughout the ages.

Where through childhood association, through a devoutly religious mother, through adolescent conviction, or through intellectual appeal from the pulpit the leaders of Argentine thought have been heavily Catholic, that influence has borne fruit in the political and social life of the nation. But there have been Argentine men of thought and action without the slightest affinity to the Church. The Church itself, as in every country in which it enjoys an official or semiofficial status, has a long history of victories and defeats in the privy chambers of state. The Argentine constitution only roughly defines the line of demarcation between those things that are Caesar's and those things that are God's. As a result there is almost constant friction between the Holy See and the Government of the republic over the appointment of cardinals and bishops, for instance. The Papal Nuncio in Buenos Aires is as busy as the steering committee at a Democratic convention. Only a generation after the constitution was adopted Argentina abolished the teaching of religion in public schools.

There are many other examples of intellectual independence on the part of the temporal authorities—a most irritating independence in some cases. It is difficult for a Protestant North American to understand the subtlety of the relationship between Church and State in a country like Argentina. It's something like the relationship between a man and his mistress just at that point when a lawyer is trying to establish common-law marriage. While the Church's best statesmen are dealing with the problems of this delicately balanced relationship its priests baptize the babies, minister to the sick and the dying, marry the young couples, and strive mightily to save as many immortal souls as possible. The result is that the subsecretary of the Foreign Office who finds it his duty to uphold the state's contention against the demand of the papal representative goes to the parish priest for solace.

Catholicism is the "official" religion of Argentina, yet any other denomination or sect can establish congregations anywhere in the land. There is complete freedom of worship and freedom of thought. Although the ritual of the Church is prominent in every state ceremony, formal relations are often strained between those taking part. All these things are understandable only to a Latin Catholic. The Church is a part of life, but since when is life a smooth course?

It is customary to talk about the attitude of the Church toward some public problem or other as if the Church were

an individual or a political organization. The Church itself
has only one attitude: that it must survive for the everlasting
benefit of mankind. And that is only implied. It may not be
strictly accurate to say that the Catholic Church in Argentina
is antidemocratic, but it can be said that most of the clergy
are skeptical about democracy. It follows that most of the
Argentine aristocracy are skeptical about democracy, since
that is the class which attends church most regularly and ab-
sorbs the attitude of its spiritual advisers. Since the policies
of the Argentine Government are in the hands of the aristocracy, it often appears to the outside world that the Church
directly dictates Argentina's course in international affairs. It
could better be said that the mental attitude of Argentina's
ruling class transmitted into international policy was developed by the Church.

Among the orders most clearly antidemocratic and most
heavily influential in creating a pro-Axis atmosphere in Argentina are: (1) The Verbo Divino, a German congregation
most active in the Misiones jungle; (2) the Sagrada Familia,
founded by Father Berthier, a Frenchman; and (3) the
Frailes Redentoristas, mostly Germans operating in the
Chaco. Among the Dominicans, the Cistercians, and the
Franciscans there are many Spanish and Italian priests bitterly antidemocratic because of the experience of the Church
in the Spanish Civil War. Priests who come from Europe
have bumped against Spanish and Italian Freemasonry and
they have been propagandized into associating these organizations and their methods with British and North American
Freemasonry—or even with the entire Anglo-American
civilization.

Catholic leaders familiar with the situation of the Church
in Germany and in the countries overrun by the Germans,
particularly Poland, Belgium, and France, were appalled to
find the clergy in Latin America had assumed a definitely

antidemocratic tone by mid-1941—and had been sold the idea that Nazi Germany was really engaged in a crusade to save civilization.

Catholics of intelligent foresight organized the CIP (Catholic International Press) in an effort to replace Nazi propaganda in the Catholic-minded press of South America with an honest news report of the course of world affairs. Father Félix Morlion, a Belgian priest, toured Brazil, Argentina, Chile, Peru, and Ecuador studying the situation of Catholic sympathies and laying the groundwork for the reception of CIP. This was in July-September of 1941.

Father Morlion found church leaders in Argentina, Chile, and Ecuador particularly blind to the persecution of Catholicism by the Nazis, and many of them actually teaching that Britain and the United States, as materialistic, godless, Freemason democracies, were a great menace to the future of Catholicism while Nazi Germany in a sense represented the survival of an orderly civilization. The part of Germany in the conquest of Spain for Franco laid the groundwork for this attitude, and subtle Nazi-Falangist-Fascist propaganda effectively spread throughout South America by thoroughly organized efforts maintained it and fed it. He found that the encyclical of Pope Pius XI, "*Mit Brennender Sorge*," was actually being interpreted in church circles as a message that Germany "might become the defender of Christianity." Father Morlion found that the great mass of people were prodemocratic in the countries he visited, but that the clergy and the youth taking an active part in church affairs were prototalitarian.

The smartest piece of propaganda work discovered was the Servicio Europeo de Información Cultural (SEIC), sent out from Berlin and purporting to be the voice of German Catholics. The language is clerical, and the "news" contents consists not of attacks on Britain but of notices of restorations of churches and development of theological studies, spiritual help to prisoners, and new cultural realizations in Germany and the occupied countries. Many parochial bulletins throughout South America printed these items in the happy faith that they were authentic. Actually, even the mailing lists were confiscated from offices of international Catholic organizations in Belgium, Holland, and France— and of course only a moment's reflection makes it apparent that news of any kind sent from Germany is sent by the Nazi propaganda center, which uses freely the names of Catholics who can't protest.

As the result of Father Morlion's study, the CIP set itself the task of proving through the dissemination of the facts of the case that Nazism is a pagan religion absolutely incompatible with Christianity—and that the deeply planted South American fear of being swamped in North American materialism is not borne out by the history of the Catholic Church in the United States. The review *Acción Católica* and some individual Catholics aware of the world situation worked desperately to overcome the already deeply entrenched Nazi-Falangist-Fascist propaganda. The visit of Father Morlion and other Belgian priests had a great deal of influence in intelligent Catholic circles.

Beginning the Lenten season in 1942, Cardinal Copello issued a pastoral which, considering the fact of a world in agony and a civilization fighting for its life, was a masterpiece of evasion of the facts. Ignoring aggression, systematic rape, murder, and starvation, ignoring the brutalization of millions caught in oppression and slavery, the Cardinal chided universities for teaching liberalism, women for drinking alcoholic liquors and for failing to wear sufficient clothing. Blandly passing over the question of guilt and the fact of deliberate attack, he set forth that the world was being punished for its sins. He called on the Lord for mercy. To many aware members of his own Church, it sounded like a man communing with his spirit while somebody burned down his house and killed his wife and kids. It is enough like the recent negative attitude of the Holy See to disappoint and irritate the beleaguered people of the democratic world, Protestant and Catholic alike.

The propaganda against what is weakest in democracy might under ordinary circumstances and in ordinary times exercise a healthy influence on our world. It is unfortunate that in seeming to ignore the agony of our fight for existence, our fight for the right to correct our own mistakes in our own way, Cardinal Copello has become an effective Axis agent in a war still being fought on many fronts by propaganda.

The Church is a property-owner, a large property-owner in most Spanish-speaking countries. Besides being the custodian of property, it is a receptacle for literature, for music, for tradition, for all the material and immaterial treasures of Hispanic life. It is like the Basque mother who has listened well as a child and in her turn imparts what she has remembered to her children. All this makes the Church conservative, so conservative that entire orders like the Jesuits have been exiled and proscribed for dabbling in social experiment, as in the Indian communes of the upper Paraná and Paraguay. Here again is the conflict between the individual priest, often human, keen, and genuinely interested in the sufferings of the individuals about him, and the Church as a continuing corporation plagued with administrative problems. As a property-owner the Church is afraid of social revolution, so afraid that, as in the case of Franco, it will back a counter-revolution if necessary. Perhaps it has good right to be afraid of revolution after its experiences in Russia and Mexico. As a custodian of the cultural treasures of the race (and for many centuries it was the only custodian) the Church is afraid of social revolution. As a going concern interested in perpetuating itself as shepherd of a wayward flock the Church is afraid of social revolution.

The formation of Argentine nationalism, if not the direct work of elements within the Church, must be considered an outgrowth of Church-sponsored insistence on the Hispanic tradition of social discipline. The underlying theme of the Church's most able preachers and nationalism's ablest exhorters is: The inner purity of the Spanish Catholic way of life and the Spanish colonial political method must be preserved against the anarchy and immorality of the Anglo-Saxon world, against Russian Communism and the pre-Vichy French slogan of Fraternity, Equality, and Liberty. To most of the faithful this seems to imply an acceptance of dictatorship as the alternative. It is becoming increasingly obvious that this is just what it is intended to imply. Certainly that is true in the cases of many nationalist leaders who aspire to be the Führers or if necessary the Quislings of Argentina.

Inherent in acceptance of the dictator idea is acceptance of Nazism. Almost all Argentine nationalists argue themselves into partisanship with the audacious shock troops of the New Order before they realize the contradiction between burning local patriotism and acceptance of the Nazi thesis of Nordic racial superiority over the "mestizo monkeys" of South America. Once the paladins of home-grown totalitarianism get caught in all these carelessly set ideological traps, they bluster their way out with screaming posters and street riots and pretend they have hardly heard of the war alleged to be currently in progress. One of the most ludicrous examples of illiterate nationalism jockeyed into a clown act by the Nazis is the speech delivered at a mass meeting on December 14, 1941, at the Plaza Once de Septiembre in Buenos Aires. Manuel Anselmo García, introduced as secretary of the

Unión Nacional Argentina and chief of the Social Argentino party, said:

It is laughable that democracy should be defended in the Hawaiian Islands. . . . The Spanish and the Italians colonized the New World. . . . England helped Chile in the Argentine-Chilean war, while the Italians helped Argentina. . . . Now the North Americans want to be our brothers. We don't accept them. We can't accept them, because we are Spanish and Catholic. The North Americans are not. Our forebears mixed their blood with the Indians of America; they built homes here and held the aboriginal population in respect. How was North America colonized? The English came to the United States dressed in silk shirts and fancy pantaloons.

Brother García blandly ignored the fact that Argentina exploited or killed its Indian population in colonial days, that Argentines still boast that their blood is "untainted" by Indian blood, that the Pilgrim Fathers lived hardships worthy of the best Spanish tradition while treasure-drunken Pizarro in Cuzco demanded a room full of gold from the Inca and cut his throat after the room had been filled. But Brother García and his confederates weren't interested in the facts of the case; they were interested one week after Pearl Harbor in stemming as rapidly as possible any sympathy that might develop among Argentine nationalists for a sister nation attacked by what should have been a common enemy. How much of the García drivel is the result of years of carefully directed propaganda, and how much was paid for in cash by the Falangists or the Nazis or the Fascists, is hard to say.

What is most startling to the casual observer in Argentina is that rightist mass meetings, printed journals, radio programs, and kindred public activities are tolerated by the Government, sometimes given police protection, while let two Communists meet over a glass of beer and they are whisked off to the jug for conspiring against the state. This is in spite of the equally startling fact that in Argentina the nationalists openly and frenziedly demand a revolution to modify the existing democratic processes of government, while most of the radicals of the extreme left talk softly of reaching the millennium through the orderly processes of the nation's existing institutions. It makes one feel like asking, with Lew Lehr, "Am I cwazy?"

CHAPTER X

SEED OF REVOLT

ARGENTINA'S revolutionary nationalist movement began in 1930 when General José Félix Uriburu seized the capital and became Provisional President. He was following tradition when he put an end to the liberal government of President Irigoyen by the most effective means at hand. He defied the constitution and nullified the operation of the nation's laws. The landowning class had begun to realize after a series of election defeats that majority rule can be distasteful when the wrong people are in the majority. The result was Uriburu, and with him the organization of a disciplined semimilitary group determined to keep authority in the right place.

At that moment when a formal organization growing up within the state declares itself to be the state, fascism is born. That is what happened in Italy, in Germany, in Spain, in Rumania. What we call fascism has come most clearly from puny bud to triumphant flower in Germany.

In 1923, when Adolf Hitler staged his comic-opera putsch and his beer-drinking companions battled the police in the streets of Munich, the Nazi organization was one of a hundred or more similar local movements throughout Germany, the inevitable result of depression, defeat, and dissatisfaction among German youth.

Nothing distinguished the sprouting Nazis from their contemporary centers of agitation until Franz von Papen, once military attaché in the United States, met Hitler, recognized his possibilities as a symbol of protest, and persuaded Hitler to seek financial support from the German industrialists, who were at that time looking for some method of stemming the threatening tide of socialization of German industries. Following the economic collapse in Germany as a result of the war, German heavy industry was forced to rely on government subsidies for its existence. As Socialist influence grew more powerful, particularly in the Weimar Republic, there was considerable agitation in the direction of halting subsidies altogether and forcing industry to surrender shares to the Government as a step toward socialization of industry, with the object of protecting the interests of the workmen. At that time Hitler made his bid for support of the industrial class; it was his good fortune that the industrialists were desperately in need of him, or someone like him.

A brilliant opportunist, Hitler, with a little coaching, succeeded in promising to industry the very thing it wanted, receiving in return enough financial backing to buy the influence, the propaganda, and the personnel to make his Nazi movement break into national prominence, and to overshadow and defeat all the contemporary protest movements based on principles similar or parallel to his. The Nazi movement grew up in Bavaria. Until the Von Papen conspiracy Hitler was the butt of German jokes, a foolish rustic of bizarre appearance, slovenly habits, and uncultured speech. Under the impetus of his new advisers, he moved out into North Germany to sell himself to the aristocratic class.

The writer has a close friend who heard Hitler speak to the leading social group of Dresden. Apparently it was the first time he had worn formal clothes. He appeared at the banquet in a dinner jacket, although the occasion called for evening dress. His hair was plastered back on his head with brilliantine. He nervously adjusted his tie, glancing self-consciously about him from time to time, obviously overawed and embarrassed by the brilliance of the company. When he began to speak, he fawned all over his listeners, promising them everything they wanted. My friend, then in his early twenties, had been persuaded by the popular emotionalism of the moment to join the Nazi cause. After hearing Hitler and realizing the intellectual and moral poverty of the man, he quit the movement in disgust.

At this time there were 7,000,000 unemployed in Germany, 70,000 of them university-trained professional men. Hitler promised them all employment. To give emphasis to his promise he used the money obtained from the industrialists, set up a national (Nazi) organization, and established centers where party members might obtain living expenses and clothing during the harsh German winter. The clothing was a cheap uniform, and the unemployed so helped thus became, perhaps unwittingly, the Storm Troopers who later spread terror throughout Germany. Actually they constituted an organized army of desperate unemployed men who were to be used to terrorize and control the working population of Germany in the interests of the industrial class.

During and immediately after the war the Jews in Germany had succeeded in largely occupying the professions. In order to obtain the very valuable support of the 70,000 unemployed professional men, Hitler had promised them that the Jews would be ejected from the professions and that they would be replaced by these same unemployed "Aryan" Germans. The reign of terror against the German Jews was inevitable if Hitler was to keep the confidence of his people and comply with his very definite promises to them.

It was apparent from the start that Hitler must have not only the support of the industrial class but the support of the militarist as well. Both militarists and industrialists believed they could liquidate Hitler the moment his usefulness to them ended. For that reason he was allowed to grow to his present stature. His fanatic and unintelligible creed was never accepted for a moment among the Junkers nor among any of the Germans of intellectual attainments, but they encouraged its imposition upon the minds of the simple Germans they wished to control, providing Hitler for that purpose with the complete propaganda machinery of Germany, a machinery organized so thoroughly and effectively as to stagger the imagination of those who did not see its possibilities.

Hitler liquidated every movement within the Nazi organization that might have liberalized National Socialism or in any way deviated from its harsh and fatal course. This is the explanation for the purge of Ernst Roehm and his companions, a purge ordered by Hitler's backers with the double purpose of eliminating Roehm and frightening other possible dissenters into implicit obedience.

The full Hitler story has, of course, not yet run its course. Hitler has not been liquidated. He is still absolutely essential in holding the German people spellbound and emotionally disciplined for the orders of their masters. When Hitler no longer serves this purpose, he will be eliminated.

Hitler is powerful as a fanatic expression of what the German people, after ten years of propaganda, believe to be their own will. He has been built into a legend by those who needed him. In turn he has shown himself shrewd enough and unscrupulous enough not only to do their bidding ruthlessly and without pity, but also to work on their own internal jealousies, rivalries, and aspirations until to some extent he controls them. The outbreak of the war gave him the tremendous personal advantage of the complete trust and leadership which a disciplined people at war must necessarily accord their Chief of State. It is this personal ascendancy of Hitler that makes interesting the question of how he can be liquidated when he has served out his usefulness to his masters.

Argentine nationalism grew in soil perhaps as fertile as that of postwar Germany, but it failed to produce at the right moment a Hitler. Uriburu himself encouraged organization of the Legión Cívica Argentina, which in more capable hands might have become the Argentine counterpart of the Nazi party. The Legión gathered in all the young, restless hotheads, organized them, drilled them for military duty, uniformed them in brown shirts, and gave them a standard to carry. In the palmy days of the Uriburu usurpation these Storm Troopers could be seen parading through the streets or standing armed guard at their headquarters. Thus was born out of the September Revolution the first organization dedicated to superseding the Argentine people. Had Uriburu or one of his lieutenants had the talents required for such a job, Argentina would have joined the totalitarian states in the same decade that produced Franco. What actually happened was that the possibilities of Argentine Fascism struck so many shrewdly ambitious men at the same time that in the fight for leadership that followed, the nationalists divided themselves hopelessly and ruinously. Directly from the Legión came Acción Nacionalista Argentina, Unión Nacional Fascista, and Partido Fascisto Argentino, whose symbol was the Roman ax and fasces.

The whole confused business today is divided into the Legión (now much less powerful); the Acción Nacionalista; the Alianza de la Juventud Nacionalista; the Federación Orientación Radical de la Joven Argentina (FORJA), which actually began as a radical counterpart to the Legión; the Afirmación Argentina, the Legión de Mayo, the Acción Gremial Argentina, the Partido Nacionalista Laborista, the Defensa Social Argentina, the Partido Nacionalisto Argentino, the Acción Liberadora, the Comité Fascista Argentina,

the Unión Nacionalista Argentina Patria, the Cruzada Reno-
vadora, and a dozen more local organizations hanging on the
fringe.

By 1934 the Legión had lost its grip through the ineptness or indifference of its original backers. It is even possible
to credit General Uriburu with intelligence enough to see
what he had started and conscience enough to abandon the
whole idea. With the descending arc of the Legión's history
and the mushrooming of its hopeful successors, the Alianza
de la Juventud Nacionalista grew into prominence and a
measure of power under testy old General Juan Bautista
Molina. The Alianza is a potential army of youngsters in
their twenties operated by older men patiently waiting the
hour of action.

Some of the members of the Alianza think they are patriots; some are simple opportunists; some are in the pay of
Nazi Germany. The Alianza uses any good slogans that seem
effective, usually falling back on the cry for liberation of Argentina from foreign capital. It is not to be supposed that
all members of the Alianza are young aristocrats with a stake
in preserving the estancia system of peonage. Nor are all of
them intellectuals afraid that liberalism will rob them of
their cultural heritage. As in all modern counterrevolutionary
movements, shock troops are recruited from the landless and
the jobless who can be persuaded that any change must be
for the better. In Argentina all these thousands of excitable,
rioting, proselyting, shouting youngsters are used by the tra-
ditionalists to offset the solid political advantage liberal and
radical elements have gained through universal suffrage and
the birth of a middle class. Most of the "first families" are
represented only in the Restauración, which has as its purpose the Falangist return to Spanish medievalism. It is a
mass attempt to ignore everything that has happened since
Ferdinand and Isabella.

All these clamoring factions have produced a sunburst of propaganda organs, among them *La Fronda, Crisol, Bandera Argentina, Clarinada, Voz Nacionalista, Combate, Nacionalismo Laborista, La Maroma, Choque, Oiga!, Camila, Nuevo Orden, Nueva Política, Fortín, El Restaurador,* and of course our old friend *El Pampero*. The prestige of the latter as a big daily newspaper under heavy German subsidy makes Enrique Osés the actual arbiter of nationalist affairs. Thus even those nationalist organizations which can't secure German financial backing are brought pretty well under Nazi control. In addition to the periodicals there is a heavy traffic in nationalist books. The propaganda army contains many of Argentina's most brilliant writers, among them Hugo Wast the novelist. Some of these writers have been to the United States, one of them on a scholarship financed by North American capital. They employ a superficial acquaintance with things *Yanqui* to make their stuff sound authentic. With the greatest of glee they have reported back to an astonished and frightened compatriot audience in turn peewee golf, the Big Apple, dog-and-cat hospitals, *Tobacco Road*, boogie-woogie, and working wives.

When writers formed the club known as ALA (Amigos del Libro Americano) to encourage the publication of books by Argentine authors, nationalist propagandists weren't long in taking it over and driving out those of democratic sympathies. Now its chief is Clemente Pellegrini, a publisher who is busy spreading nationalist and fascist propaganda through a widespread and effective book-distribution system. ALA is a successful concern under Pellegrini. The German and Italian Embassies place large orders through its luxuriously furnished and well-staffed offices. ALA reprinted Theodore Dreiser's book, *America Is Worth Saving,* and made it into Nazi propaganda by omitting certain passages. It published a Spanish edition of Virginio Gayda's book

What Italy Wants and distributed it through the Italian Fascist organizations in Argentina. Other busy outlets for this kind of propaganda are the Editorial Mazorca connected with *El Pampero,* and the Rosas Institute for Historical Investigations, which will investigate anything tending to prove Argentina should be under nationalist discipline and out from under the *Yanqui* yoke.

Nationalists, and particularly nationalist leaders, are perfectly aware that disputed purpose and disputed leadership have made them sterile. Although estimates of the man power of all nationalist groups combined run from 300,000 to 500,000—a dangerous proportion of the adult male population of the country—nationalism is an immediate danger only because of the propaganda it disseminates and the confusion of mind it produces. Three or four of the most energetic little Führers are trying to overcome the impasse by offering themselves as supreme leaders. Among these are Osés, General Molina, and a political derelict who calls himself Adalid but who is registered on the baptismal records as Manuel Fresco.

Molina was presidential secretary to Uriburu, with the military rank of lieutenant colonel. He was associated with the notorious Lieutenant Colonel Kinkelin, who first dressed up the Legión in brown shirts, trained them in the practice of arms, and taught them the Fascist salute. Molina always considered himself the rightful successor to Uriburu, but he lacked the energy and the sense of timing that distinguishes the true nationalist leader. After considerable intrigue he succeeded in getting control of the newly organized Alianza. In 1941 he threw the nation into an uproar by attempting to register himself with the Argentine Government as president of a Supreme Council for the entire nationalist movement. Fifteen collaborators made up the proposed board of control. Either the public outcry or opposition from other aspiring nationalist chiefs persuaded the authorities to deny Molina's application, and the old General's star seems to have set since.

Dr. Fresco, once governor of the province of Buenos Aires, has been kicking around political organizations for several years trying to get a hold. He might have succeeded had he been able to hide his limitless ambition. He was forced to organize his own party, Patria, with a subsidy of several million pesos he got who knows where. His nickname, Adalid, means "tribal chieftain." At about the time he adopted it, Osés began calling himself *Primer Camarada*—First Comrade. They both got their idea from Franco, who calls himself *El Caudillo*, which is Spanish for *Il Duce* or *Der Führer*. The fact that nobody in Germany, Italy, Spain, or Argentina doubles up with laughter at the spectacle of these grown men naming themselves like kids in a neighborhood gang indicates the intellectual poverty that has descended upon those unfortunate countries.

In muscling in on the Alianza, General Molina had to compromise with another aspiring nationalist leader, Juan Queralto, a short, insignificant fanatic filled with what he believes to be patriotic fire. Co-organizer of the Alianza with Queralto was Hector Bernaudo, who had been sent to Italy by the National Cultural Committee to study Fascism. Bernaudo brought back the results of his study and began applying Fascist principles to Argentine labor. He was instructor for the new Alianza, repaying the nation that sent him abroad to study by organizing to overthrow its institutions.

These propagandists, agitators, demagogues, and organizers have in mind the removal of the machinery of democratic government and the substitution of a dictatorship. But that is all they have in common. They range all the way from the almost idealistic FORJA tinged with share-the-land and share-the-wealth elements to the darkly Falangist Restauración bent on restoring pure feudalism. There are so many leaders and so many divergent purposes, such a heavy turn-over in organization and in printed periodicals, that the nationalist movement is buried in its own complexity. They have succeeded in confusing democracy by spilling demonstrators through the streets and plazas to shout down every constructive proposition put before the people. They have seized upon and worried every political mistake, every disclosure of graft, every unsavory by-product of popular government, until they have succeeded in identifying in many minds the national Congress with corruption and ineptness. They have operated as a destructive rather than a constructive force.

In the almost ludicrous array of attitudes struck by these homespun political Pagliacci it is inevitable that some should be repeated many times. One of the most popular of these is the cry for the return of the Falkland Islands. It seems that Great Britain dealt with various Argentine governments both legitimate and impromptu in the formative years of the republic. In the course of armed invasions, quarrels over repudiated debts, and other acts of international friction the British occupied and kept the Malvinas Islands, now called the Falklands. This naval base dominates the southeast coast of South America and the Strait of Magellan. A century later, the seizure of the Malvinas is still a fertile subject for nationalist speakers and writers—to the extent that a We Want the Malvinas Back society actually functions, prints booklets, and sends lecturers about the country. So popular is this appeal to the proud Argentine that many level-headed and essentially democratic leaders of national thought have been induced to subscribe to the society and its aims before they discovered it was being used as anti-British propaganda not for its own purposes but in order to help the penetration of Nazi Germany into Argentine nationalism.

Another popular theme used for nationalistic purposes is

the Return to Rosas. On a few hours' notice you can find half a thousand enthusiastic demonstrators for a Return to Rosas any one of whom would have been shot at sunrise by the tyrant himself if there were some way to conjure him back from the gaucho Valhalla. Get a half-dozen nationalists together to discuss Rosas over a table in the back room of a *boliche* and you will get an amazing divergence of opinion on who he was, what he advocated, and what his place is in history.

Herein lies the great weakness of nationalism. Some believe Rosas or his ghost will restore the straying colony of La Plata to the Spanish Crown; that fits in with the Falangist scheme. Some think he would like to give the country back to the Indians in the spirit of the Aprista movement of Peru. The aristocratic Criollo families are certain Rosas was for them and that reverence for his memory represents the longing of the Spanish landowner for his soil and the peon for his benevolent master. All of them in the nationalist movement want the strength and discipline only a dictator can bring them, but the aristocrats want at the same time a side agreement whereby they are guaranteed perpetual ownership as a permanent oligarchy. Meantime, Rosas says nothing from the grave.

It would take a Philadelphia lawyer to chart the movement of Nazi German influence in the Argentine nationalist hierarchy. There is no question that some nationalist associations were organized by the Nazis, financed by them, and directed by them. Toward the end of 1940, when General Molina was at the height of his enthusiasm for the Nazi military victory in Europe, he organized a luncheon celebration at the exclusive stone-fronted, dark-paneled Jockey Club for Ambassador von Thermann. In attendance were the cream of the nationalist leaders and most of the pro-Nazis prominent in public life. Among them were five generals, including Rawson and Jones, an admiral, three Senators, Dr. Fresco, and assorted characters. Nationalism includes everything from these shouting converts to totalitarianism to little patch-breeches committees meeting in the dimness of the Bacigalupi Wine Cellar in Rosario. Nazi Germany claims them all. Karl von der Eichen, Nazi chief, said:

We have in South America nationalist societies with party chiefs who apply methods of discipline analogous to those used by the National Socialists. When our powerful fleet and invincible Army and our triumphant Air Corps move toward South America, not only will we not encounter anybody to offer us serious resistance but we can count on those who will receive us with open arms.

From time to time frightened nationalist boys arrested in flagrant acts of rioting and terrorism have confessed to being led by Germans. As far back as 1934 members of the Legión Cívica under the command of Johann Wilcke, a Nazi employee of the Banco Germánico, were imprisoned for trying to toss a bomb into the Teatro Cómico, where a democratic play was being staged. As the nationalist movement has reached deeper and deeper into public life arrests for breaches of the peace have been fewer. In the university city of Córdoba a gang of nationalists succeeded in breaking up a meeting of the Radical party and wounding several with pistols. A little later two students were killed in a Fascist-inspired street fight. Similar acts of violence have occurred in every part of Argentina and in near-by Brazil, Uruguay, Paraguay, and Chile. It is the technique used by Hitler in Germany and in all the countries taken by the Nazis.

Argentina has been on the verge of armed revolt at least twice in the past two years as a result of this breakdown of self-discipline within the nation. In addition to those nationalists willing to lay down their lives for an ideal there is an active fringe of extremists ready for any kind of putsch that offers excitement and change. If Nazi Germany is as well organized and well prepared as is indicated by the thoroughness of its cell-and-block system within the German population of Argentina, these extremists of the nationalist movement constitute an auxiliary corps of shock troops of important proportions.

Equally important are the nationalists in public life who, influenced by anti-British and anti-United States propaganda paid for by Germany, directly or subtly influence official Argentine policy against co-operation with the other American nations.

In January, 1942, the republics of this hemisphere met at Rio de Janeiro for the purpose, among other things, of controlling subversive activities endangering all of us. The conference reaffirmed "the determination of the American Republics to prevent individuals or groups within their respective jurisdictions from engaging in activities detrimental to the individual or collective security and welfare of the American Republics." It recommended that suitable legislative measures and regulations be adopted to ensure that "the Governments of the American Republics control, within their respective national jurisdictions, the existence of organizations" of "subversive character," and that they "proceed to terminate their existence if it is established that they are centers of totalitarian propaganda." Argentina officially subscribed to this resolution.

The last week in January the Argentine Government created by decree of the Minister of the Interior a new department called the Sección Vigilancia y Represión de las Actividades Anti-Argentinas, under the direction of Dr. José Conrado Castells, Undersecretary of the Interior. Dr. Castells was authorized to arrange meetings of federal and local officers to co-ordinate all activity against the totalitarian fifth column. Accordingly, a conference was held at Mendoza the week of March 23. This conference resolved to exercise the strictest supervision over all foreigners, both immigrants and transients, recommending that constitutional guarantees be withdrawn in cases of illegal entry; it recommended strict control of associations and organizations composed of foreigners, and prohibited the transfer of land to aliens where such transfer might be prejudicial to national security; it recommended also strict nationalization of education. On April 2, Acting President Castillo dictated a decree approving the resolutions of the Mendoza conference. The provincial governments began taking individual action in accordance with the resolutions.

On April 11, by executive decree twenty-seven Argentine citizens and twelve aliens were arrested in Buenos Aires and eighteen individuals were arrested in Córdoba. All were "invited" to leave the country under the alternative of deportation in the case of aliens and transfer to remote sections of the country in the case of citizens. The courts upheld the legality of this decree under the terms of the state of siege already proclaimed by Castillo. Dr. Miguel J. Culaciati, Secretary of the Interior, advised the Buenos Aires press that action had been taken in this case on receiving the advice of the chief of police of the federal capital that the arrested men had been engaged in collecting funds through prodemocratic organizations for "certain belligerent nations" and in this manner cloaking Communistic activities which endangered the security of the republic. Among those arrested was Dr. Augusto Bunge, representative in the Congress for the Socialist Labor party and president of the Democratic Commission for Aid to the Democracies.

Argentina set in motion the machinery conceived at the Rio de Janeiro conference and used it to stop collection of funds for the Allied nations, on suspicion that some of those doing the collecting were Communists. National Deputy

Solari, secretary of the special investigating committee, screamed for similar action against Nazis, Fascists, Falangists, and Japanese bent on destruction of democratic Argentina from within, but he was discreetly ignored.

The entire nonco-operation program of Argentina as unveiled at the Rio conference was hailed with immense delight by Enrique Osés and *El Pampero*. For days the front page of the paper was plastered with news pictures of Acting President Castillo and the Argentine delegation to the conference. The Argentine flag was printed across the page in colors the day Argentina blocked the demand of the other American nations for unanimous repudiation of the Axis.

La Prensa, one of the world's greatest newspapers both as an example of journalistic excellence and as an influence on the minds of men, had already printed a pointed editorial which said:

Although in the case of Communism an endeavor is made to prevent disturbing plots, which are mostly imaginary, there exists on the other hand an extremist movement in the opposite direction which does not even take the precaution of disguising its activities, and openly abuses democratic institutions, working to pull them down and replace them with a system founded on principles which are antagonistic to the state and to individual rights. We would like to see the same energy displayed where this movement is concerned.

Under the terms of the state of siege, the Government rationed newsprint to the various dailies, and editorials of this kind disappeared.

In the difference between the attitude of the responsible, established Catholic *La Prensa*, representing orderly if slow social progress, and the irresponsible, nationalistic, Nazi-financed *El Pampero*, whose editors are always either on their way in or on their way out of jail, lies the strange story of Argentina caught in the ideological currents of the world.

CHAPTER XI

A NATION SICK

LIKE most Latin American nations, Argentina is vulnerable from within and from without. It is vulnerable to ideological penetration and to armed assault.

From a military standpoint, its long coastline is undefendable, and its jungle approaches lie open. With only a quarter of a million men in its army, all Argentina's tradition of armed valor is useless against a first-class Power. In modern times there is nothing a nation of 13,000,000 people can do against a big, determined, capable aggressor. Because of its cultural leadership and its superior economic condition, Argentina can influence its small neighbors, Chile and Paraguay —perhaps even Bolivia—toward a defensive alliance. Otherwise its flanks are unprotected. The Argentine Air Force is small, unable to get the equipment it needs. The Navy is efficient, but entirely inadequate to protect the long Atlantic shore.

Argentina needs modern motor highways before it can fully utilize modern defense equipment. Its communications system and most of its military branches are in the hands of German experts. The country lacks the industries necessary to maintain a long war. Its civilian population is unprepared technically and psychologically. The entire southern half of the country can be nipped off by a landing on the coast or an incursion from southern Chile, where German colonies make up the bulk of the population. In the upper reaches of the jungle rivers alongside Paraguay and Brazil, Argentina

148

barely maintains its sovereignty, even at the moment. There the German and Nazified Ukrainian settlers live their own lives and police themselves with little recourse to the institutions of the land.

Buenos Aires has been captured by gaucho bands, by revolutionists, by a small British force. The capital has no natural protection. Today it is a great, sprawling city like those in Europe that have fallen before the advance of land, air, and sea forces.

This complete physical vulnerability helps produce the state of mind that holds Argentina aloof from the more belligerent councils of its sister nations. Helped along by deliberate Nazi terroristic propaganda, particularly newsreel pictures of panzer armies wiping out small defenseless nations, the situation gives pause to the Elder Statesmen like Castillo who are aware of the constant public pressure for a declaration of solidarity with the rest of America. It makes Argentina think of self-protection at a time so many of the world's people are gambling their very existence for an ideal.

But the possibility of external aggression is the least of Argentina's worries. Its real danger lies from within.

The fact that General Molina after a career in the German Army and a tour as attaché to the Argentine Embassy in Berlin, after acting as military adviser to the German Embassy in Buenos Aires, can manipulate a pro-Nazi state within a state should and does give pause to the most casual observer. The fact that he is aided and abetted by other Prusso-Argentine militarists like General Basilio B. Pertine is enough to give a fair indication of what to expect in Argentina within the next few years. General Pertine studied in the Spandau military school, was military attaché in Berlin, followed the First World War from the German lines, was Minister of War in Argentina under President Agustín P. Justo. He is president of three important Argentine firms, Cardimex,

Agfa Tudor Varta, and Electro Metalúrgico Sema, and director of the powerful Siemens-Schuckert. All these concerns are German.

As late as 1941 high-ranking officers of the Argentine Army were being arrested and disciplined for conspiracy to overthrow the Government. Again, only lack of intelligent, determined leadership among nationalists saved the country's democratic institutions. During the winter three of the principal air bases were placed under armed guard and a dozen offices were seized in a dramatic raid understood to have prevented an uprising of the Army Air Corps. The nation was never informed of the nature of the danger that had been averted. There was simply the brief notice of the arrest of the officers and their subsequent release. No two government officials, no two private citizens, will agree on what happened. If, as the Administration maintained in newspaper interviews, nothing happened and nothing would have happened, it was ridiculous to grab the ringleaders and ground the Army's planes. If there was something afoot, it was dangerous to release almost without discipline those involved. What is most dangerous is that the people of Argentina were never told the truth about the supposed conspiracy.

The Argentine Army has been propagandized thoroughly by Nazi Germany and by those nationalist elements in sympathy with or on the pay roll of the Nazi Government. This propaganda has made a deep impression on many of the highest-ranking officers and upon hundreds of subalterns anxious for promotion and recognition under a military dictatorship. German instructors in military science, German advisers in the Army's technical branches, and German attachés have sold the ideals of Prussianism to many professional soldiers. German newsreels and short military pictures used ostensibly for technical instruction are shown to units of the Argentine Army just as fast as they can be rushed across the

Atlantic from the propaganda bureau in Berlin. These films have their effect.

As early as October 3, 1937, the Nazis were busy with the Argentine Army. On that date Bernard Kesser and his Deutscher Reichskriegerbund organized a solemn act as a memorial to the German Soldier. Immediately following the Argentine national anthem, the Nazi *"Horst Wessel Lied"* was sung. Speakers attacked democracy and personal liberty, praising Hitler as the coming St. George about to slay both dragons. Kesser himself attacked internationalism as the curse of mankind and pointed to the presence of many officers of the Argentine Army as proof that "Argentine soldiers love their country as we love ours." Actually in the audience were General Molina, Generals Guillermo José, Francisco Reynolds, Martinez Pita, Juan Esteban Vacarezza, Colonels Carlos von der Becke and Sanguinetti, Major Vitale, and Captain Sirito. Ostensibly gathered to honor the German dead of the last war, they were preparing their nation to accept the role of Germany as the champion of nationalism and social discipline in the coming war.

While Germans are busy trying to Nazify the Army the Falangists are making an effort to restore the prestige of Spanish soldiery. Since Falangism was forced on Spain by Moorish cavalry, Italian infantry, and German mechanized corps and across the dead bodies of the men and women of Euzkadi, Andalusia, Catalonia, and New Castile, it has been a hard job to sell Franco's soldiers as the Spanish prototype. Nevertheless there has appeared in Buenos Aires within the last year a dramatic motion picture *All's Quiet in the Alcazar* which restores in one tremendous, vicarious experience Spanish pride in Spanish arms. It is typical of the subtlety of Franco's people that this film skips very delicately over the ideological questions involved, presenting the heroism of the Spanish soldier without direct reference to Falangism.

While nobody is selling the Argentine soldier democracy but everybody is selling him a substitute, the Nazis have gone deep into the Argentine educational system so as to get the next generation ready for acceptance. So flagrant have become these abuses in the halls of the colleges and the universities that student riots and demonstrations are common. On April 7, 1942, Professor Carlos Astrada, noted for his totalitarian bias, appeared in the chair of contemporary philosophy at the faculty of philosophy and letters, University of Buenos Aires, and thus touched off a disturbance that required a strong squad of policemen. After an hour of excitement during which the students refused to hear Dr. Astrada, refused to leave the room, and refused to listen to the exhortations of the dean, twenty-three of them were carted off to jail in the Black Maria. (Intervention of the police inside the sacred precincts of learning is a scandal in Argentina, where education is respected beyond other earthly goods.)

Not all Argentine students have the strength to resist Axis propaganda. The Unión Nacionalista Argentina is made up of students of fascist tendencies. It was originally proposed as the Sindicato Universitario Nacionalista Argentino. It acts exclusively in university circles, where it places candidates for student offices and serves as the central clearinghouse for totalitarian ideas and actions. Many acts of violence between fascist and anti-fascist student groups have emphasized the thoroughness with which both learn their ideological lessons. Conflict is particularly pronounced at the University of Córdoba, which was graduating doctors of philosophy before the Pilgrim Fathers ate their first turkey dinner.

Under the governorship of the notorious Dr. Fresco, fascism was pushed into the schools of Buenos Aires Province. Teachers were obliged to accept an *Educational Guide* which implanted in the classrooms the antidemocratic spirit. Teachers were "encouraged" to join nationalist organizations "in the spirit of patriotism." The figure of Rosas was exalted, while children almost forgot the real heroes of Argentina: San Martín, Sarmiento, Moreno, Rivadavia, and Alberdi. Students weren't taught that Rosas bathed his country in blood for twenty years, that he made bonfires of books, that he turned the schools over to the Jesuits and withdrew state support from the universities as useless time-wasters, that he killed or exiled every real intellectual, that he revived the feudal system. They were taught that Rosas was the strong man sent by Providence in the nation's hour of need, like the dictators of Europe.

Evidences of the existence of a program designed to sap Argentina's democratic strength from within are plain, so plain that they march with the Army, go to school with the youngsters, speak from platforms and pulpits and through microphones, scream from downtown newsstands and from billboards. Documentary proof has been presented to the Government, concrete denunciations have been made in the public press, judges have pointed out the facts from their benches, books have been written about the Nazis and their methods, about the nationalists and their activities. It has been proved that this program reaches into local police stations, provincial offices, government bureaus, into every phase of public life and into every private home in one form or another. It has been shown over and over again that totalitarianism has spread throughout the nation, disguised under many names and claiming many virtues.

In spite of this pitiless publicity, in spite of exhaustive investigations made by competent authorities and reported to higher authority, in spite of the experience of the conquered and enslaved European nations who refused to listen to the same evidence, the program continues in Argentina almost flagrantly in the open. In spite of inter-American conferences at Havana, at Lima, and at Rio de Janeiro designed to combat this slow poison eating its way through the viscera politic, the whole movement of penetration goes forward almost undisturbed. The work of the Axis and its little nationalist echoes goes ahead with meetings, drives, slogans, publicity, awards, and all the rest of the technique of mass persuasion. The scurrilous little journals still print jibes at democracy and freedom, still collect their expenses from the German Embassy, still sow the mildewed seed of race hatred, still lie about the courageous and the honest, still aggravate the peaceful in the interests of confusion, still circulate through the mails at the expense of the people they are busy doping into confusion or insensibility.

On March 27, 1942, National Deputy Juan Antonio Solari said:

It is impossible to ignore that the danger is general on this continent and it is absurd to crawl into our shells like snails and refuse to meet with our neighboring republics of America and act against the common danger from within. We must never lose sight of the fact that Nazi Germany is attempting to hide its infiltration into our country by making use of others. Falangism is actually the mask of Nazism and in many cases acts for it. The Japanese—about whose activities the Brazilian Government has learned plenty—are acting with the Nazis. All this indicates the urgency of forgetting good intentions—the kind with which the road to Hell is supposed to be paved—forgetting speeches and conferences, and going into immediate action.

That was in March.

Deputy Solari, after a year of official investigation, knew what he was talking about. He understood that the future of Argentina hangs not on the ability of the nation to defend its frontiers against an attacking army but on the strength of its people to resist the termites in the woodwork. He knew that the woodwork itself, like the Wood of Dunsinane, might get up at any time and walk.

The propaganda of dictatorship says there is no such thing as fair play, no such thing as gentleness and consideration for the weak, no such thing as the Golden Rule. The fascist says that people who believe in such things are soft. He knows the world is not for the dreamers, but for him. He wants to live dangerously and for the moment, for tomorrow we die. It means nothing to him that hearts are broken and bodies are starved and raped and left to rot under the beaks of vultures. All that is part of the fast, new, hard, cold life the human race is going to learn to live. That is the New Order he is bringing to the world. If he can bring it to the world without having to fight, so much the better. In Argentina he is trying to bring it to a people difficult at the moment to reach with his ships, planes, and guns. He is trying to bring it from within, as he brought it to Italy and Germany.

CHAPTER XII

THE NAZI TECHNIQUE

THE people of the democratic world have made a practice of ignoring the facts of life. They were guilty of it as early as a decade ago when Japan moved into Manchuria "to restore law and order." By the time total war struck them they were as confused as a girl out of a convent on her first date with a sailor.

Argentina has resisted the facts of the totalitarian penetration into its national life. Skillful propaganda has parried the warnings of its daily press. Political opposition has nullified the warnings of its enlightened and aroused representatives. Official silence has greeted with equal frigidity the shouts of impassioned prophets and the studied, cold figures of methodical investigators. It is a familiar story in the United States, where through many years we have resisted the facts about the world-wide assault on democracy.

The plain truth about the thorough, systematic conquest of Argentina now in progress is clear enough everywhere but in the minds of those most deeply affected. The Axis penetration into schoolroom, church, bureau, regiment, office, and home is a carefully executed movement on the pattern perfected through the thrill-packed years since the German reoccupation of the Rhineland. The record shows how with patient preparation and consummate skill the forces of invasion have acquired and used the tools with which to paralyze their victim—tools such as political parties, terrorist societies, radios, newspapers, government officials, military leaders, tech-

156

nical channels, and industries. There can be no doubt that the Axis has tended and encouraged the trickling fountainheads of Argentine nationalism, guiding them into rivulets of popular protest and then into roaring streams of domestic Falangism threatening to sweep Argentina and half of South America into a Western version of the Spanish Civil War—and thus into the lap of the Axis itself. There is no doubt that a complete army of German Nazis stands organized with political and military leadership, with supply corps and signal corps, with Intelligence and General Staff, ready to throw off business suits and peasant costumes and march into any emergency in the land of their adoption. Into the American nation tied most closely to Europe in aspirations, in racial make-up, in ethics, in culture, in trade and investment, has been poured the same deadening, defeatist philosophy, followed by the same glittering offers of salvation, the same yeasting social excitement, that carried Europe screaming to destruction.

If Buenos Aires is the bridgehead into America, the logical step once the Axis had decided on total war was to seize and hold that bridgehead at all cost. This tactics is fundamental in the technique of invasion, whether it be assault by mechanized death or the attack by paralysis at the nerve centers. Since the day of Alexander's phalanxes it has been axiomatic that an aggressor with a new weapon is a doubly dangerous foe. Newer and more effective than the deadly spearhead of planes and tanks is the technique of conquest by political twilight sleep. The Ausland Organization moved first into Buenos Aires with the utmost care, building slowly and thoroughly on its primary landing-force until it was fairly certain resistance had been blocked at the source. While the German settlers were being coerced or forced into Nazi cells and blocks in anticipation of future events, the philosophy of non-resistance circulated thoroughly through every government office to which the early Axis agents could gain access. Official Argentina, like official France, found at the moment of crisis that it had been overcome by a strange lethargy like the kind of nightmare in which the muscles refuse to move the body out of the way of an oncoming express train. This lethargy took the form of wondering whether a change in the kind of government might not be stimulating as long as the right people could be sure of staying in power; of wondering whether or not the Nazi threat might have been exaggerated out of all proportion to its true dimensions; of doubting the character and the capacity of fat, stolid Great Britain and rich, pleasure-loving North America in the face of determined attack. These themes were played with Mozartian variations by all the fiddles and wood winds of the Nazi propaganda orchestra until the chambers and corridors of state were filled with music.

It is unfortunate that the first civic awakening rudely to deny and break this daydream of happy security made the newspaper headlines almost simultaneously with the German attack on Russia. It is unfortunate because those militant members of the Chamber of Deputies who first yelled to high heaven that the country was under totalitarian invasion were most of them political radicals. Aristocratic Argentina looks on political radicalism as a form of Communism and on Communism as a city matron looks on a garter snake in a picnic basket. As in most countries of Europe, it is hard to tell in Argentina where liberalism ends and radicalism begins, and where radicalism ends and Communism begins. That makes all liberals suspect.

As soon as the Argentine Chamber of Deputies leaped on mild-mannered Dr. Culaciati and dragged him through the daily news with his spineless answers to questions about Nazi penetration, the Nazis claimed a Communist plot. That was the obvious move, and it worked. At least it worked among the aristocrats, the bureaucrats, and all the others who were afraid of Communism. During the month of June, 1941, it was impossible to arouse even the vigilant metropolitan dailies to a state of excitement about undercover Nazi activities in Argentina. The entire investigation undertaken by the Chamber of Deputies and prompted by the questioning of Dr. Culaciati as spokesman for the Ministry of the Interior came close to dying on the vine. Public apathy was thick enough so that Ambassador von Thermann and his well-dressed confederates must have stepped out of the big bank building and down to the Siegfried Room of the Jousten Hotel for schnapps and anchovies while congratulating each other.

For a few days keen, ambitious Damonte Taborda kept his committee in leash while its board of strategy sized up the situation. Adolfo Lanús, Juan Antonio Solari, Silvio Santander, full of energy and a kind of youthful enthusiasm not described in the Nazi pamphlets on tottering democracy, called in a half-dozen anti-Nazi Germans, took down names and addresses, brought themselves up to date on the framework of Axis infiltration. Then on July 1 they dropped in on the Gambrinus beer parlor in the serene little suburb of Florida. They came back with a truckload of evidence showing how the outlawed Nazi party and Nazi Labor Front had been operating under their culture-and-charity cloak, and how the German Embassy managed the whole business through its special attachés and secretaries sent from Berlin for that purpose.

There were thirty German Nazis meeting in the Gambrinus at the time of the raid. They comprised a unit of the Charity and Culture Circle, District North, Zone Florida. Among the trophies carried away were documents, books, files, maps, membership credentials, swastika arm bands and badges. Questioning of the surprised Nazis provided the committee with its first glimpse of the network in action. It

established for the first time that the phony cultural groups
and labor unions were actually under the strictest supervision
and direction of Berlin despite an attempt at assuming a local
character. Heinrich Frohlig, Heinrich Korn, Friedrich Wagner, and Georg Bein (that Leipzig Fair drummer again!)
freely admitted their identities and the character of the "cultural federation" of which they were officers. When confronted with maps seized in the raid, they confessed that
they had divided their particular district into the zones and
blocks indicated by the chart. Herr Wagner said the zone-
and-block system was worked out by the Nazis for metropolitan districts only and that it wasn't used for party organization in the interior. He said the fact that Florida was heavily
populated by Germans explained the thoroughness of the
mapping system used there. Herr Korn's account book
showed that the 14,800 pesos collected from Nazis in his district in the fiscal year 1939-40 had been increased to 30,500
pesos in the next period, apparently due to increasing pressure
from Berlin.

The immense detail of family data required from each
new candidate into the "cultural circle," the five full-face and
two profile photographs, the references required within the
Nazi party, all indicate the importance as well as the true
nature of the organization. Records showed that members
were given an identification booklet like a passport, but only
after repeating the oath: "I swear allegiance to my Führer,
Adolf Hitler, and promise obedience at every moment to
those leaders he places over me."

A study of the correspondence of the local indicated intense
activity and rigid attendance requirements, giving the society
almost a military aspect. Absolute obedience was required and
enforced. One letter seized by the raiders reported to the
metropolitan chief of the German Labor Union: "In the past
year we have divided the local group into small cells and

blocks in order to make easier the work of group leaders. Among the latter I wish to commend for their zeal Comrades Weinzierl, Dr. Christ, Gold, Beeser, Strasser. The others are working too, and I am sure of good help in the coming year. Heil Hitler." It was signed by the section delegate. There was uncovered in the Gambrinus headquarters a complete file of the Gestapo noting the ideological bias, degree of loyalty, and personal characteristics of suspected Germans within the district.

It was apparent that every kind of check was made on individuals, down to citations for misdemeanors, indicating that police control was being exercised by the Nazi party rather than by the proper Argentine authorities. There were complete instruction books for rituals and procedures governing all public Nazi ceremonies, including funeral services for departed comrades, plays, monologues, pageants, and all kinds of spectacles designed to keep alive the spirit of Nazi sacrifice among the members. A second instruction book brushed up the faithful on the subject of politics, instructing them in Nazi ideology, pointing out the rules laid down for living and working in a foreign land, comparing the Nazi system to Italian Fascism and pointing out obligations to the party. Another booklet dealt with the Versailles Treaty, with the Four Year Labor Plan, the social structure of the Reich, and the importance of the Labor Front. Another contained the latest decrees governing the Strength through Joy movement, the NSDAP, and other party units.

Almost overnight it dawned on the nation that it was harboring a nest of international criminals and showing them all diplomatic courtesy. Damonte Taborda engineered the Florida raid without consulting the Acting President of the Republic or any of his Administration. In doing so he avoided the usual leakage of information whereby Nazi agents forestalled capture or loss of confidential papers. The police of

Buenos Aires are answerable to the Government through executive appointment of their chief. In failing to consult administrative authority Damonte Taborda assured the enmity and nonco-operation of the executive branch of the Government. All police authority was denied the Chamber committee; it looked for a few days as if the entire investigation were dying again.

When Judge Vásquez stepped up and offered to hear evidence and to send out on his own authority police properly armed with warrants and properly protected by the law, he became a sort of national hero. Public opinion, pushed a little by the newspapers with newly awakened conscience and imagination, swung slowly but solidly to the side of the committee, its resourceful chairman, and its self-effacing membership. As a matter of fact, Damonte Taborda, Solari, Lanús, Santander, and Fernando de Prat Gay, Guillermo (Bill) O'Reilly, and José Aguirre Cámara were found to be solid citizens, not Bolsheviks as at first supposed. Each one has experienced the satisfaction of public acclaim for a job that began under the worst kind of suspicion.

The co-operative attitude of Judge Vásquez put the committee again in a crusading mood, and greatly to the surprise of the Nazi supreme command, now certain of immunity, the police moved in on Labor Front headquarters at 1250 Calle Alsina and the party headquarters in Calle Veinte-cinco de Mayo, carting away tons of important files. In this raid, carried out so effectively that among the seized documents was an unopened letter arrived an hour earlier from Berlin, a carload of Nazi agents were captured and jailed. They were Alfredo Mueller, Wilhelm Wieland, Josef Schmolz, Jan Ziegele, Rudolf Jahre, Walther Bendfeldt, Wilhelm Ullmann, Karl Heinz Sandstede, Ferdinand Eifler, Wilhelm Keller, Karl Schade, Heinrich Vollberg, Otto Brunner, Otto Bechler, Wilhelm Arnold, Paul Wuttke, Walther Altern-

kemper, Joachim Uflerbaumer, Hans Hillebrecht, Hans
Kauser, German Schuckardt, Friedrich Frohwein, Fernando
Ellerhorst, Curt Appelhans, Rudolf Obermüller, Phillip Alt,
Walther Boese, Karl Klingenfuss, Hans Sandkuhl, Biercamp,
A. Schmidt, W. Krankenhagen, E. Schriefer, all officers of
the "cultural society."

Among the many interesting items taken from the headquarters of the Cultural Federation was a book inscribed
"Gottfried Brandt, His Property." It was an account book
filled with a list of members of the society. Each name was
marked with two numbers; one number indicated the member's order in the Nazi party in Germany, with date of induction, while the second number indicated the member's
order in Argentina, with the date of induction into the Argentine party. This was the most direct proof obtained in
Argentina of the clandestine existence of the outlawed Nazi
party. The book revealed that in Argentina Nazi organizers
use the identical system of division for administrative purposes used in Germany, tabulating not only party members
but outsiders. Dr. Brandt's book classified party members according to their duties within the Nazi discipline, leaders
being noted as *Blockwart* (block leader), *Zellenwart* (cell
leader), *Pressewart* (press chief), and so on. The book indicated that the "charity" organization operating within the
phony federation was a collection group specializing within
the structure of the NSDAP. Among its assets was a special
savings fund guarded in Germany and used for the benefit
of members of the SA (Storm Troops) and the SS (Security
Troops) injured or sick in the line of arduous duty. The
membership cards of the German Labor Union bore the signature of Dr. Robert Ley, Nazi Labor Chief, and were
marked with the two numbers indicating the member's order
in the Arbeitsfront in Germany and the Trade-Union in
Argentina. It was observed that these cards were transferable

from country to country, but always indicating membership in the parent Labor Front in Germany.

There were 12,000 Argentine members listed. One of the account books of the Culture and Charity Federation bore names of 1,261 minor officers, listed with key numbers. In other books the numbers only were used, up to 64,319, together with the amount collected from each individual corresponding to the number. The names of block and cell leaders were written in longhand in the margin alongside each ten numbers. This account book of collections indicated Nazi organizations in Avellaneda, Belgrano, downtown Buenos Aires, Colonia Liebig, Florida, Hurlingham, Misiones, Quilmes, Tucumán, Vicente López, and many other districts known to be heavily populated by Germans. There was also the Agrupación Teutonia, whose job it was to organize and keep track of members outside of the principal settlements. The subdivision of these apparently innocent organizations into squadrons or blocks and the assignment of a chief to each, the care with which contact was kept between groups by means of modern communication and transportation facilities, the careful selection of leaders, the rigorous discipline of members, the complete personal responsibility of group captains, the espionage system in force within the groups and the energetic action taken in cases of indifference or hostility or failure to meet payments or other requirements, the perfect co-ordination of activities with those of other strategic corps—these led investigators to the conclusion that they were dealing with a thoroughgoing organization of military type controlled directly from Berlin.

They promptly notified the Chamber of Deputies of this fact, and on August 29 they published in booklet form an account of their findings, along with facsimile reproductions of the evidence. This first public report of the findings of the Damonte Taborda committee caused an international sen-

sation, startling the United States and bringing down Nazi
reprisals upon the heads of Argentine citizens caught in occupied France. The private life of Damonte Taborda was
immediately impeached in the Nazi propaganda publications.
The air of hostility within executive government circles grew
more ominous.

Immediately, the committee went to work on the real
source of infection: the German Embassy. Here it was on
even more sensitive ground, more sensitive because it had
been the central clearinghouse for the entire Nazi intrigue
against Argentina and because a public accusation against the
German Embassy is a public accusation against the Reich itself. But the committee, by now rather sure of itself and
basking in the glow of public approval, wanted to know what
might be the connection between the skyrocket of Embassy
expenses, the fantastic increase in Embassy personnel, and the
intense pressure for perfection of the Nazi state within Argentine territory. It wanted to know what diplomatic immunity sheltered in that tremendous granite dovecote between the Avenida Alem and the Calle Veinte-cinco de Mayo.

As experienced democratic politicians, the committee knew
that tyranny of any sort breeds its own enemies. The committee went to anti-Nazi Germans familiar with the operation of the Embassy. Following their lead, it went to the account books of the two German banks. Once the financial
structure of the Embassy was laid bare, all its activities began
to show in bright relief. In its second report, September 5,
the investigating committee announced it had been able to
prove that the money used to corrupt Argentina by political
and ideological penetration was being siphoned through the
Embassy itself. Not only the financial transactions of the Embassy but almost its entire activity were found to be dedicated
to breaking down democratic government in Argentina and
replacing it with a totalitarian state.

The increase in volume of banking done by the Embassy (multiplied by seven in two years) indicated an increase in official activities out of all proportion to the commercial, industrial, and numerical importance of the German community in Argentina. The two Nazi banks, the Banco Alemán and the Banco Germánico, carry all the Embassy's business. In the Banco Alemán there were three accounts of special significance: account "K" and account "L," both in the name of Dr. Richard Burmester, and another account in the names of Ludwig Meisz, Karl Freitag, and H. Sens. There were four accounts in the Banco Germánico: a special account in the name of Meisz, Freitag and Sens; an account in the name of Hermann Metzger; an account in the name of Dr. E. O. Meynen, Counselor of the Embassy; and a fourth account in the name of Prince Stephan zu Schaumburg-Lippe. All of these names were of Embassy personnel. The Prince and Herr Meisz were also treasurers of private enterprises, as was established by a careful check of other accounts in the bank.

From July 1, 1940, to June 30, 1941, the Embassy took in a total of 6,157,400 pesos, and deposited that sum in these accounts under their various names. The funds which the German Embassy had at its disposal for use at its own discretion, and without regard to the proper offices of an Embassy accredited to a friendly nation, came from payments made to it by virtue of the Argentine-German trade treaty and from collections made within Argentina from German industrial and commercial firms and their employees. There existed an open account by which Germany and Argentina maintained the balance necessary for an exchange of manufactured goods and raw materials between the two countries.

In May, 1940, the Minister of Foreign Affairs communicated to the Minister of Finance the German desire to use the Reich's favorable trade balance to pay through this open account the necessary salaries and expenses of the interned crew of the battleship *Admiral Graf Spee* scuttled a little earlier in the Plata within sight of Montevideo. The Germans wanted also to use 50,000 reichsmarks a month out of this fund for general expenses of the Embassy in Buenos Aires. The Central Bank of the Republic, handling this fund, observed that according to the terms of the trade agreement the funds available in this account must be used by Germany only for the purpose of buying Argentine products, but added that at the moment it was impossible for Argentina to export goods to Germany because of the British blockade. Despite the decision of the bank, the German Embassy was granted permission to dispose of its balance in the manner requested.

Later the question of the *Graf Spee* sailors became one of the most aggravating problems confronting the people of Argentina in dealing with the Reich. How the battleship's survivors got to Buenos Aires after the sinking at Montevideo is a story not yet fully available. Somehow tugs got to the scene of the scuttling and in the full glare of the burning ship took off 1,046 men for transfer to Buenos Aires, although they were plainly the prize of Uruguay. As a matter of fact the mariners were "hot" in the language of international law, and it is likely Uruguay was glad enough to have them stolen from under its nose. In Buenos Aires the German colony idolized these good-looking heroes, and Argentine citizens certainly felt no rancor toward them. After the suicide of their captain they were offered parole and freedom of movement, but all declined. They were interned in April, 1940. Germany was charged with the cost of their keep in accordance with international custom.

Six months later twenty-nine officers and thirty-nine petty officers had escaped from the river island of Martín García, leaving only one of each in "token" internment. The rest were scattered throughout the republic by government decree, some taking jobs with German firms or on German estancias.

By March, 1942, about four hundred had escaped from Argentina. These comprised the technical staff of the battleship, likely to be of use to Germany later. Of those electing to remain in the country, eighty were living in a community house leased for the purpose in a suburb of Rosario. Here they lived like fraternity brothers. They scattered Nazi propaganda through the district and found sweethearts among the neighborhood families. The easy escape of the technicians and the open Nazi activities of the remainder were common knowledge by the time the Damonte Taborda committee made its report to the nation on the banking practices of the German Embassy.

The committee discovered an interesting kind of banking procedure at the otherwise quite careful and thorough German Embassy: the practice of issuing checks made out only to "Bearer." Ordinarily this type of check is used only for small transactions of a limited character. Larger checks are usually made out to individuals, for the protection of all parties. But the committee learned through a scrutiny of the accounts that in one year the Embassy had issued bearer checks in the amount of 2,000,000 pesos and in one ten-day period alone it handed out ten bearer checks totaling 500,000 pesos. Although the banks involved admitted that this was extraordinary procedure and "bad banking practice," the result was that the committee found it almost impossible to locate the most highly paid and most dangerous of the Nazi agents operating directly with the Embassy.

While this fancy bookkeeping was going on, the German Embassy grew to a staff of fifty-nine individuals with diplomatic immunity. This can be compared with eighteen at the British Embassy and fourteen at the Embassy of the United States. This was in spite of the fact that Germany had only 36,000,000 pesos invested in all Argentina while Great Britain had invested 5,500,000,000 and the United States nearly

2,000,000,000. It didn't escape the notice of the committee that Germany was employing four times as many men covering an all-out attack on Argentina and its institutions as Britain was employing to look after the tremendous investment it has made in a brilliant future for Argentina. It's no wonder German-inspired propaganda among Argentine nationalists has trumpeted away at the theme "Save Argentina from foreign capital!"

It is typical, too, of the cynicism of the Nazi attack that at the same time paid Nazi demagogues were crying for expulsion of the Anglo-Saxon capitalists its Embassy was quietly maneuvering to gain control of the Belgian, French, and Netherlands investments whose home offices and stockholders had the misfortune to fall into the hands of the Gestapo on the occupation of the Low Countries and France, or whose managers had relatives in the power of the Nazis in those countries. A great many of the public utilities of Argentina have been organized with capital from these countries.

Since the proper operation of utilities is vital in wartime and since Nazi Germany has moved in on the home offices of these companies in Europe, Argentina finds itself more deeply than ever before in the hands of its hidden foe. The committee pointed out to the nation in its second report that forced changes in policy and management in Paris, Amsterdam, and Brussels gave Germany control of more strategic enterprises, despite the pitifully small amount of German money invested in lighting, powering, and transporting the Argentine people. Of the 1,500,000,000 pesos invested from these three captive countries, 80 per cent is in public-service corporations.

Another financial ace up Germany's sleeve is the manipulation of shares in Argentine corporations held in captive Europe. A major disaster on the Argentine bolsa—and it might easily result from such manipulation—would throw the country into the kind of disorder the German High Command likes to see in countries earmarked for invasion.

Investigators of the Chamber of Deputies looked into the German Chamber of Commerce, another office in the remarkable building on Veinte-cinco de Mayo. It appeared that the chamber had gone into the collection business, taking from Germans and German firms in proportion to their incomes, from 4 per cent to 32 per cent. Heinrich Vollberg and Wilhelm Dosch admitted on close questioning that although the contributions were "voluntary," the Nazis knew how to apply enough pressure to make them unanimous and complete. Actually this amounted to a levy by threat and force within the boundaries of another sovereign country.

The money collected was turned over to the German Embassy for the Winter Help Fund. It is interesting that that chamber's contribution to this fund grew from 12,000 pesos a year in 1933 to about 200,000 pesos in the year 1941. This demonstrates how bad the winters were getting. The money was gathered during the heat of the Argentine summer in each case, a farsighted arrangement made, no doubt, after reading the fable of the grasshopper and the ant. Karl Schmits, president and manager of the chamber, denied that his organization had anything to do with collecting Winter Help funds but returned immediately to correct himself when the investigating committee made arrangements to inspect the books of the chamber. The Schmits boys had other business: they collected a neat fee for the issuance of trade certificates issued free by all other foreign chambers of commerce in Argentina. With the disappearance of German-Argentine trade this side business disappeared, also any excuse for maintaining such an organization.

But with the disappearance of trade not only was there no indication of closing the chamber, but a second office opened:

the Office for Stimulation of German Trade in Argentina. Heinrich Vollberg operated this. Like the Chamber of Commerce, it existed and exists only for the purposes of Nazi infiltration. It gives out Nazi propaganda and keeps in line German businesses. Heinrich Vollberg himself was kept busy conferring with and lecturing to German businessmen. His salary was paid by the Association of German Chemical Industries, a most important unit of the Wirtschafsgruppen, which is the Nazi party extended into business. Not only are the directors of this group named by the German Ministry of Economy, but they must be approved by party leaders.

Vollberg, far from being engaged in stimulating the non-existent trade between Germany and Argentina, was busy as a beaver stimulating the Winter Help collection and getting them as quietly as possible into the hands of Prince Stephan. On the side he was director of the Federation of German Charitable and Cultural Societies, so engrossed in cultural affairs and the German Chamber of Commerce, so busy with commercial things. Vollberg admitted he took in 1,337,723 pesos (better than $250,000 in United States money) in winter relief for the German Embassy during the fiscal year 1940-41. Vollberg's office for Stimulation of Trade paid to the newspaper *El Pampero* 103,800 pesos from March 3, 1941, to May 12, 1941, a quick glance at the books of the Banco Central showed. During that period *El Pampero* was busy as usual cartooning and libeling President Roosevelt, sneering at Yankee-inspired Pan-Americanism, warning its readers that Nazi Germany was about to swallow the world, demanding a militant Argentine nationalism to "once and for all put an end to the insipid joke called democracy."

Thus is modern trade stimulated. The whole proposition was so fantastic that Vollberg made every effort to convince investigators that the funds for maintaining *El Pampero* as an organ of Nazi propaganda did not come from his office but were actually sums of money left by German subjects who had been called suddenly home, and administered for them by other individuals. Vollberg said his office handled only 5,000 pesos a month. A further study of the accounts left no doubt as to their origin. Some of the checks bore the name of Vollberg or of his secretary, Rosa Obleten. Others bore the names of German firms but were issued following deposits made in their favor by Vollberg or Rosa. Somewhere in the picture there circulated many of the "Bearer" checks issued by the German Embassy. One of the interesting banking transactions brought to light by the investigating committee involves a quaint character by the name of Johann Solbrig, a man very careless with money. The following dialogue took place August 8, in the committee's offices in the national Congress building:

Damonte Taborda. Do you frequently visit the Office for Stimulation of German Trade?

Solbrig. Once in a while; when I have business.

Damonte Taborda. What kind of business?

Solbrig. Business connected with getting representatives in Germany. When we want to get a representation.

Damonte Taborda. Do you advertise in the papers?

Solbrig. Only in *El Pampero.*

Damonte Taborda. There has appeared a check for 15,000 pesos more or less made out by the Compañía Rheinmetall Borsig May 12 of this year. Do you remember the check?

Solbrig. Yes, sir.

Damonte Taborda. Do you remember also that on May 9, the Office for Stimulation of German Trade in Argentina deposited to the account of Rheinmetall Borsig 14,000 pesos?

Solbrig. I remember the deposit, since I made it myself.

Damonte Taborda. Is your name Rosa Obleten?

Solbrig. Ah! No.

Damonte Taborda. Because the deposit was made by a young lady of that name.

Solbrig. I didn't actually take the money to the cashier's cage myself, but it was deposited in my name.

Damonte Taborda. Is this young lady an employee of yours?

Solbrig. No. One morning I was in Mr. Vollberg's office waiting to transact some business with him and I asked this lady to deposit the money for me.

Damonte Taborda. Did you send a check or the cash?

Solbrig. Cash.

Damonte Taborda. Does the house of Rheinmetall Borsig usually allow outsiders to deposit such large sums for it?

Solbrig. No; since I was in the bank building and didn't want to go downstairs, I asked the lady to go out and deposit the money for me.

Damonte Taborda. But I ask you if your firm uses outsiders for depositing money in such sums.

Solbrig. Never.

Deputy Lanús. Why didn't you take the sum directly to *El Pampero* rather than depositing the money, then making out a check to *El Pampero?*

Solbrig. We wished to make the transaction in the name of Rheinmetall Borsig, but the firm didn't make the deposit of 14,000.

Deputy Lanús. Then who made the deposit?

Solbrig. I.

Deputy Lanús. Where did you get the money?

Solbrig. I had some funds available. Actually it was money left me a year and a half ago by a Mr. von Pappen, a representative of our firm in America. This gentleman left unexpectedly.

Deputy Lanús. You deposited this money in the Banco Germánico?

Solbrig. No, I kept the money in cash. As this gentleman traveled a great deal, I always had funds at his disposition at the factory, funds which were not accounted for in the books.

Deputy Lanús. How long ago was the money left with you?

Solbrig. In January, 1940.

By a curious coincidence Georg Bein had the same experience. A Herr Scolmayr of the German Manufacturers' Association left him 10,300 pesos, which he took to *El Pampero* "in payment for advertising." A little later Vollberg explained to the committee another matter of 20,000 pesos which a certain Herst Niehl left in his care on being called suddenly to Germany. Vollberg remembered in the midst of questioning that the sum was not 20,000 but 77,000 pesos, of which he turned over 30,000 pesos to the German Embassy.

Day after day it became more plain to the investigators and to a now attentive nation that behind it all was the German Embassy. The various offices and societies which pretended to be of a private or commercial character operating in co-operation with the Embassy were simply focal points of agitation and propaganda busy boring into Argentina and jeopardizing its relations with friendly states. The lavish funds at their disposal despite the modest nature of their own official budgets, the complete absence of bookkeeping, and the freedom with which they spent pointed again to the Embassy. Only the most vague and unsatisfactory replies were made to questions directed at those whose business it was to administer these funds.

The German Ambassador himself became vague when questioned about the radio transmitter he tried to send as "diplomatic baggage" to Lima. The Damonte Taborda committee kept a record of the contradictory public statements made by Von Thermann following seizure of the secret sending set from the baggage compartment of a Pan-American plane at Córdoba. First the Ambassador said the packages containing the radio set were "diplomatic baggage," then he called them "diplomatic mail or correspondence," then he decided they constituted "diplomatic mail in transit." First he said he didn't know the contents of the package, later denying there could have been "any document inside the transmitter," referring this time to a set of instructions for use of the radio in sending secret messages. The instructions had been discovered by the committee on examination of the transmitting set.

Nor did the investigating committee like the part played by the Embassy in converting the outlawed Nazi party and Labor Front into the fake cultural society and labor union. Receipts made out to these new Nazi units were signed by the Ambassador and employees of the Embassy. One member of the Embassy staff was treasurer of the cultural group, despite the obvious impropriety of claiming diplomatic privileges and immunities for an officer of a private organization. If the organization was not private but official, the committee pointed out, it was unable to deny that it functioned in Argentina at the orders of the totalitarian regime from which it sprang.

Taking all these facts into consideration, the committee proposed to the Chamber of Deputies that it memorialize the executive branch of the Government on the ground that the German Ambassador in exceeding the proper functions of his office had made himself unwelcome. With but one dissenting vote, the Chamber passed the resolution, and precipitated another feud with Acting President Castillo and his Cabinet. The Ministry of Foreign Affairs felt its dignity slighted, and the executive branch felt its prerogatives stepped on. While various Ministries and bureaus were sounding off about their rights, the penetration directed from the stone building in Calle Veinte-cinco de Mayo went steadily forward. A conference of Nazi leaders in contact with the Wilhelmstrasse decided to sit tight. But public pressure, uninfluenced by the official Argentine attitude of indifference in the matter, grew so strong that Von Thermann arranged a vacation trip home—an excursion from which he never returned to Buenos Aires. Thus the dignity of the executive branch was preserved, the public clamor was answered, and the conclusions of the committee of the Chamber of Deputies were justified.

When the investigating committee published its third formal report, September 17, Argentina got its first clear glimpse into the brain of Dr. Goebbels. The Nazi propaganda administrator had said (March, 1933) that German news agencies, radios, and theaters must "give out propaganda on internal, economic, and social policy, but also external policy" and he had followed that declaration with the decree providing that German journalists who lived abroad must form part of the Landesverbande and thus place themselves under actual physical discipline of the Nazi state. The committee without a great deal of difficulty followed the strings from Dr. Goebbels to the complex German news organization operating through Buenos Aires into all southern South America. Lest it be accused of tampering with the free opinion of German journalists, the committee prefaced its third report with a quotation from the lips of Adolf Hitler of November 27, 1936:

Since the advent of National Socialism I have given a limit of four years to literary and artistic criticism for conforming to National Socialist principles. . . . In view of the fact that during 1936 literary and artistic criticism has not improved sufficiently, as from today I prohibit the continuation of literary and artistic criticism in its present form.

In retrospect it is astonishing that after the frank statements of Hitler and Herr Goebbels anybody could have accepted the truth or even the honest intent of anything written or spoken by German newsmen anywhere in the world. Yet Argentina until September, 1941, was accepting without question the thousands of poisoned words pouring daily across the Atlantic from Berlin and the other thousands being manufactured at home by Germans sent to Argentina for that purpose.

After false starts and contradictions, Walther von Simons and Emil Tjarks, managers of the Transocean news agency, admitted to questioners that their organization, masquerading as a legitimate commercial enterprise, lost 77,000 pesos in the first six months of 1941. But a study of the agency's books showed that its receipts were only 1,015 pesos in that period while its expenses were 214,179 pesos. The deficit made up by the German Government was 213,163 pesos. It is greatly to the credit of the public accountants drafted by the committee that they were able to arrive at definite figures of any kind. Actually Transocean kept no accounts, despite the German reputation for thoroughness and despite the fact that the agency had spent well over 1,000,000 pesos in the preceding four years. The accountants in their report to the committee said wistfully: "This company does not keep accounts and there exists only a series of annotations without rational order."

Von Simons and Tjarks said they had no copies, nor did they know of the contracts made by the agency, or of the general balance sheets or of the statements of profit and loss made by the home office in Berlin. Von Simons admitted he had no idea whether his company was operating at a profit or at a loss in Latin America, although he was Latin American manager of the concern.

The committee wondered what kind of a business concern Transocean must be if it kept no books, had no idea of its profits or losses, and seemed not to care. After discovering that the Nazi Government made up the company's losses, it learned that the managing directors, Karl Schulte and Friedrich von Homeyer, were in reality officers of the Reich Ministry of Propaganda, and that the directorate included half a dozen reigning Nazi industrial princes, all of them important in the Hitler regime. In the four-year period during which Transocean collected a total of 23,512 for its services, the Nazis sent bank drafts for 814,955 pesos from Berlin. Despite this fact, Manfred Zapp, director for Transocean in the United States, told the Dies Committee of the House of Representatives that Transocean's losses in the United States were compensated by the company's profits in Argentina. The accountants at work on Transocean's books in Argentina believed that if a proper bookkeeping system had been maintained it would have shown even greater losses sustained by the agency.

Of course Transocean lost money, because it was not a news service in the strict sense of the word, but a propaganda agency subsidized by a warring nation as part of the machinery of attack. Transocean never bothered to make out bills for news service to *Bandera Argentina, El Pampero, Crisol, Deutsche La Plata Zeitung, Il Mattino d'Italia,* and *Diario Español* in Buenos Aires. More than that, it was discovered the news agency was actually paying these newspapers sums of money for advertisements that were never published. But immediately the investigating committee began to look into the Transocean books and bank accounts there appeared contracts with all these newspapers, contracts signed not years ago when the service began, but in August, 1941, when the investigation began. Right in the middle of August the committee found an exchange of letters offering Transocean services to these newspapers, and letters of prompt acceptance. These transactions were so naïve as to send into hysterics the business representative of a legitimate news agency who knows what are the delays and difficulties of selling service.

When the committee got into the accounts and records of *El Pampero,* it found the same astonishing condition: operation at a tremendous loss and nobody much interested in the losses. This propaganda organ had a deficit of 421,251 pesos in the last half of 1940. It is an interesting commentary on the comparative conditions of conscience of the boards of strategy of Transocean and of *El Pampero* that the former offered the committee's accountants free access to the books which revealed nothing while the latter hid all its books and defied a court order to turn them over to the committee for review.

Lest the nation assume that elimination of Transocean might solve the problem, the committee in its September report listed and analyzed the many other "news" channels from Berlin into Buenos Aires, including the Deutsches Nachrichten Büro, the South American Journalistic Post, and the allied agencies of Italy, Japan, and Vichy France.

CHAPTER XIII

CHILDREN OF THE NEW ORDER

"IL DUCE. All Italian children love Mussolini; *Il Duce* directs the New Italy and works without rest for the good of the country. The austere face of *Il Duce* is illuminated with tenderness when he looks at children."

This quotation is from a *First Reader* taught in an Italian school in Argentina.

National Socialism is a gift of God to all peoples. Its culture is superior to all others. Argentina is a Communist country which we must conquer. Democracy in Argentina is a stupid lie. Every Nazi must fight it and replace it with the blessings of the present regime in Germany.

This quotation is from the *Nazi Decalogue* reported to be circulated among German schools in the territory of Misiones.

The more deeply involved the Chamber of Deputies investigators got in the totalitarian penetration into Argentina, the more certain they were that its most dangerous manifestation was the hold it had on growing, learning children. The *Berliner Tageblatt* of August 10, 1938, listed 203 German schools in Argentina serving the children of 236,755 Germans and people of German descent. At the same time serving an Italian population of better than ten times that number there were only four private Italian schools in Buenos Aires and none registered outside in the territories.

Careful study of the German schools proved to the committee that:

1. The Reich's educational system extended, like the Nazi party itself, into foreign countries.
2. The private German schools in Argentina were a part of this system, were controlled by the present German regime, and took orders from Berlin's diplomatic representatives in Buenos Aires.
3. The teaching and administrative faculty of these schools acted in militant Nazi circles, were selected and appointed in Germany after a careful apprenticeship, and must demonstrate to the proper authorities fidelity to Nazi principles.
4. The textbooks were edited in Germany, and the character of their teaching was contrary to the laws and institutions of Argentina, tending to sow in the minds of children the seeds of violence and racial intolerance.
5. The teaching methods employed produced an atmosphere opposed to Argentine sentiments and to Argentina's history and its position geographically, politically, economically, and socially.
6. The operation of private Italian schools, although not such a pressing danger, should be carefully watched by the authorities.
7. The nation should improve economic conditions and provide better public educational facilities in the interior, and should immediately control the subject matter taught in private schools.

In its recommendation for more public schools in outlying districts the committee hit upon an Argentine weakness that was taken advantage of by the Germans, as a good field army capitalizes on the mistakes of an enemy. In concentrating wealth and advantages in the city of Buenos Aires a prosperous country had neglected some of its country children. The inevitable German answer to criticism about Nazi-controlled schools was "That is the only way we can educate our young." While that statement wasn't entirely accurate, it served as an excuse to hold the children of German colonists bound to the language and tradition of the homeland, and after the rise of Nazism to the ideology of the party. As long ago as the time of Sarmiento these foreign schools had been a stumbling block in the development of a unified nation. The public school system had contributed toward breaking the influence of foreign-language schools, had succeeded fairly well except in the case of the race-proud Germans. Nobody knows better than Nazi educators what it means to an ideology to get hold of children and teach them through the formative years. They have had the example in their own country of the denunciation of slacker parents by fanatic kids whose affections and mental processes have been warped by the mass hypnotism exercised by Nazi party instructors.

In the past ten years the death agony of the Old World civilization, translated into social upheaval, has deeply agitated those American nations like Argentina which have their roots deep in the old soil. This agitation has been deliberately intensified by the Axis in its effort to hold Argentina as a European wedge driven into America. Germany, because of its advantage in claiming a closely knit national unit within Argentina's boundaries, has undertaken to bring up the children in the New Order even though they may have been born as free as the plumed rhea of the Chaco. It has been demonstrated that Germany has officially intervened in the lives of Argentine children and forced them by every kind of pressure known to the Nazis into German schools, where they become in the course of time potential Storm Troopers or mothers of Storm Troopers.

How zealously these little citizens are bent into the forms of human life decreed by the Nazi state is generously demonstrated by the quality and character of the instruction given them; the real intensity and drive in the educational program; the anxiety to pattern the curriculum exactly after that in vogue in Germany; the prolongation of the educational period among those most apt for party work; the airy dismissal of everything Argentine; the exaltation of Nazi heroes and all their deeds.

In the month of August, 1937, when the Nazis celebrated in Germany the twentieth anniversary of the founding of the Ausland Organization, Dr. Kroh of Tübingen spoke on the *Unvolking,* the psychology of the adaptation of peoples to new national surroundings and patterns. He said:

A young man obliged to pronounce sounds other than those of his mother tongue is deprived of a part of his personality transmitted to him by the generations. In cities promiscuous contact with a foreign population implies a danger to the pure racial community. Intellectuals run the same risk. Moreover, in seeking to restore throughout the German community the force of instinct— the principal heritage of man—National Socialism helps to awaken the natural resistance of Germans living abroad.

This bizarre morsel out of the Nazi philosophy of culture sounds like a perversion of some of Oswald Spengler's shallowest thinking. But it can't be ignored if we are to understand the fanatic effort to keep Argentine Germans from learning anything about America, its languages, or its ideals. Not to be out-Spenglered, Prof. H. J. Beyer proclaimed at the same Ausland meeting:

"Germans must conceive of their country as one continuous current, since this conception permits the creation of a unified historical conscience."

All this professorial double talk leads up to the primary aim of the Ausland Organization: to convert and hold all Germans living outside Germany to the national racial cult, to keep all German blood pure, and to help Germans resist assimilation into the national life of their new homes.

Ausland Chief Wilhelm Bohle, on the occasion of his appointment as assistant in the Ministry of Foreign Affairs, sent a message to all the *Volksgenossen*, his race brothers living abroad, in which he crowed about the growing military might of the Reich and invited them to collaborate in the Nazi program as Germans in the eyes of God. Later he complained:

There are still some Germans living abroad who decline to become Nazis and yet claim to be Germans. For these so-called Germans who say they are sincere and yet stupidly help the enemies of the Reich we have only one designation: traitors to the Fatherland. We know only totalitarian Germany. Every German who declines the totalitarian concept weakens the Reich and lessens it in the eyes of foreigners.

Under these auspices were the German schools in Argentina brought into the fold. Two hundred masters of German schools abroad gathered as Ausland Organization guests at the Stuttgart celebration were camped apart from the rest. They wore uniforms and underwent special instruction designed to impress on them that every German abroad must be a Nazi, that they must be subject to Nazi discipline, that they must buy German products exclusively and teach others never to buy Jewish products, that they must counsel others to send their children to German schools, that they must employ only Nazis and do everything possible to get work for unemployed Nazis. At these Stuttgart festivals from 7,000 to 10,000 Germans from abroad gathered each year until war made it impossible.

What most aggravated the Chamber of Deputies was that in submitting Germans and particularly German children abroad to Nazi discipline the party directors in Berlin simply ignored the authority of the lands in which these people were growing up as new citizens under hospitable laws. December 1, 1936, the Reich laid down statutes governing the Hitler Jugend (Hitler Youth), which are followed closely by youngsters in Buenos Aires. Baldur von Schirach, chief of the HJ, decreed that all leaders abroad should lay off local politics and use their time to keep the closest possible contact between German youth abroad and German youth at home. In Argentina the Hitler Jugend is called the German-Argentine Boy Scouts and the League of German-Argentine Youth. These excited little corps march about in uniforms, arm bands, badges, and all the other bright gadgets professional boy-organizers foist onto their charges.

The committee's fourth report to the Chamber of Deputies describes a rustic scene reminiscent of the grotto camp of the Fascist Balilla I watched on the hills above Florence in August, 1939. By chance, both ceremonies were held the same year. The Argentine encampment was on one of the green jungle islands of the Paraná River across from the city of Rosario. With the strained, unnatural solemnity dictators require of children, boys of the German school of Rosario gathered under a profusion of banners to the note of trumpets. Standards bore the symbol of the Hitler Jugend. On a rustic altar reminiscent of the ceremonies of Teutonic mythology the chiefs sat on great stones. Before the altar files of boys stood in military formation. Over the great river the white cranes flew in startled silence. Into the New World hard faces and brown uniforms were bringing the hereditary fevers of the Old World.

The German Minister of Sciences, Education, and Public Instruction administers the German schools in Argentina through the German Embassy in Buenos Aires. The Minister in Berlin sends the schoolmasters who are to teach the Argentine children of German parents. One of the most important requirements of a schoolmaster about to be sent abroad is his complete identification with the procedure and the ideals of the National Socialists, which is to say with militant, modern Germany. Like the teachers, the scholastic materials come from Germany. The Humboldt Schule reported in its summary of operations for the year 1940:

"The Reich readers [printed in Berlin] for use in various classes arrived in three shipments; they have proved their worth for the use of German schools abroad."

They were the same texts used in corresponding schools in Germany. German schoolteachers in Argentina have been circularized regularly with up-to-the-minute instructions from the Ministry of Public Instruction in Berlin. Most of these are reminders that children in their charge must be taught the ideology of the new Germany and must become familiar with conditions of life now regnant under the New Order. One circular says:

"Following the latest decrees of the Reich Government, Germans both young and old are required to give the Nazi salute with bare heads and right arm upraised while singing the Argentine and German national hymns."

In order to corroborate this evidence, the committee called before it Gustav Adolf Messer, teacher and director of a German school in Buenos Aires and vice-president of the Association of German Schoolmasters in Argentina. Maestro Messer not only confirmed the fact that the activities of teachers were overseen by Nazi authorities in Berlin, but he admitted his credentials were German rather than Argentine, that he had to apply in Germany for permission to come to Argentina to teach, and that he would be pensioned by the German Government at the completion of his service in Argentina. Instructions to schoolmasters appeared over the signature of Hermann Metzger, cultural attaché of the Embassy in Buenos Aires and director of the German Cultural Council. One of these circulars establishes the fact that in order to receive pensions and enjoy other privileges schoolmasters must put themselves strictly under Nazi discipline.

In a text written particularly for the guidance of German

schoolmasters, Reichminister Bernhardt Rust explains that in
order to create in the soul of his people one single political
and ideological will, Adolf Hitler has put into effect a "new,
ingenious, and intelligent" system of education:

Long before the National Socialist state was able to take over
public instruction, an organic and complete system of educating
youth grew up outside the official spheres of education and the
public academies; there was crystallized in the spirit a new sense
of values not through the medium of public instruction but
through the experience of the common struggle for a political ideal
which affirmed and developed those ideals of character inscribed
on the party's banners. Nazi youth was the spokesman for the
new education long before it received its special mission from the
state.

This statement contains the philosophical elements of totalitarianism in purest essence. Here is the implication that
not a people but a political organization is the German state,
and that the political party has designated itself custodian of
the culture, tradition, racial memory, religion, and spiritual
longings as well as the physical existence of all the people
within the boundaries it has determined upon.

One of the first acts of the triumphant Nazis in Germany
was to organize the NSLB, the Association of Nazi Teachers.
This organization is kept busy preparing courses of study,
camp meetings, and seminars for the purpose of keeping its
members shot full of Nazi ideals and methods of instruction.
The Ministry of Education through the NSLB maintains two
permanent camps staffed by selected teachers who serve for
several weeks at a time in order to maintain the continuity
of instruction. The NSLB organizes conferences in which
teachers and school inspectors get special ideological training.
This training is obligatory. It surpasses ordinary academic
procedure, as the investigating committee discovered while
looking through the documents of Hermann Schrammen, a

German instructor who taught in a suburb of Buenos Aires.

Judge Flores of Paraná seized a sheaf of interesting documents belonging to Schoolmaster Schrammen. He found a letter of instruction from the German Foreign Ministry advising Schrammen in Germany of the political requirements he must meet before he could leave Düsseldorf and return to teach school near Buenos Aires. Another document certified that Schoolmaster Schrammen had completed his Storm Trooper training with the Army of the Lower Rhine as of August 3, 1935. This document was covered with seals and countersignatures of officials of the Nazi party. A third paper notified Schoolmaster Schrammen February 1, 1936, that he had been accepted as a teacher by the Düsseldorf Scholastic Association, "in the name of the Führer and by order of the Reichministry of Education." Then follows correspondence between the teacher and Nazi authorities over the proposed service in Argentina, and in conclusion an order for cabin space on the *Monte Oliva* sailing from Hamburg April 3, 1936.

Schrammen had been director of the school in Argentina in 1933 and 1934, and had gone home to get the further credentials required by the Nazi party, which had organized the German educational system abroad since he had left the Fatherland. Having fulfilled the requirements and returned from Hamburg, Herr Schrammen, whom we must picture as a slightly bent man with receding hair and a pair of spectacles, occupied his first post until December 12, 1940, when he got permission from Herr Metzger at the Embassy to go to the Crespo Institute at Entre Rios. There was a clause in Schrammen's contract with the Institute that said: "The German Embassy in Buenos Aires is sole referee in any dispute arising over the terms of this contract." Other documents showed that the Embassy in Buenos Aires acted as intermediary between Schrammen and the two Ministries in Berlin that licensed him to teach in Argentina.

The committee was able to gather a great deal of evidence proving the complete dependence of German schoolteachers in Argentina on the Reich and their complete submission to the Führer. All of them as members of the Deutsche Lehrerverein in Argentinien were rounded up in 1936 by Dr. Wilhelm Keiper, predecessor of Metzger, and forced to swear allegiance to the Hitler regime—despite the fact that they were earning and living by virtue of the hospitality of their adopted land. The oath of obedience was exacted in the German Embassy. Since that date no German schoolteacher in Argentina has been excused from the oath. This thorough control from Germany is in spite of the fact that students of Argentine birth outnumber the students of German nationality better than six to one in the German schools. In order to keep a solid block of race, language, and culture under discipline in Argentina, the Nazi regime reaches into every home of German origin, disregarding every consideration but the demands of the German state, denying individuals the right to breathe the free air of a new land, preventing their assimilation into the country of their choice, holding them willy-nilly for whatever pompous plans of conquest may wheel through the brainpans of the High Command at home.

The Chamber of Deputies committee charged that official inspectors whose duty it was to supervise methods and subject matter taught in private schools were in general sympathetic or negligent. In their report to the Chamber there was aired the accusation that officials notified the principal of the Humboldt Schule that he would be inspected next day and he'd better get the portraits of Adolf Hitler off the wall.

An intimate glimpse into this same Humboldt Schule revealed that youngsters were being taught that Germany had been robbed of its colonial empire and was justified in fighting to get it back; that the English, the Jews, and the Freemasons were trying to prevent the development and expansion of Germany; that Hitler has declared the future of Germany to lie in its youth; that German children must train themselves as warriors and keep themselves valiant, faithful, and sincere for the combat; that all Germans must think in German terms; that the preservation of German songs and the German tongue was a duty of Germans abroad. "The beat of our heart must ever be for Germany" was one slogan repeated often. Throughout the copybooks of the children sounded the familiar Nazi propaganda in the form of simple themes about Germany's part in the war, about the beauty of Nazi discipline, about the exciting moments in the Nazi party's seizure of power in Germany. Pupil Georg Krankenmann had submitted the following theme:

War was declared September 3. First England declared war on Germany, then the French; Germany had no alternative but to fight. That's why there is war in Europe. The Poles are very bold, but their boldness has not helped them and Germany has taken Danzig and conquered the Corridor. The Poles were to have been helped by the English but nothing has been done. Here in a foreign land there are many lies and we can't believe the news. . . .

And so on and so forth. All of this and similar exercises found in the notebooks of the school's youngsters tell a story of childish minds fed a steady diet of military and political propaganda until they parroted back all the sterile phrases of their masters. Here were children taught not the Golden Rule nor love of their fellow men, but a credo of hatred and recrimination for wrongs, real and imaginary, committed before they were born into this bright world.

The Humboldt Schule was ignoring Argentine law, which

decreed that all schools must teach the principles of the nation's democratic institutions and explain the rights and guarantees of the national constitution. It was openly defying the law which forbade the teaching of political or racial ideologies, and another law which made it mandatory to teach from textbooks written expressly for Argentine children.

A peek into the Goethe Schule showed first off a swastika on the wall of the principal's office. A look into the *Second Reader* revealed the following chapter titles: "Hitler Gets Work for Everybody"; "Oh, Happy Day" (the arrival of Hitler); "The Voice of the Führer"; "How Dieter Saw the Führer"; "Heil Hitler"; The Banner on House Number 8 (describing the room in which died Horst Wessel, once pander, now Nazi hero); "Ode on the Birthday of the Führer"; "Prayer" (for Hitler); "The Helping Hand" (collecting for the Brown Shirts). The reading about Dieter is a little gem:

We travel to Kladow. Uncle Karl told me once that the Führer often goes to Kladow. My father says: "The man at the helm has a heavy labor." A woman runs past the corner shouting in a loud voice: "Heil Hitler! Hitler! Hitler! There in the auto!" Dieter has seen Adolf Hitler. "Where has the Führer gone?" asks Gerhard of his father. "The Führer visits Dr. Goebbels here often at his pretty house near town." Now everybody has arrived at the gate. "Heil Hitler!" all cry. The Führer approaches and smiles.

The committee in reporting to the Chamber of Deputies pointed out that the National Educational Council had already passed resolutions demanding that the Humboldt, Goethe, and Ludwig Uhland schools be closed and their teachers be disqualified. Nevertheless they were still in operation and without any apparent change in ideology or curriculum.

And while this was going on in Buenos Aires in full view of police authorities, government Ministries, and the Argentine press, German schools in the remote interior provinces were having a real field day. As far back as 1938 the governor of La Pampa, E. Pérez Virasoro, complained that German schools in Santa María, Santa Teresa, San Rosario, San José, Médanos Blancos, and Hucal were of pure Nazi character, teaching not just the German language and religion, as they professed, but totalitarian politics as well. He reported that the walls of these schools were covered with the insignia and maps of foreign countries rather than the prescribed symbols of Argentine democracy. He objected that students saluted with arm upraised in totalitarian fashion and shouted "Heil Hitler!" Virasoro's successor, Governor Duval, complained August 9, 1940, that despite the earlier denunciation and decrees of the National Educational Council:

"Nothing has been done to relieve this problem of foreign schools in our country, aggravated today by ideological and racial propaganda resulting from the war in Europe."

The schools in La Pampa Province were simply headquarters for instruction in Nazism. They were maintained by subsidy from Buenos Aires under orders from the German Embassy. Despite every complaint of local officials and educational leaders they were allowed to continue their labor of creating a totalitarian state within a democratic state they despised, until Governor Duval warned that "our own schools are losing out, dying, and in their places are growing up these exotic rivals directed by manifest enemies of our country." He too asked the Government to close these schools.

The problem was even more acute in the territory of Misiones, where of a total population of 187,000 there were 22,000 Germans, 17,000 German Brazilians, and 23,000

Poles and Ukrainians. The Argentine educational authorities came close to throwing up their hands and letting Misiones take care of itself. This is a tropical land, its emerald jungles cut by cataracts, gorges, and rivers pregnant with the freight of the wilderness. There are few true Argentines in this rich, humid area. The population is Paraguayan, Brazilian, and European. In the department of Iguassú on the river Alta Paraná 27 per cent of the children themselves are foreign-born. They are Paraguayan, German, Danish, Swiss, Russian, and Polish. In this area there are 34,000 school children attending 302 registered schools and 20 "home schools" not authorized by the Argentine authorities.

This is where German contempt for things Argentine grows in uninhibited crescendo. Former Governor Venasco of Misiones told the investigating committee:

The propaganda is immense; it is distributed by means of newspapers, pamphlets, books, and lectures in German. In one of the reports there is a shorthand transcription of a lecture given in German in which are expressed opinions prejudicial to the Argentine authorities. One of the paragraphs of this lecture says that all Germans in the colony must prepare for joint action and make every effort to educate their children, because from among them will come the future rulers of Argentina, because those in power now are of an inferior race and can't go on governing.

A typical German school of Misiones is the Escuela Germana of Eldorado. A look into the copybook of an Argentine boy being "educated" in this school brings to light the. following lesson:

January 30, 1933. The President of the Reich, Hindenburg, calls Hitler to Berlin and makes him Reichschancellor.

February 27, 1933. Night burning of the Reichstag.

March 5, 1933. Reichstag elections. National Socialism gains a majority. The banner of the swastika is Germany's new flag.

March 21, 1933. Day of Potsdam. Spring begins. Gala inauguration of the new Reichstag. Hindenburg and Hitler place crowns on the tombs of Frederick the Great and the Soldier King.

May 1, 1933. Great national feast of the German people.

Beginning in 1933

1933. Dissolution of parties. Expulsion of Jew employees of the state. Beginning of reconstruction of automobile highways.

1934. Introduction of Work Service. After the death of Hindenburg, Hitler is Führer of the German people.

1935. Return of the Saar to the Reich. Introduction of compulsory military service.

1936. German soldiers again in the Rhineland. The number of unemployed goes down to a million.

1937. Great buildings. Friendship with Italy. Visit of Mussolini to Berlin. Demand for the return of our German colonies.

The most apt scholars of the Misiones schools were sent on excursions to Germany until the war began. In Germany they were housed with children of German descent gathered from every part of the world, including the United States. They wrote glowing letters home describing the thrill of close contact with things of the Fatherland.

The German encirclement of Buenos Aires was completed with the heavy settlement of the provinces of Entre Rios and Santa Fé. Schools here showed the same characteristics. In 1916 Entre Rios was already a thorn in the side of Argentine educators. One of these, Ernesto Bavio, reported that in the Russo-German schools of that province there was no attempt to teach anything Argentine:

The textbooks, which should be the most effective element in the process of nationalization, are printed in Germany, and the themes and exercises are completely foreign to our country. If the language, reading, and writing are in a foreign tongue, it is clear that the concepts of geography, arithmetic, and the rest will be the same. As far as geography goes I saw none taught in the schools I visited, but I observed wall maps of Germany and unfortunately none at all of Argentina.

Even the conservative Bishop of Jaso, Gregorio Romero, complained of the schools of Santa Fé that he saw maps of Italy and by their side mutilated maps of Argentina with the entire area of Patagonia cut off "as if it were *res nullius*, a land belonging to nobody and fair prize for the first settlers who wished to occupy it."

Repeated reports and complaints about the character of instruction in these outlying foreign schools have resulted in occasional bursts of energy in Buenos Aires, particularly among members of the national legislature. But Argentine school decrees have been evaded as neatly as have the decrees outlawing the Nazi party and the Nazi Labor Front. It is to be doubted that these decrees have been so much as noticed in the deeper interior points up the Paraná and Uruguay rivers. The establishment of a few Argentine public schools in the area of trouble resulted in a campaign among Germans to keep their youngsters out of them and in the private schools. As long as German schools operate openly in Buenos Aires under the jurisdiction of Nazi educational authorities and utilize all the approved methods and curricula of the Reichsministry of Education, it must be difficult to frighten into submission German schools tucked away in the jungle where the name Argentina rings only academically in Teutonic ears.

In times of peace the problem of a numerous, energetic, and unabsorbed racial group can deliver enough headaches to a national government. But the Germans living abroad are at war; they have been at war since their bodies and souls were seized by the militant, conquering Nazi party in 1933. One of the primary objectives in the Nazi ideological war is the forging of a spirit of German nationalism in the minds of children of German descent in every part of America—against the day when the continent can be conquered physically or ideologically or both. Every textbook, every copy lesson, every lecture, sent from the German propaganda offices in Berlin to the German schools of Argentina has been created for that one purpose. The schoolroom assault has brought Argentina up against the alternatives of ignoring the problem as too complex or closing every private German school, disqualifying every German teacher, and sending every German lesson book back whence it came. In order to make its objective, the latter course must in addition include a revision of the nation's system of public education, eliminating from it all pro-Axis elements and greatly expanding it to absorb the work now done by Axis agents in scholars' gowns. The Argentine Chamber of Deputies is enthusiastically in favor of closing German schools and eliminating once and for all the Nazi pipeline into Argentina's next generation.

CHAPTER XIV

ARGENTINA FIGHTS BACK

AFTER three months of labor, including the most exhausting kind of inquiry and cross-examination, a running fight with the executive authority of the Government, and the publication of four dramatic reports to the nation, three of the investigating committee's membership joined a group of legislators bound for the United States on a goodwill visit. Raúl Damonte Taborda, president of the committee, Adolfo Lanús, and Fernando de Prat Gay made up the touring party, leaving the committee in the hands of Dr. José Antonio Solari, one of the bright young men of Argentine politics. In setting out for the north, Damonte Taborda and his committeemen defied the opposition press, which, led by *El Pampero*, wanted now to discredit the entire investigation as Yankee-inspired and Yankee-financed. Many impartial critics appeared who believed sincerely that the committeemen were making a mistake in visiting a nation interested in the committee's proceedings.

Damonte Taborda had become thick-skinned in the course of his long fight against fascism in its many Argentine forms. He wanted to visit President Roosevelt and assure him that the people of Argentina, no matter what the official attitude of their Government, were democratic in sympathy and deeply loyal to the hemisphere we call American. Damonte Taborda as a young, stubborn, aggressive legislator was used to getting what he wanted. He knew, too, the caliber of his temporary successor.

Many believe the fifth, edited by Dr. Solari, to be the most thorough, accurate, and convincing of all the committee's reports. Dr. Solari is forty-two. He was elected National Deputy on the Socialist ticket in 1932. He has served ever since, representing the politically radical city of Buenos Aires. He has been publisher and editor of *La Vanguardia*, the official organ of the Socialist party. His books on politics are standard. His interests are deep in the social structure of his country. He is unique, almost revolutionary, among Argentine family men because of the intelligent activity of his wife, the writer Herminia C. Brumana.

Hardly had Dr. Solari warmed the presiding chair at the committee table when he was involved in a battle with the Ministry of Foreign Affairs over the request for information on its personnel. The fact that the committee should imply by the most subtle means that there could be disloyalty within the Foreign Office hurt Foreign Minister Dr. Ruiz-Guiñazú beyond the power of words to describe. He promptly and categorically denied the right of the committee to peek inside his offices, and the matter was closed with a widening breach between the Congress and the Administration. The committee, denied access in this direction, turned to other Ministries and solicited information about the personnel of the Post Office Department and the State Oil Corporation, and propaganda circulating through those mediums.

In an earlier investigation the committee had run across the name of a woman employee of the municipality of Buenos Aires among those who had taken the oath of allegiance to Adolf Hitler as members of the Nazi party. Dr. Solari sent a note of inquiry to the Mayor of Buenos Aires, Dr. Carlos Alberto Pueyrredón, asking information about this employee and what measures might have been taken in the case. It also asked information about the rest of the city's employees.

The Mayor replied as regards the National Socialist employee:

The Committee will no doubt understand that I have limited myself to giving the employee in question a severe reprimand, because, as this office has already informed you in our letter of November 12, this case was unforeseen, and the writer therefore could not violate the guarantees provided for in Articles 18 and 19 of the National Constitution, which establish that punishment cannot be given for unforeseen reasons, nor can anyone be deprived of what the law does not prohibit. I have consequently been greatly surprised that you, in the name of the committee over which you preside, should have considered yourself entitled to lay down rules of patriotism. You, Mr. Deputy, should know that my family has been Argentine for many generations, and that every one of them has rendered our country valuable services before, during, and after our war of independence.

The Mayor went on to say that on many occasions he had expressed publicly his sympathy for the Allies (Great Britain and allied countries), but that his high post prevented him from meddling in politics.

The acting president of the committee replied that he shared some of the patriotic points of view of the Mayor, but that the fact remained that a municipal employee had been given only a remonstrance for belonging to a foreign party opposed to Argentine democratic institutions and for having given an oath of loyalty to Hitler rather than to the country where she lived, with the aggravation of not being German by birth, since she was born in Switzerland of Austrian and German parents.

Then the investigating committee asked Federal Judge Dr. Miguel Luciano Jantus for information regarding the lawsuit against the directors of the newspaper *El Pampero* for repeated disrespect toward national authorities and offense against the Congress. The Fiscal, Dr. Caraballo, had shown himself willing to accede to the committee's request for information, but the Judge refused to supply it. The data which the committee wished to obtain referred to the number of cases that had been demanded against the administration of the newspaper, who had started them and on the mandate of what officials, who were the persons accused and on the grounds of what articles published, and finally, who was attorney for the defense.

Commenting on the refusal on the part of Judge Jantus to facilitate the information requested by the committee, the newspaper *La Prensa* published an editorial:

A REFUSAL TO GIVE JUDICIAL INFORMATION THAT IS UNJUSTIFIED

The arguments put forward by a judge when refusing to supply the Investigating Committee of the Chamber of Deputies with data, which to a large extent is at the public's disposal, are inconsistent. Taking our national life in general, it is opportune to point out that this is hardly the moment to find excuses in the law, nor to weaken the spirit of the citizens, seeing that it is a question of defending the very existence of the Argentine state.

La Nación expressed the opinion:

The resolution made by a Federal Judge of the Capital to refuse to reply to a request from the Committee Investigating Anti-Argentine Activities for certain information necessary for the development of its work has produced general surprise. Any difficulties that arise in connection with tasks of this nature should be judged unfavorably only in cases where such judgment is founded on convincing reasons of public interest. In the case which we are referring to, no such reasons existed, because inconsistency of the arguments on which they were founded is demonstrated by its very terms.

Further on the same newspaper went on to say that:

The assertion that the requested information "does not fall within the scope of the investigation" cannot be defended in view of the similarity between the accusations lodged with the federal lawcourt and the matters which are being investigated by the parliamentary committee. As concerns the doubt that the Investigating Committee enjoys "jurisdiction and faculties," the judge could not know that it acts on the delegation of the Chamber, with all the prerogatives held by the Chamber. In Article No. 2 of the resolution voted by the Chamber it authorizes the committee to "obtain the most ample co-operation possible from the national and judicial Government," and Article No. 4 irrevocably adds: "The Honorable Chamber of Deputies of the Nation expressly delegates to its Investigating Committee all the faculties that are its exclusive right, and which are established by the Constitution, etc."

And it concluded by saying that "it is deplorable that the federal lawcourts should not have taken these points into consideration and should have adopted such exaggerated reasons for refusing such a lawful request."

The 277-page fifth report of the Chamber of Deputies investigating committee appeared November 28, 1941. With its publication ended all doubt about the clandestine operation of the Nazi party and its official and semiofficial appendages in Argentina—a patent and insulting violation of the prohibition imposed by President Ortiz in 1939. The report bared the workings of the Deutsche Arbeitsfront (the DAF) as the chief political instrument of the Reich and the Nazi party. At the time of the prohibition imposed by the Argentine Government, Erwin Schriefer was chairman, Hans Schulz treasurer, Karl Fleischer secretary, and Kurt Lange assistant secretary of the DAF. Members of this German Workers' Front were given a carnet containing their own personal data, subscriptions, and instructions, and some quotations from Hitler on the nobility of labor. The emblem

of the DAF was a wheel inclosing a swastika. Accounts of
the organization were kept in the Banco Germánico under
authorization of Eckhardt Neumann and the four officers
just named.

With the legal disappearance of the DAF and the immediate appearance of the German Trade-Union in its place,
it was startling to learn that the German Trade-Union also
used the abbreviated form DAF, operated also at 1250 Alsina Street, and used the Banco Germánico and the funds
left by the Deutsche Arbeitsfront, and that its officers were
Erwin Schriefer, chairman; Eckhardt Neumann, vice-chair-
man; Franz Hartmann, secretary; Wilhelm Schumann, assistant secretary; and Karl Fleischer, treasurer. The official
magazine of the Deutsche Arbeitsfront, *The German in Argentina*, appeared again miraculously as the official magazine
of the German Trade-Union, without the slightest change
of content. The emblem was now a wheel inclosing the
initials ULG for Unión Alemana de Gremios (German
Trade-Union). In the new association's bank accounts entries
appear in favor of the German Trade-Union—DAF.

Lest the public founder in German initials designating the
various units of the Nazi party, the committee listed the
following:

AK—Comrades in Work
BDM—League of German Maidens
DAF—German Workers' Front
HJ—Hitler Youth
KDF—Strength through Joy
AMK—Mother and Child
NSBO—National Socialist Firm Cells
NSFO—National Socialist Women's Group
NSFK—National Socialist Aviation Corps
NSKK—National Socialist Motorized Corps
NSLB—Nazi Schoolmaster's League

NSV—National Socialist Social Help
PG—Party Comrade
SA—Storm Troops
SS—Security Troops
WHW—Winter Help
NSDAP—National Socialist Party of German Workers

The fifth report brought to light a document indicating the lighthearted attitude taken by the Arbeitsfront chiefs toward what was to have been a shutdown of their activities. One of the paragraphs of a circular issued to the faithful shortly after the President's decree says:

With regard to the situation of the DAF, in order to face the continuous rumors of a prohibition of our organization and the loss of rights of all the comrades in work, I make it known that no danger of this kind exists. In the decree of the Government dated May 15, there is nothing that would cause such a supposition, but there does exist the necessity for a reorganization, which has in principle already commenced. I request you therefore to answer pertinent questions this way.

Other circulars advised how best to use the name of the organization and the emblem in public notices and advertisements so as not to run counter to the decree. Secretaries of units were notified not to use the ordinary words and phrases designating officers and locals of the Arbeitsfront. There is overwhelming evidence presented by the committee now under Dr. Solari to prove that throughout Argentina there was no doubt in the minds of Nazis themselves as to the identity and function of the German Trade-Union.

After investigating the discovery of a cache of arms on German property in the Apóstoles district of Misiones the National Gendarmerie questioned Robert Suntheim, local Nazi chief, about operations of the outlawed German Workers' Front and got a picture of the busy calendar of the organization. Suntheim said the Trade-Union was an extension of the Workers' Front designed to unite all German workmen from day laborers to intellectuals, that it met regularly to discuss community problems and the war, that it celebrated Nazi holidays with special programs, and that the German national anthem was sung. This is exactly what the government decree was formulated to prevent. The Nazis had not the slightest intention of abiding by the spirit of the decree, nor had they any fear of consequences of their defiance.

Although there was nothing in the statutes of the German Trade-Union to give them official status, there existed throughout the German business houses and other enterprises, including hospitals, banks, and the German Embassy itself, Work Groups incorporating all workmen engaged at one particular plant or in one firm. In Buenos Aires one of these units existed in each of nine separate businesses, making it easier to group all German employees, collect their dues, and keep track of their activities.

The committee found evidence of the military character of the so-called union. Severe discipline is the hallmark of all Nazi organizations. All Nazi units of any importance are marching units. They are developing their own tradition and customs, in which the members are taught to take pride. In order to forge Germans into a closely knit group, Nazi leaders insist on celebrations and demonstrations of a military nature often enough to keep alive the necessary spirit. In Argentina one of these was the Langemarck Procession in commemoration of the loss of crack German regiments in the Battle of Langemarck in the First World War.

Until 1939 this was a public spectacle in Buenos Aires. From the suburb of Banfield thousands of men of the Arbeitsfront marched. Boy Scouts stepped along to the roll of drum and the shrill of pipes, boys emotionalized by the occasion. Motorcars of the Nazi sanitary corps moved past with swastikas fluttering in the wind. Special cars full of the families of marchers rolled through the neat suburban towns. The sports section of the NSDAP and the marching Work Groups were colorful. Down dusty roads and tree-lined avenues they marched and motored, arriving in disciplined formation to the place of the celebration, where stood Ambassador von Thermann and a staff of Nazi group leaders on the decorated platform. Then began the Ambassador's speech, moody and full of the threat of future triumph.

The Arbeitsfront provided a pool of skilled labor for Germany to fill pressing shortages in war industry at home. The teaching of crafts and professions was and is one of the important functions of the Labor Front. German youths of from fourteen to sixteen in Argentina were being carefully selected for skill, then sent to Germany for apprenticeship. While this seems on the surface a legitimate enterprise, the political teaching to which these apprentices were subject made them more than simply finished craftsmen. Although they were to be expert mechanics, draftsmen, carpenters, and metalworkers, one of their three finishing examinations was titled "World Conception." That is simply graduation in Nazi ideology.

The German Trade-Union, according to its statutes, "proposes to protect the interests of its members; give them aid in case of unemployment, sickness or urgent necessity of any kind; give them instruction in Spanish and in elementary and professional subjects; organize and maintain libraries and recreation rooms; create information bureaus and employment agencies; plan excursions and recreations and provide any other assistance within the limits of society and the laws of the land." Publicly, this is an organization bent on helping people. Nevertheless the committee found that every act of the Labor Front in Argentina contradicted these expressed principles. Like other German organizations in Argentina under Nazi control, it protested full compliance with the institutions of the country at every moment it was utilizing to discredit or replace them. Hard at work spreading the propaganda of Berlin was the Labor Front's magazine, *The German in Argentina,* which published a full cover portrait of Adolf Hitler the same month (May, 1939) it was in theory outlawed along with its parent organization. The title over Hitler's picture was "Our Führer." In the same number Hitler was quoted:

Germany is once again a World Power. What World Power will tolerate silently the shame that at its very doors millions of people who are its own are ill-treated? There comes a time when a nation which recognizes its own power will not consent to be stared at any longer.

There follows the adhesion of the Arbeitsfront (or Trade-Union) to Hitler:

We, the members of the German Workers' Front (or Trade-Union) in Argentina send to our Führer on the occasion of his fiftieth birthday our most cordial congratulations.

Another item describes one of the innumerable public acts organized to keep the business of Nazi Germany on the move among these people in Argentina:

On January 24, all the district directors and officers of the Arbeitsfront, Buenos Aires Circle, met in a comradely reunion in the Germania House to say good-by to the examiner of the district, Work Comrade Klausmann, and at the same time to our director for the entire group in this country, Work Comrade Schriefer, who is paying a short visit to the Fatherland for business reasons.
Work Comrade Klausmann made a speech on this occasion in which he greeted his country and the Ausland Organization, saying that he had found to his joy excellent social contact within the local group.

Then the article goes on to describe the formalities of handing over the gavel of office to a successor, the farewell speech thanking the comrades in work for their happy collaboration. The whole thing sounds like an Amos 'n' Andy lodge meeting.

The magazine continued to publish. In the June, 1941, issue the committee found an article describing how in the presence of the German Ambassador members of the Trade-Union (formerly Labor Front) and the Cultural and Benevolent Circle (formerly the NSDAP) met in the German Club to celebrate May 1, and to demonstrate their loyalty to the New Germany now engaged in war. Speeches were made by Werner Grelle and Harry Wilkening. After music, Wilhelm Dobler lauded German labor, referred nostalgically to former May Day reunions, and described the struggle of German labor against Reds and Socialists. He referred to the New Order of Hitler as "the Order of Humanity, of Work and of the Duties of the People." He wound up praising the German soldier and their Leader: "In this way, then, the whole people comes before its Führer and pledges him once more absolute fidelity as the Maker of their destinies. To the Führer and the First Worker of his people!" The meeting finished with a speech by the Ambassador destined for the ears of the Führer himself. The committee reported in one of its few lapses into Spanish irony that "it has been unable to establish whether the Führer ever heard it."

Some of the titles found in the magazine between the two dates cited are: "The Führer Celebrates Christmas with Soldiers at the Front"; "The German Folk and Their Führer in the Changes of 1939-40"; "Hermann Göring to the German People"; "The Führer to the Party"; "Radio Talks by Dr. Goebbels"; "The Führer's Great Speech of January 30, 1940"; "The Führer Calls the German People"; "Armistice with Defeated France"; "The Historic Session of the Reichstag July 19, 1940"; "The Last Appeal of the Führer to Common Sense"; "Social Improvements in Germany"; "Social Work after the War"; "The Great German Empire"; "What Does the United States Want?" "Lightning Economic War"; "Economy after the War."

After reading these, the committee called in the magazine publisher, Otto Karl Gartz, and asked him to express in a few words the aims and objects of his publication. He said: "It is of a workingman's social and cultural nature. It is informative."

In the philosophy of disciplined labor as it has developed in Germany and Italy, managed recreation has an important role. In Italy the Dopolavoro takes care of the workman's time after he has labored all day for the state. Dopolavoro, which means Afterwork, has its Nazi counterpart in Kraft durch Freude, Strength through Joy. Hitler himself said: "The National Socialist Strength through Joy Community is destined to occupy the free time of the workers in order to mitigate the bitterness and sadness of the people, and to prevent their giving themselves over to idle political discussions which constitute a danger to the state." In other words, Strength through Joy as a planned recreation managed by the Nazi hierarchy keeps people's minds off their troubles and keeps them so occupied they won't look too closely into the source of those troubles.

In practice, as the Chamber of Deputies committee discovered, Strength through Joy is not an opportunity for workingmen and their families to grow spiritually and intellectually through intelligent and wholesome recreation; it is a method of ideological discipline arrived at through planned leisure. Like its sister Fascist organization, it is designed to appeal to simple, tired people who are looking forward to a little restful fun after toil. It has been found simpler and cheaper to provide this kind of recreation than to combat restlessness and despair. It draws individuals more tightly into the orbit of the state and teaches them to identify the Nazi party with fun and laughter.

Strength through Joy has no more place in Argentina than it would have in the United States. The German conception of fun distilled in Nazi laboratories and dispensed by party leaders about as human as charity case workers is a very sad affair. Nevertheless it is a big business in Argentina, forced on German families by the Labor Front, to which it is officially an appendage. In the 1940-41 fiscal year it took in 46,678 pesos and spent 64,660, which comes closer to making it self-supporting than are most Nazi activities in Argentina. As a Labor Front unit it maintains a common accounting with the outlawed organization through the Trade-Union.

The Strength through Joy encampment at Punta Chica stands across the street from the suburban station, which is one of the noisy, bright-colored stops on the interurban between Buenos Aires and the rowing clubs at Tigre. When the train grinds to a standstill alongside the platform, big-ankled German girls in shorts carry lunch baskets and tennis rackets off the dull-green coaches. They are the pimply-faced Brünnehildes of Adolf Hitler's new Valhalla on the Rio de la Plata. A few white sails stand scattered and forlorn out on the choppy water, blending into the gray distance of the Uruguayan shore. The station bell rings, the train snorts twice, draws away from the platform and the graveled yards, and disappears into the green river shoreland where willows stand disconsolately in the shallow wet. A knot of young Germans forms by the dark stone station where the yard-square timetables are pasted one over the other in a monotony of white paper and tiny black type. The blonds drift toward the entrance gate of the Strength through Joy camp and filter through to the small, dank cabins by the artificial lake.

If it is one of those rare days bright and warm along the river, an overpowering lassitude overtakes the Strength through Joyers after lunch and beer, and they lie back on coats or blankets to contemplate the blue sky through a hanging filigree of delicately traced leaves. The humidity is like a sodden weight upon the spirit, the moody German spirit slipping back into inertia after the exciting stimulus of the party pamphlets and the brisk, triumphant talk of Herr Heinrich Arnold, the district leader. In the perspiring evening the green coaches click-click along the tracks, stop at the Punta Chica station, and pick up the tired Strength through Joy remnants to carry them back to the city and another week of sacrifice for the Führer.

There are more Strength through Joy camps: one at Quilmes on the German beach where it joins the Rambla; one at Burzaco, the sports camp; one at Tornquist, the Casa Funke inaugurated by Ambassador von Thermann himself in 1940. In Córdoba Province across the pampa there is the German Holiday Home of Rumipal.

Before the Easter holidays in 1941 the Trade-Union, over the signatures of Herren Fischer, Christ, Lutz, Ledeburg, Czierski, and Weinzierl, circularized employees of German firms in Buenos Aires about the coming fun:

To the delegates of firms:

To the comrades who due to professional matters cannot participate this year in our first outing to Calamuchita of the Strength through Joy, we offer the opportunity of passing a cheap vacation in a second journey which we have organized for Córdoba between March 21 and March 30. As usual, those participating in these common outings will have a chance to know the marvelous Córdoba hills. We ask the delegates of firms to use their influence with the management in order that the work comrades may be given the opportunity of taking part in this vacation outing of Strength through Joy. As this excursion will take place during

Holy Week, it will not be difficult for the various firms to accede in view of the various feast days.

The last reference is to the accepted holiday character of Easter week in Argentina, where the early autumn days of March lure so many to vacations or devotion that most business houses run on a skeleton schedule.

Strength through Joy outings are cheap—usually the equivalent of $10 or $15. They are advertised extensively in the German newspapers and through special publications like the Trade-Union magazine. Despite the prohibition of 1939, Strength through Joy continues to operate at full program and in public view, as a subsidiary now of the Trade-Union. Until the war made transportation precarious for Germans the Argentine Strength through Joy organized excursions to the Fatherland, offering bus service in Germany at club prices.

When questioned by the inquisitive committee, Herr Schriefer had a very simple and naïve explanation for the organization of which he was an executive:

Deputy Solari. What is this suborganization which is called Strength through Joy?

Schriefer. It is not an organization; it is a motto.

Deputy Solari. Then it is just a statement, a theory?

Schriefer. Yes.

Deputy Solari. It has nothing to do with the one in Germany?

Schriefer. No.

Deputy Solari. You are very original; you take the title of the organization in Germany but do nothing that the other does.

Schriefer. In my opinion, Strength through Joy is an international motto. You know that in 1936 Argentina sent delegates to a Strength through Joy Congress.

Deputy Solari. It was in 1938. That which you call a "statement" held a congress. To do this there must be some organization.

Schriefer. It was not like that. It was an international matter, and at least among us it is not an organization.

Deputy O'Reilly. We already know it is an international organization. You deny that it is an organization and say that it is more an emblem, a symbol.

Schriefer. That is so.

The committee believed it odd that a motto had a bank account running into the tens of thousands of pesos and organized outings and programs for thousands of people in all parts of the republic. It believed it odd that an emblem presented theatrical and musical programs, educated men and women in the National Socialist ideology, owned and operated athletic clubs, regulated the esthetic surroundings of workmen so as to stimulate them to greater efforts, maintained groups of "superior" workers within various firms to teach the others and transmit Labor Front orders, provided recreation for soldiers' homes.

The Strength through Joy Community is so powerful and far-reaching an organization that it might be considered parallel to rather than subsidiary to the Arbeitsfront and the NSDAP. This situation is not unusual in the intricately thorough Nazi system, where discipline overlaps constantly. It must be difficult for an enthusiastic National Socialist to find enough hours in the day and enough mental and physical energy to keep in step with all his departments.

Only by studying the characteristics of the German Workers' Front as a political instrument in Germany was the Chamber of Deputies able to understand completely the significance of its continued functioning as a Nazi political instrument in Argentina. The power of this organization over the individual is hardly to be conceived by non-Germans living outside the Reich.

The German Workers' Front, founded on May 1, 1934, reached a definite organization with the regulations dictated by the Reich on November 29, 1934, and January 18, 1935. In accordance with these, all workmen employees and employers of German nationality had to form part of one organization, "the object of which is to put an end to class strife, and regulate relations between capital and labor." In order to attain this objective all the associations formerly composing the central organization of the syndicates, including the Catholic ones, were suppressed and replaced by the new organization, divided into two large sectors: the General Union of German Workers, which grouped together manual laborers; the General Union of Employees, which included employees and professionals, as also employers. The first is divided into eighteen groups and the second into nine. The members of these organizations, who before the reorganization were a part of the German Workers' Front, were divided into two categories: individuals and corporate societies.

Simultaneously with the creation of this organization, there were abolished the right to strike, syndical liberty, and collective contracts. On defining the objects and significance of the German Workers' Front, the Chancellor of the Reich, Adolf Hitler, stated in the preamble of the decree of October 24, 1934, that it represented

the organization of the German who works with his head and with his hand; in it are grouped together the members of ancient syndicates, of ancient employees' associations and ancient employers' associations, all with equal rights. . . . The German Workers' Front must assure that the workers have peace, through the medium of the directors' possessing understanding of the just demands of the workmen, and that these latter respect also the situation and possibilities of their factories. . . . It is not permitted that there be constituted organizations other than this.

The German Workers' Front has nothing to do with questions dealing with the assignment of salaries, dismissals, professional conflicts, workers' insurance, or other problems of a similar kind. It represents no interests; its only purpose is to bring about the fusion of all German workers. It has not as an essential object the defense of salaries and working conditions, but the formation, spiritual and political, of the German people, principally by means of the Work Service, and Strength through Joy for leisure hours.

The private companies and public services are ruled by a working statute which is governed by the laws of January 20 and March 23, 1934. According to this law, every firm constitutes a judicial unit directed by a "conductor," who is assisted by a "second" made up of his staff. The head of the company or the owner is the "conductor" and the workmen the "second." If the number of workers or employees is over twenty, they delegate to go before the "conductor" such "men of confidence" as shall be detailed for co-operating with him. In order to be a "man of confidence" it is necessary that the candidate be over twenty-five years old, have worked at least one year in the establishment and two in the profession, be in possession of all his civic rights, belong to the Workers' Front, and have shown by his previous behavior that he has decided to "work without reserve for the benefit of the National Socialist State." Yearly, the "conductor" of the company in accord with the local representative of the "cells of National Socialist companies" prepares a list of the "men of confidence."

All the members of a "community company" are subject to a special code of honor, which is watched over by the Treuhand, charged with informing the Government about the disposition and needs of the workers and the prevention of social conflicts. The Treuhand members intervene in all differences that come up between employers and workmen, fix all kinds of sanctions, including fines, dismissals, and even imprisonment.

The direction and administration of the German Workers'

Front is in the hands of a central office, at the head of which is Dr. Robert Ley. This central office is divided into six principal sections: Section 1 is subdivided into: (a) administration, which looks after technical and administrative work; (b) legal matters. Section 2. Staff. Section 3. (a) Organization of the German Workers' Front, including that of the National Socialist Strength through Joy Community; (b) aviation; (c) Army; (d) foreigners; (e) press office of the Workers' Front; (f) instruction; (g) social matters; (h) propaganda; (i) public health; (j) professional education and management of firms; (k) legal assistance; (l) youth; (m) women; (n) home; (o) economy; (p) institution of scientific work; (q) information; (r) social responsibility; (s) technical science, and (t) community of firms. Section 4. Finance. Section 5. National Socialist Strength through Joy Community, with the following subdivisions: (a) spare time; (b) excursions and holidays; (c) sport; (d) beauty of work; (e) popular education; (f) community of firms. Section 6. Supreme Court of Honor and Discipline.

The smallest unit of the German Workers' Front is the block, composed of from forty to sixty members; it is under the direction of a chief whose mission is that of spreading National Socialist ideology, clearing up questions related to the German Workers' Front, and collecting subscriptions when this is not done by the firms themselves. The unit next after this one in order of superiority is the cell, made up of four to eight blocks in charge of a head. The work of this unit consists of vigilance in carrying out the decrees of the superiors of the organization, the instruction of block chiefs, and so on. The head of a cell is disciplinarily subordinated to the head of the party cells. After him comes the local group, which is the "leaning post" of the party, also in charge of a head. Then comes the circle, then the regional administration, and finally the central administration.

In the totalitarian idea the representation of opinion and interests gives way to the idea of an administration, of a "leadership." In the heart of the society, as a result of a process which travels from above to below and not by a majority vote, the heads are those who retain the power. These men have the mission of telling the state of the structure and working of the society, and they impose all political decisions.

Within this idea, the block is the basic organization, not only of the German Workers' Front but also of the party, and its importance is exceptional. The idea of the universal conception of National Socialism is the tendency for each German to be an active participant in the construction of society, economy, and the state. For Nazism, this would be the true democracy, obviously conceived sui generis, since its formation and expression are not the result of an act of spontaneity and free will, but the product of a coactive force imposed by chiefs with discretional power. For National Socialism, the block is the image of its conception of the world. So is expressed the principle of the Führer, and with this it is desired to show that the conduct of the groups is determined by the orders of their heads, and not by the discussions of a majority.

To quote Dr. Ley on March 7, 1935:

The Workers' Front is a perfect unit with a central administration; its foundation is the community of firms. In order to better look after those who enter this community, there have been established blocks and cells. Various communities of firms are joined together in a local group, and a series of these groups constitutes a circle belonging to the administrative unit of Prussia. In the country and in the provinces the circles made the regions. In all these units, organized according to the National Socialist Workmen's party of Germany, there are workmen, employees, and employers. In its structure as well as its jurisdiction, the

Workers' Front is directed by the National Socialist party as regards organization, staff, and above all, politics.

Official reaction to the fifth report of the Damonte Taborda committee was negative—as in the case of each report since the committee had begun its work. A masterful job had been done in the structure of the thing that menaced Argentina's existence as a democratic nation. Yet there was no move to end the operations of Nazi Germany within the fabric of Argentine national life, nor even to hinder them. It is true that in some cases of open and flagrant violation of the law there were indictments in process of working their tortuous way through the courts, but while habeas corpus and other legal procedures were moving to prevent an injustice to the Nazi corps, the infiltration was going ahead as usual. The real resistance was coming from the people themselves, some of them roused by the committee's revelations, some of them long aware of the temper and the determination of the foe through contact with him on the soil of Europe.

CHAPTER XV

BRAZIL AND URUGUAY VERSUS THE NAZIS

MOST wholeheartedly anti-Nazi of all the nations of South America are Brazil and Uruguay. They got that way through long experience with Nazi Germany, its agents, its methods and its poorly concealed attitude of contempt. With Argentina these two states bordering the South Atlantic make up the continental area most coveted for German *Lebensraum* and most intensely settled and propagandized under the Reich's long-range Latin American program. The arc that begins at São Paulo and swings widely through southern Brazil, touches Paraguay and Uruguay, and points between the jungle rivers directly at Buenos Aires, is deliberate strategy based on the geography of the region and on the heavy German settlement that acts as anchor.

The heart of this arc in population and in activity is the southernmost Brazilian state of Rio Grande do Sul where Captain Aurelio da Silva Py, chief of state police, investigated the ramifications of the Nazi system of political penetration. He discovered that as a complement to the Nazi party itself there was a network of Nazi organizations thrown across all the Americas, and that in Rio Grande do Sul its principal factors were the German Workers' Front, the German Women's Foreign Union, the German Girls' Overseas Society, and the League of German Veterans. He discovered, as the Chamber of Deputies discovered in Argentina, that the German Trade-Union was the spearhead of the Workers'

Front and that its place was foremost in the program of infiltration into Brazilian life.

Captain da Silva Py confiscated the records of the Trade-Union and uncovered the pattern of its structure under the excellent organization of Herr Straskajan and Ernst Dosch, who built this thing under the noses of the Brazilian authorities. He discovered that the Arbeitsfront enjoyed complete autonomy and that its activities were independently parallel to those of the party itself. Its propaganda was constructed and distributed separately and its small local groups throughout the state were dependent directly on the Arbeitsfront headquarters. Nevertheless it was spiritually a part of the Nazi party. Beneath the official insignia of the Deutsche Arbeitsfront its officers had inscribed the following subhead: "Union of Benevolence and Education." These officers were contemptuous enough of the Brazilian authorities to try at first to convince them that this subhead expressed the real purpose and character of the organization. It was the same technique they used in Buenos Aires when confronted with the evidence of their own records. The Arbeitsfront in Brazil had tried to hide its identity and escape investigation by using the name Bund der Schafenden Reichsdeutschen (League of German Producers).

Captain da Silva Py warned his Government not to be surprised if the Strength through Joy, once outlawed, appeared again in Brazil under a new name. One of the principal weapons in the hands of the Germans in this area of Brazil was the boycott, effective because Germans controlled business through their numerous commercial houses. Under National Socialist organization, business is an effective element in political penetration.

Although Brazil was driven to a declaration of war against Germany because of the continued torpedoing of its ships at sea, its temper had been shortened by the activities of its

German colonists. It is characteristic of the German settler in South America that once under Nazi domination he forgets that the "subject races" around him are both intelligent and sensitive. This was a bad error for the Nazi to make in Brazil and Uruguay; both nations are possessed of both qualities in high degree.

Deputy Julio V. Iturbide carried out an investigation into Nazi activities in Uruguay and reported back to the House of Representatives in the session of July 17, 1940:

As Klein and Holzer represent among us economic Nazi infiltration, so does Hoerler represent, according to the documents of Patz, penetration; Huners, press penetration, and Patz himself penetration through intermediary of instruction to children and adults.

They also have their leader abroad, on whom depends the organization of National Socialist cells in the Workers' Front. And this organization, directed by Dr. Robert Ley, guided by the authorities of the National Socialist party, groups together the workers of the building industry, the printing industry, foodstuffs, factories, lumber, textiles, masons, leatherworkers, agriculture, commerce, offices, navigation, and German female employees.

On this National Socialist organization of cells of the Workers' Front depends the filing system which has absolute control of all German workmen and German-speaking employees, who are obliged in Uruguay to join the Workers' Front, an organization of such a perfect character that even though the Germans are in obvious minority in working circles, it creates a veritable problem for workers of the country on the staff of German houses.

This National Socialist organization of the cells of the Workers' Front, called the Third Army, since it deals with the German National Socialist Work Service, is under the control of military organization. This Workers' Front, whose members wear military uniforms with the swastika thereon and whose structure is almost exactly the same as that of the Storm Troops, has its press section which gives out all the pamphlets, which arrive in the country

in thousands, and the newspapers printed in German, which ar-
rive in Uruguay in a considerable quantity. We may offer a proof
of this to the House, by showing the periodicals: *For Domestic
Servants, For the Workmen in the Paper and Bookbinding In-
dustries, For the Builders' Industry, For the Metallurgic Industry,
For Commercial Employees, For Employees in Public Service,
For Young Commercial Employees, For the Lumber Industry,
For Textile Workers, For Leatherworkers, For Those Who
Work in Banks and Insurance Offices, For the Wine Industry,
For the Food Industry, For the Liberal Professions.*

This Workers' Front has a legal office which deals with all
matter and problems which come up among the National Socialists with regard to our laws.

This Workers' Front has an organization called "Strength
through Joy," which has an educative task, with sections for travel
and holidays, but whose object, as in all the other cases, is to in-
culcate into the masses the Nazi ideology.

Among the documents belonging to Patz, we found the announcement of an excursion to La Floresta, put out by the Workers' Front Strength through Joy. Therefore among us the Workers' Front is established, which organization since 1934 has been
under the direction of the German Minister of the Interior.

To mention this authority is to point out the military character
of the organization itself. The structure of this army of workmen
is exactly the same as that of the Storm Troops. A few posts have
had their names changed in order to hide its character, but under
other names there still reigns the military hierarchy. The militari-
zation of the working class, under police vigilance, has given
origin to a community divided into sections of organization, education, travel, esthetics, work, help, lodging. . . . But beneath
all this the idea of imbuing into the masses National Socialist ideology is triumphing. And the authorities of this Workers' Front
are elected from among selected functonaries in the Assault and
Protection sections.

A proof of the work being done by the members of this Workers' Front is given in the statements made before the committee
by two former employees of the firm of Quincke. All workmen

speaking German, whether Germans, Hungarians, Austrians, or Swiss, were obliged to fill up a form on which figured the date of their birth, the names of their parents, their addresses, nationality, and origin. These workmen were permanently in reception of all Nazi propaganda, which was received in profusion from Germany, and once the war started, were obliged to meet at certain points to listen to the speeches of the Führer.

They were also obliged to make the Nazi salute, to contribute to the "Winter Help" collections, a resource of exceptional significance for Nazism, and to observe the one-dish meals.

Nonacceptance of discipline, nonmembership, and failure to submit to all the instructions of the Workers' Front signified dismissal from the German houses in the country, even in the case of those whose owners had proclaimed that they, old residents in the country, had nothing to do in their commercial life with the party activity of Nazism.

There was also found at the house of Patz (obviously) insulting correspondence regarding Uruguay. There was also found graphic documentary evidence as to the manner in which they [the Nazis] were grouped together in the interior, and how along the national highways the Brown Shirts of Hitler parade and march in their uniforms, all of which goes to show a great disrespect for our sovereignty. We find ourselves face to face with criminals guilty of the crime of *lesa patria*.

These soldiers cannot be considered as defenders of our democratic ideals, as they are educated in tendencies contrary to our own, and if, as is a logical conclusion to arrive at, they are organizing themselves to fight against us, all these members of foreign military forces, who figure in photographs easily recognized, should receive the sanctions which are the lot of those who, in a foreign land, have endeavored to form themselves into a legion under a leader of their own nation, and who in consequence constitute by their absolute military character a veritable danger for the safety of a country which opened to them, with generosity, its doors, believing them to be worthy and honest persons. . . .

Our justice will say the word as to whether, in a democratic land, the verses of the anthem which the Nazi legions sing, can become a reality: "Free the streets for the Brown Battalions, free the streets for the Storm Troops!"

In the report of the Damonte Taborda committee to the Chamber of Deputies November 28, 1941, the troubles of Brazil and Uruguay were aired for the benefit of the Argentine public. Throughout its series of investigations and reports the committee was desperately trying to build up public consciousness of the nation's pressing problem so that the Government itself might be forced to act. The press of Buenos Aires filled in this program with revelations of the discovery of a Nazi plot to overthrow the Government of Chile, a plot which followed too closely on the heels of the Belmonte revelations in Bolivia for coincidence. The entire political structure of South America, from the Amazon Valley to the Strait of Magellan, was wobbly and had been since the Ausland Organization went into action among South American Germans. Opportunist politicians were having a field day, confident of being able to bargain with the organized Nazi minorities. Nationalist parties were being strengthed by direct subsidy and by propaganda encouragement, and new ones were springing up to challenge their leadership among the restless. Military cliques were conferring and gauging their strength against the day when they might call themselves in "to save the nation from anarchy."

The entrance of the United States into the war in December cleared the air at last, gave the democratic majorities a rallying cry, and brought to an abrupt halt the open, insolent activities of the Nazi party and its auxiliaries and outriders in every country except Argentina, Chile, and Paraguay. Brazil seized scores of radio spies sending secret messages to Germany from stations hidden along its coast. Venezuela, Colombia, Ecuador, Peru, Uruguay, Brazil, and Bolivia closed the flagrant centers of Nazi activity operating as Legations and consulates. Agents were moving out of these countries like bedbugs out of a mattress at the first whiff of disinfectant. For the first time since democracy was challenged by the brilliant and bewildering weapons of totalitarianism, a common purpose and determination seemed to move the peoples and governments of the continent.

The story of the survival of the democratic principle in South America, where it has never been universally accepted by the ruling classes, some day will mark for special distinction the people of Brazil and Uruguay. With Mexico, whose clearest voice in international affairs has been the fire-eating idealist Ezequiel Padilla, they form a closed circle against every kind of totalitarian penetration. It is in those countries whose people have fought longest and most tenaciously for political self-expression that resistance to the Nazi idea is strongest. Nobody pretends that all the Latin American nations have attained perfection in representative government as the Anglo-Saxon sees it. In both Brazil and Uruguay extraordinary powers have been assumed by the Chief Executive in times of stress. As in the United States, democracy there is in the process of evolution. It is evolving out of the Portuguese and Spanish colonial systems. It has had to contend with economic and racial difficulties of serious proportions, in addition to natural political barriers. Frequent and dramatic changes of government in many of these republics have been the result of the pressure of the democratic ideal against the incredible rigidity of social and political tradition handed down from Spanish Empire days, as earthquake and volcanic eruption rend the Andean cordillera when the weight of mountain masses bears too heavily on the hard crust of the earth. And as the earth cools and establishes its permanent form, so Latin democracy is settling toward its final and definitive stage.

CHAPTER XVI

FREE PEOPLE FROM EUROPE

IT IS true in Argentina, as elsewhere in the world, that those men and women of the voiceless majority who sincerely want liberty and freedom of conscience have not yet learned how to unite themselves in a common purpose. In addition to wanting liberty and freedom of conscience, they want so many divergent things that even were they politically apt enough to cope with totalitarianism, they are unable to agree on objectives. Some of them want capitalism as it was; some want Communism; some want Socialism; some of them don't know what they want. The totalitarian Powers and their blocks and cells abroad want only one thing: fascism. They want only the all-embracing state under their discipline. It is difficult to fight an enemy who knows exactly what he wants and how to get it.

In Argentina the move to preserve freedom for humankind is a strong movement. But it suffers from the same handicap that paralyzes the Argentine national movement into inaction: It is not a unified movement. Even the anti-Nazi Germans are divided into two camps. There are the Black Front followers of Dr. Otto Strasser, who believe in action, even violence if necessary. Then there are the thousands of honest, intelligent people who call themselves the Other Germany and believe in fighting totalitarianism with the weapons of democracy. Argentine chief of the Black Front Germans is Bruno Fricke, an active, nervous, imaginative man of the type that made up the subordinate leadership of the Nazi party itself in its smashing rise to power in Germany. Membership in the Black Front in Argentina is rather closely limited to men of his kind. Das Andere Deutschland is an organization of students, professional, and laboring men with leanings toward Socialism of the kind that failed to consolidate its strength sufficiently to hold Germany after the collapse of monarchy. This Other Germany movement includes some Communist elements, but it is free from affiliation with international Communism. It is not militant, but it is active, numbering 4,000 affiliates throughout South America. This is not a large proportion of the German population of South America, but it is to be remembered that each member is a hero, since he calls down on himself the inevitable persecution of the party and the Gestapo. It is safe to say that up to outbreak of the war there were not 4,000 active, convinced German Nazis in South America...

When there is peace and the peoples of Europe look again for leadership, it is likely to come largely from the exiled Spaniards, Germans, Italians, French, and Central Europeans now scattered across the American continents. That fact explains most of the misunderstanding and suspicion between on the one hand the many energetic, ambitious individual leaders of the "Free" movements in America and on the other hand the political philosophers and old Socialists genuinely interested in the political salvation of their people at home.

Strangely enough, it is among the democratic Italians of South America that the anti-Fascist movement is strongest, most highly developed, and freest of little individual ambitions. It would be poetic justice if the race which first experimented with Fascism should light the way to its universal defeat and rejection.

In Argentina and in Uruguay, where Italian blood is close to being dominant, faith in democracy is high among the people. Buenos Aires and Montevideo are southern headquarters for the anti-Fascist organization Italia Libre (Free Italy), growing in every part of the three Americas. Sigfrido Ciccoti is general secretary of the Free Italians in Argentina. These in turn are ready to recognize Count Carlo Sforza in New York as supreme chief. Count Sforza's program for reclaiming Italy after the Fascist disaster is embodied in eight points:

1. The Italian people shall choose their own political institutions once they have been liberated from Fascism.

2. All Italians shall abide by the results of a free plebiscite. It is certain that the choice will be some form of democracy.

3. Free institutions are nothing without adequate leadership. Free Italy needs men who know how to defend democracy, provide the highest form of social justice, and impose strict respect for the law.

4. The ancient humanist civilization of Italy will find its best expression in the spirit of liberty and in the economic organization of the nation. Decentralization based on Italy's best intellectual traditions will help create an atmosphere of complete liberty of thought, speech, and religion.

5. A completely independent judicial system will usher in a new era, with the most severe punishment for those in high places who betray their solemn vows. Severe justice makes it possible to pardon those who break the law through fear or ignorance.

6. The new Italian government, because it will be composed of men who hailed the Atlantic Charter of 1941 as a generous message of human justice, will have authority to insist on the fair distribution of prime materials needed by the Italian people.

7. The Italians understand that these and other social and economic problems can be solved only in a world based on international accord, in which there will be no room for anarchy of nationalist states.

8. The Italians will co-operate valiantly and serenely in the solution of all international problems that concern them, on the

one condition that there shall be no discussion of Italian problems as such, but only of Italian aspects of European problems.

It is this people with new enthusiasm for real democracy that has driven Mussolini's Fascist army to cover in South America. Free Italians have helped the Government of Uruguay ferret out the Fascist infection points: Dopolavoro, Casa de Italia, Escuela Italiana, Sociedad Italiana de Socorros Mutuos, Sociedad Epicurea, Círculo Alpinista, Asociación de Ex-Combatientes Italianos, Comitato Italiano, Cruz Roja Italiana, Sociedad Recreativa Assolana, Círculo Italiano, Asociación Nacional Alpinista, Asociación Democratica Italiana, Italmar, Italcable, and others managed by the Italian Embassy.

Bahía Blanca and Rosario, the two cities that south and north close the heavy population line along the river and the sea, are Italian centers. Italians are in the majority in Bahía Blanca with its 100,000 people. This is one of the oldest Italian colonies in South America, founded by a group of stalwarts from Brescia who managed to escape after participating in the Ten-Day Revolt. They were joined by other patriots who survived the revolutions of 1848. Some of them founded a short-lived colony called Nuova Roma, along with General Silvino Olivieri, famous for his Legione Manara and his defense of the Roman Republic. The Nuova Roma colonists moved into Bahía Blanca, and with them came immigrants from Genoa, from the Romagna, and the Basilicata. Northerners, as almost everywhere in Argentina, predominate.

The democratic-patriotic tradition of the founders of the Italian colony in Bahía Blanca was kept alive through the years of its growth by community leaders such as Luis C. Caronti, who founded in 1882 its first and greatest library, and Daniele Cerri, Genoa-born general in the Argentine Army.

When Fascism launched its campaign to "conquer" Italian immigrants in Argentina, its efforts in Bahía Blanca met with failure, thanks to resistance organized by the Italian Liberal Center and a number of mutual societies. Against the wishes and over the bitter opposition of the Fascist consul, a monument to Garibaldi costing 24,000 pesos was erected in 1928 by the Italian community of Bahía Blanca. Later, the city council granted the petition that a street be named after Giacomo Matteotti, the only case on record in South America of the Italian martyr's being so honored.

In addition to the Italian Liberal Center, which has constantly kept alive in the last fifteen years the flame of freedom in the Italian colony, there is now a large branch of the Free Italy Committee, with subcommittees already organized in the near-by localities of Punta Alta and Ingeñero White, and others in the process of being organized elsewhere. Italian workers are employed in large numbers in the railroads and cold-storage plants which are under British or North American management. Free Italy organizers have made great progress among them, and are now the largest single nationality group in the local anti-Nazi prodemocratic movement.

Organizers for Argentine co-operation with Italia Libre found an enthusiastic reception in Rosario, the grain and meat metropolis north of Buenos Aires on the river. Here the Italian population alone is 75,000. Immigrants are mostly from Piedmont and Liguria, but there are also Southerners, the Abruzzians and the Sicilians. With their Argentine-born children and grandchildren these courageous, liberal-minded men constitute a great stumbling block to the Nazification of this rich area of Argentina.

It was not hard to persuade these Italians that their salvation lay in active support of such a movement as Italia Libre, which had existed for some time before the end of 1941, but largely as a vehicle for radical political expression. Once the direction and tone of the Free Italy movement was changed under the leadership of Count Sforza, it began to attract adherents in large numbers. In September, 1941, Italians of Rosario for the first time in many years staged a public, open-air celebration of the Twentieth of September. Italia Libre headquarters were opened in the downtown district. Local newspapers like *La Tribuna* turned over their columns to this movement for announcements and propaganda. Government censorship of Free Italy's radio texts prevented a similar arrangement with broadcasting stations.

The Free Italians in Rosario, as everywhere in South America, faced the prospect of fighting the Italian consular organization. This is not an easy thing for nationals living abroad. Commercial firms depend on consular offices for goodwill and for permission to trade. These businesses always constitute the backbone of the Fascist organization abroad. They are subject to continuous pressure; none of them can stand the consequences of resistance. In Rosario the Italian Fascist units, such as the Fascio itself, the Dopolavoro, and the veterans' organization—all hit by the Argentine decree of 1939—still operate in the disguise taught them by the Nazis. Now they are the Casa de Italia, a central clearinghouse for all organization and propaganda in favor of Fascism. The Dante Alighieri School here, as elsewhere in Argentina, is a focal point for propaganda. The school's administrative offices are in the same building with the Italian consulate. The school is under the patronage of wealthy Fascists, mostly importers and exporters. The school not only holds frequent social events where parents are brought together and taught Fascism, but it also boasts a full-fledged Spanish department under a Falangist instructor. In Rosario, Fascists listen to their own radio broadcasts and read the Buenos Aires newspaper *Il Mattino d'Italia*. All the Italian social and welfare clubs are of course under Fascist control, down to the Italian Red Cross. This is inevitable where pressure can be applied from Rome. Wherever Fascism is operative in South America among Italian settlers, it is because of this pressure. The bulk of membership in the Fascio is always made up by clerks and minor employees of the firms that can be brought into line by threat of economic reprisal.

The Fascists, like the Nazis, have learned to use farmers' grange organizations as a rural counterpart of the business houses under control. Throughout the Entre Rios provinces, where small farming is more common than elsewhere in Argentina and where the German and Italian populations are heavy, farm groups are well organized. The natural independence of men of the soil tends to retreat before the benefits of both economic and social organization. This is particularly true where farmers settle a strange country and learn a strange tongue; they are easily persuaded to join with their countrymen in fighting loneliness and all the strange new problems of price and production. It is everlastingly to the credit of Axis organizers that they saw at a glance all the possibilities inherent in this condition among the farmers of the river country of Argentina. The advantage held by the totalitarian Powers in this vital part of South America (perhaps the most vital now that Brazil is in the war) was gained while democracy slept.

Free Italians count on the recently organized Youth Section to carry in the years to come the burden of mass persuasion in Rosario. The fact that Italian immigration into Argentina came with a tremendous rush, then quit almost entirely at the close of the last century, makes the young Italian Argentine the key figure in the dramatic counter-attack of democracy along the river Plata. His are the shoulders upon which Argentina's future must rest. He is the backbone of the trades and crafts, small business, farming. He and his fellows will constitute the middle class as it rises out of the estancia system.

If the Italians are the flesh and blood of democracy among Argentina's European nations, its backbone is the Spanish Republican movement. The victory of Franco in Spain, of course, merely postponed the inevitable day of complete Spanish democracy. Those Spanish patriots who fled Franco vengeance on the collapse of resistance in Spain have been sown broadcast from New York to Buenos Aires, where their seed flourishes in a burning desire for eventual triumph. It is fortunate for Argentina that in the last hundred years its Spanish immigration has been largely from Euzkadi, Galicia, and Catalonia, where love of liberty is like thirst and hunger. There are 3,000,000 of Basque descent in South America, most of them in Argentina and Chile. There are 80,000 true Catalans, and their children are uncounted. Until a generation ago the Galicians were so numerous and so distinct that their name came to represent the entire Iberian Peninsula in Argentina.

The Basques will never rest until they have made their homeland a free, autonomous country participating with dignity in the new council of nations. Acción Vasca, Emakume Albertzale, Laurak Bat, Euzko Txokoa, the Basque section of *El Centro Republicano Español,* and all the other newspapers, periodicals, and active political units of the Basques in Argentina labor for that end. When former President Aguirre of the Basque Republic visited Buenos Aires and Montevideo after more than three years of Odyssean wandering, he was met in the style of a monarch on royal progress through his realm. His final settlement in the United States has turned the eyes of free Basques northward as the eyes of Italians are on Count Sforza. A Basque without liberty is like a lion caged. He rests neither day nor night. Herding sheep across the crags of Patagonia or taking his maté in the shade of an ombú like an island in the pampa, he is a machine working toward the day when he and his people will stand up again free beside their free neighbors.

The Spaniards, like the people of all broken, mountainous countries, feel patriotism as a local sentiment. Unconsciously they resist not only internationalism as represented by the Communist ideal and later by the Nazi dream of New Europe, but they resist the conception of Spain as a homogeneous nation. No Irishman singing in exile of the vales of Killarney or the hedgerows of Skibereen brings his nostalgia closer to his own fireside than the Spaniard away from the hills of home. The Spaniard who hates Franco for rejecting provincialism and forcing the state down his throat finds it difficult to co-operate with the movement for a unified Republican Spain. Until all elements agree on a formula for a Union of Spanish Democracies there will be no common channel through which can flow the energy to carry Spain to freedom.

The Spanish problem is in miniature the problem of Europe. It is the problem of the United States in its first seventy-five years of independent existence. It is inconceivable to a Catalonian—in whose blood is the blood of a Raimundo Lulio or a Berenguer, on whose tongue is the language of the troubadours, in whose heart is the sweep of the northern valleys to the sea—that he should be subject to a bureau in Madrid, or a monarch in Madrid, or an office of the Falange. He has less in common with the gypsies of Seville, despite an attempt at a common tongue, than he has with the burghers of Avignon—yet he is not by any means French. Barcelona has fought with a bloody sword for a thousand years to be Barcelona. If there is now someone to deny it, it will fight for another thousand years. That is the spirit of the Spanish unconquerables. To suppose that they have bowed to Franco or that they will accept democratic rule that fails to understand their character is to miss the entire point of the Spanish struggle for freedom.

International Communism, as impersonal in its ideals as medicine or psychology, failed in Spain, as Falangism must fail, because it couldn't understand individuals. The conception of the world as a beehive where workers move in an everlasting line to their job of constructing cells and more cells on into the infinite is no dream for a Spaniard. He can't stomach it with the tantara of Falange hautboys accompanying the fairy story of Gothic splendor. Nor can he get it down with the oily dressing of comradeship on the lips of whiskered intellectuals just out of Russian prisons.

The Spanish Republican Front in Exile makes its principal headquarters in Mexico City, where flourish in dignity, like Alfred among the Saxon cottagers, the Socialist party; the National Popular Front; the UGT (Unión General de Trabajadores de España); the PCE (Communist party of Spain); the JSU (League of Socialist Youth of Spain, and of Catalonia); the PSUC (United Socialist party of Catalonia); the PSU (United Socialist party of Spain); and the individual trade-unions or syndicates of Spain.

The most notable document to come out of this boudoir of unhappy bedfellows is the Xochimilco Pact, signed February 16, 1941, among the floating gardens of the Vale of Mexico. The pact, in the form of a pledge to the Spanish people, says:

We commemorate on this sixteenth day of February the fifth anniversary of a democratic victory of our people against the forces of reaction which had taken possession of power. On February 16, 1936, the Spanish people, with magnificent unity in the Popular Front, defeated in a historic election the reactionary forces of our country, to obtain once more the popular liberties which had been taken away and a Government which, faithful to our democratic regime, had interpreted the program of the Popular Front and, with it, the fundamental interests of Spain.

But the Spanish reactionary forces—the most backward and sanguinary that any people can know—in league with Italo-German Fascism, could not consent to the electoral triumph of February, nor that the Spanish should live under a republican regime, by means of which might develop a democratic revolution permitting the social progress of Spain, in relation and in harmony with other peoples. Great church dignitaries, great landholders, financial oligarchies, a caste-ridden Army, with the support of international fascism, organized to deal a deathblow to the Spanish Republic and to our people, who were making sure progress toward a regime of liberty and democracy.

On July 18, 1936, the reactionary forces, encouraged and supported by Italo-Germans, rebelled against a legal and democratic regime, and came out against what had been the result of the national will expressed by means of popular elections. The Spanish people, thanks to its unity in the Popular Front, fought against the uprising in thirty-two months of heroic struggle for their national independence, for liberty, and for peace. Spanish fascism, with the decided support of Italy and Germany, has not been capable of conquering the forces of Spanish democracy, in spite of the latter's having been abandoned by the so-called democratic Powers with their infamous "nonintervention." The example of thirty-two months of struggle is the clearest proof of the unity which animated the Spanish people in their struggle for the independence and liberty of Spain. Only the unspeakable treason of Casado and all those who aided him in supplanting the Constitutional Government with the so-called Council of Defense, by means of a rebellious force which had already gone over to the enemy, was able to put an end to our Republic, delivering our people up unarmed to the most frightful sacrifice, and thus permitting fascism and international reaction to win a transitory victory which opened the way for the unleashing of the present horrible conflagration.

By means of a policy of merciless repression and extermination of the people, the reactionary forces, headed by Franco and the

Falange, have tried and are still trying in vain to still all the traditional longing of the Spaniards for liberty and to strengthen the bloody Falangist regime. But the victories and benefits won by the working class, the farmers, the middle class, by the whole people, with the Republic; the experience gained by the latter in its heroic struggle for its freedom lives on for better days, and the perennial memory of them constitutes the most effectual incentive for their resistance and struggle.

The Spanish workers, farmers, and petty bourgeoisie, the best of the intellectual class, including some nuclei of the rural clergy and certain middle-class elements—all wholesome forces, all honorably inclined people; in Catalonia, in Euzkadi, in Galicia, in Asturias, in indomitable Madrid, in every corner of Spain—show their opposition and repugnance to a system which has the most abominable exploitation, reaction, and crime as its foundation.

Again, as after the reaction following October, 1934, there is being forged the unity which in February, 1936, won a great victory for democracy and liberty.

In resistance and in the anti-Franco struggle there is being developed the process of unity in all social strata and among the different political tendencies of our Spain.

Socialists, Republicans, Communists, Syndicalist forces, Catholics, Nationalists, men who have never had a party or organization, honest elements and true patriots of the Army and military institutions, intellectuals and men of science—all are struggling and contributing to systematic action, impelled by an irresistible force, against terror, hunger, the entrance of Spain into the war; for a general amnesty which would liberate prisoners and thousands of refugees, families, husbands, sons, fathers, who suffer and fight for the liberty and independence of their country in their exile. All forces are merging their aspirations and longings in [the winning of] a victory, in the reconquest of a popular and democratic Republic which would return their liberties to our people, secure the right of Catalonia and Euzkadi to liberties, peace, work, and well-being for all.

The signers of this document, members of the Spanish democratic progressive parties and organizations, men who have held positions of responsibility in the Republican regime; intellectuals, chiefs, and officials loyal to the Spanish Republic, on this sixteenth day of February, the anniversary of the triumph of the Popular Front of 1936, issue a call to the Spanish people, to those who in prisons and concentration camps are enduring the ferocity of the Franco regime; to the farmers of our Spain, despoiled of their lands, to the workers of industry, to public officials, to soldiers, to Army elements faithful to the Republic and the people, to the women, to heroic Spanish youth, to all those who have struggled and are still struggling for the Republic against Franco and re-action and against the traitors to it, to all worthy sons of demo-cratic and popular Spain, in order that on this sixteenth day of February you may redouble your efforts combined with those of the victims of repression, in order that you may strengthen the bonds of unity, in order that you may intensify your efforts for the new Popular Front which shall rise from the very heart of the Spanish people inspired by an unquenchable faith in the victory of the people.

We likewise issue a call to Spanish Republican emigrants, to those who suffer in the concentration camps of Franco and Africa, and to those who tirelessly work and labor all over the world in order that, with the memory of February 16, 1936, and the heroic liberating war of our Spain, they may be worthy of those who fell in the struggle and be inspired by those who continue the struggle with sublime courage, and by those who at every mo-ment of their loyalty to our cause of liberty defy death, and that they may redouble their aid in favor of those who continue strug-gling in every town in Spain.

The very wording of this document, the pat phrases of the professional radicals, raises the gorge in many true demo-cratic liberals who want none of recrimination, who have no desire for another Spanish civil war, who believe that only through the courage and faith of individuals without man-aged fanaticism can men win their way to freedom. The pact disappointed many politically oriented Spanish republicans because they thought it failed to recognize adequately the national aspirations of Catalonians, Basques, and Galicians. This dissent was so sharp that representatives of the PSU and PSUC refused to sign the document, turning a deaf ear to the very eloquent plea for unity. This split widened the breach between the true world Communists, insisting on the international character of the revolution, and the Spanish Socialists interested in the individual happiness of the Spanish provinces seeking regional autonomy.

Somebody with a Rabelaisian sense of the ridiculous may be sitting among the Olympian gods laughing to himself with great belly laughs—because Juan Comorera, general secretary of the PSUC, when he headed south to explain to his fellow Catalonians why he couldn't subscribe to the Xochimilco Pact was thrown out of Argentina as a dangerous Communist. It is likely that Comrade Comorera, along with many other Catalonians, would have deserted Communist leadership over the question of autonomy had he been given a chance to move around and discuss the matter with his fellows. In persecuting him, the Argentine Government very likely kicked out of his head any soft ideals that may have been growing there in the direction of a peaceful approach to the problems of Spain.

In general, that is how militant Bolsheviks are made. The true strategist never makes the mistake of uniting all opposition elements against him. In fighting Communism, as in fighting Nazism, the governments of many American republics often abandon the principles of strategy. The average liberal is open-minded about political action. He knows what are his ideals, but he doesn't know the technique of arriving at them. He is constantly being wooed by extremists who tell him all governments are capitalistic, reactionary, and unsympathetic toward the great problems of the common people. In South America, as elsewhere, the failure of constituted authorities to keep abreast of the mentally active citizen tends to clinch the argument put forward by the extremists and build within the body politic a united revolutionary spirit led by its most active, and therefore most dangerous, elements.

When Germany and Soviet Russia agreed to divide some of the spoils and keep the peace, Communists became suddenly silent about the Nazi menace. For a year preceding the German attack on Russia Communist organs maintained a neutral tone in dealing with the war. They were strict isolationists. There was an air of official unconcern over the massacre of Poles, Czechs, and other Soviet neighbors. Communist newspapers in Buenos Aires were busy as can be publicizing the deplorable wages and working conditions in American-owned beef-packing plants, British-owned public utilities, capitalist-owned industry of any kind. Within twenty-four hours after German troops moved across the Soviet border the newspapers were screaming bloody murder, calling the enemy Prussian butchers and making love to the American beef-packing plants, the British-owned public utilities, and anything or anybody connected with what are now the United Nations.

There is reason to doubt that the Soviet Government itself ever took any particular notice of the erratic activities of these self-styled Communist agents. Communism, like religion, can be operated as a racket. There are sincere believers in communal ownership among all peoples the world over. And there are frenetic agitators the world over who have nothing more to offer than the half-baked political slogans hatched by a few pale-eyed Mensheviks as they starved to death in the Czar's prisons back in 1908. In Latin America somebody, probably the Church, has persuaded governments to hunt all of them down indiscriminately with special police, beat them in horror chambers, ride them out of town in disgrace, and turn their children over to the juvenile authorities.

Of the hundred-odd ways to refute the Communist argument, this is about the only one that is invalid.

Only among the Spanish republicans is the Communist element important in the prodemocratic community of Argentina, although it has some influence in most of the other national groups.

An increasing factor in Argentina and throughout the rest of Latin America is the Free French movement. There are more Lorraine crosses in evidence than swastikas in most communities from Mexico City to Tierra del Fuego. There are 10,000 Free French in Buenos Aires alone, and it is claimed that their bulletin circulates to 80,000. Free France is strong in Chile, Bolivia, Uruguay, Peru, Mexico, and the Central American nations, although it doesn't have official branches in all these countries. The Free France movement, largely De Gaullist, is the most sophisticated, enthusiastic, and self-sacrificing of all the Free movements among European peoples in America. Albert Guérin, hero of the First World War, gave up his important business in Buenos Aires to lead Free France in Argentina. With Vichy controlling French diplomatic and consular establishments, it is obviously impossible to stay in a French business and follow De Gaulle. Albert Ledoux, important French diplomat in Montevideo, resigned his post on the fall of France and personally organized Free France in Uruguay, Chile, Peru and Ecuador, making his own inspection trips and attending inter-American conferences such as that at Rio de Janeiro.

There are similar movements among Austrians, Hungarians, and Rumanians in Argentina, but the same elements of confusion and cross-purpose that brought their homelands to disaster have weakened the effort of exiles and immigrants in Latin America. There are Communists and monarchists, secret societies and countersocieties—with the Hapsburgs and King Carol thrown in for good measure.

FREE PEOPLE FROM EUROPE 241

A bright contrast is the democratic singleness of purposes to be found in the large Polish community of Argentina, where all but the Ukrainian Poles are bitterly anti-Nazi. There are only about 40,000 real Poles in Argentina. Most of those in Argentina are laborers or farmers, with a small professional and intellectual class. The majority live in Buenos Aires, La Plata, Rosario, Santa Fé and Córdoba, where they are laborers in the meat-packing plants and on the railroads. The greatest Polish farm community is surrounded by Germans in the Misiones territory. Despite some local antagonisms, the Poles in Argentina are intensely patriotic, and willing to sacrifice themselves to see the defeat of fascism. Polish volunteers flow out of Argentina in a steady stream to the Polish armed forces in Great Britain.

The Poles are united in the Federación de las Sociedades Polacas, which combines many smaller groups. Their daily newspaper is the *Kurier Codzcenny;* there are three weekly papers—*Glos Polski* and *Gazeta Polska* in Buenos Aires and a Catholic weekly in Misiones.

The Polish Government in London misses few bets in South America. Minister Arciszewski, accredited to Argentina, is prominent in the diplomatic world. He was Polish representative to the League of Nations. Ministers have been appointed recently to Bogotá, to Montevideo, and to Lima.

The power of democracy among all these European-born South Americans is a growing power, and it will in time have its tremendous influence in shaping the destiny of Argentina. If it lacks adequate leadership, it is because it is hardly yet aware of its own strength and purpose. If it is alternately shouted down by the Nazis and pushed around by the fire-eating radicals within its own ranks, it is because it is still developing politically. Not to have faith in its ultimate triumph is not to have faith in the future.

PART THREE

"HE THAT REGARDETH THE CLOUDS SHALL NOT REAP"

CHAPTER XVII

THOSE PEOPLE, OUR NEIGHBORS

AS A BOY I was struck by the fact that the villain in any given Western story—later in any given Western motion picture—was likely to be a Mexican. In those rare instances in which the villain was an Anglo-Saxon renegade, his most vicious henchmen were Mexicans. At the same time the bad girl of the story—and later of the picture—was a Mexican girl named Lolita or Conchita or Pepita or what not. Usually she worked evenings in a cantina just across the border (somehow the border was always near by), filling out her pay check by prostitution or by tipping off the bandit boss that the Bar-X cattle were going to cross the San Pedro at eleven o'clock that night.

I used to read the stories with a growing sense of rebellion against the author, who most likely lived in White Plains or Jersey City and showed up once a week at his office on Fifth Avenue. I rebelled because my short life in southern Arizona and California had taught me already that the best citizens of the district were Mexicans. When the family was gypped out of an orchard and later other assorted real estate, it was by Yankees. After a long ride on the range it was the Mexican adobe with a short tallow candle lighting up its calcimined walls that offered bed for the night, and "Welcome, paisano." My best friend was an old Mexican who sat philosophically through the afternoon hours leaning against the ranch house making rawhide quirts for the movie cowboy trade. The Mexican girls I knew were more reserved than

245

the blonde tarts who "picked up" at the first honk of an automobile and drank gin until they couldn't see. The Mexican girls mostly married and had fourteen kids, while a lot of the other girls got lost in alcoholic spinsterhood somewhere between the Armistice and Coolidge Prosperity.

Later in Japan I watched American tourists making the rounds of the geisha houses, the *sukiyaki* parlors, and the Imperial gardens. When they filed back full of sake to their ships, they usually burbled over with happiness about the daintiness of it all, the local color, the happy way of life, the innate sense of piety and propriety that distinguished the Nipponese. Nobody saw in them a dangerous, implacable enemy masking their cold efficiency behind pretty manners.

Attending motion pictures and plays, and reading more stories, I arrived at the conclusion that Englishmen were aloof, uninterested, dressed in tweeds, tall and bony, addicted to smoking pipes, of a strange speech heavily interspersed with "ah" and "oh-ah," consciously superior to Americans. I had to go to them to find out I had been looking at a caricature of a half-dozen of London's funniest characters—and mistaking them for the English people.

In the course of time it has come to me that North Americans may be congenitally unable to understand the people of any other country. Our literature has become the Sunday newspaper comic page and our geography has become the Hollywood movie. We don't look for Englishmen in Dickens or for Russians in Dostoevski, or for Frenchmen in De Maupassant. We've got them all in the funnies and in the pictures, so to heck with it. If we come out thinking Alphonse and Gaston are Frenchmen, Micha Auer is Russian, and Sir Cedric Hardwicke is English, well, all right.

It is no wonder Argentina is unknown to the average North American. Even those who go there to do business come back with a most remarkably superficial conception of

Latin life, gathered at the Tabaris night club or over cocktails at the apartment of the Livingstones who went to
Buenos Aires two years ago from Omaha (he is with Con-
solidated Motors) or at the race track where, my dear, we
saw a man who looked just like César Romero, you know,
in the movies? Most North Americans who make the long
trip south in order to learn something about South American
life learn about the rumba from the game steward on ship-
board and remain intellectually exhausted after this feat. Few
of them can carry on an intelligent conversation in Buenos
Aires. Most of them are without knowledge of Rubén Darío,
the great poet of Spanish America. Most of them never read
La Gloria de Don Ramiro. Most of them don't know De
Falla from Debussy. For them, the profound pattern of
Latin culture is as remote as the Upanishads. An Eskimo in
the Knickerbocker Club couldn't be any more out of place
than a salesman from New York or Detroit in the salon of
Señor Hipólito Artigas Menéndez on Avenida Alvear.

If this is true of the globe-trotter, how much more true of
the stay-at-home who doesn't know just where to look for
Buenos Aires on the map. And if this is true of Latin culture,
which is fairly simple to look into and begin to understand,
how much more true of the deep-rooted Latin folk life which
moves the people of Argentina inexorably along certain behavior paths yet is complex and difficult for outsiders to
grasp.

It is almost impossible to find a North American in the
interior of Argentina. But what is worse, it is almost impossible to find one of the 5,000-odd North Americans in Buenos
Aires anywhere but at the amusement centers or partying
within the select circle of their own people. There are some
exceptions.

You can't do business with people you don't understand;
you can't understand people unless you live with them or

study from intelligent observers who have lived with them. And unless we understand Argentina or something about Argentina the slogan "Continental Solidarity" is just wishful thinking.

Stop a North American on the street and ask him to describe an Argentine and he will admit ignorance, or start out: "Well, he's a dark, Spanish-looking guy wearing a kind of baggy pants, a flat-brimmed hat, a wide leather belt, and a scarf around his neck." This individual is describing a music-hall gaucho character popular about 1914 in Paris. He has seen Rudolph Valentino in *The Four Horsemen*. This is very funny, like describing a German as a man in Bavarian yodeling costume. Or an American as a tall old man with a white goatee wearing red-and-white striped pants that fasten under his boots.

There is nothing wrong with ignorance frankly admitted. But when a nation of 130,000,000 ready to step into a role of world leadership at a time when its people are waiting in agonized hope bases an important part of its international policy on ignorance—then failure to attempt to overcome that ignorance becomes a sin against mankind. The fact that the people of Latin America are willing to accept a large measure of United States leadership after being caricatured unmercifully in our art and literature demonstrates the desperation of the people of the world, and punctuates the tremendous, sobering responsibility come to rest on our shoulders.

With the beginning of the Good Neighbor policy and pressure on Hollywood and the pulp magazines to "clean up" Little Mexico, the villains in the pictures and stories ceased to be García and López. It turns out now (our mistake) that García and López are pretty fine folks, and while Vice-President Wallace gets south of the border for a tamale feed out in Chapultepec Park or somewhere we are busy bringing out happier Mexican caricatures, but still caricatures. The Latins

are now our friends, and their tropical rhythms are all
through our blithe popular songs. Leo Carrillo has now come
into his own, and is sometimes saving the heroine from a
fate worse than death at the hands of a blond bandit from
Duluth. Carmen Miranda is singing her Brazilian Negro
songs and Xavier Cugat is working his string and percussion
section like a shipyard swing shift. Walt Disney is galloping
Mickey Mouse and Donald Duck across the pampa on a
spotted *pingo* while women's clubs are hearing lectures on
"The Culture of the Incas," with slides.

There is nothing wrong, certainly, in wanting to be good
neighbors. But first we must understand our neighbors.

The first handicap to getting acquainted is a dull sense
of geography. We know more about Europe than we know
about America. We lump everybody south of us from Mexicans to Patagonians in one vague, dark-skinned mass. A quick
glance at a good map should show us some of the obvious
differences—the mountains, the tropical jungles, the warm,
dry highlands, the low plains, each producing through the
course of the centuries variations in dress, speech, social structure, industries, and all the web of life. A look into racial
origins makes immediately plain other differences between
these many highly individual republics and between the
larger districts within those republics. A superficial study of
the foreign trade of the United States begins to bring out
new lights and colors, economic zones, commercial routes,
growing industrialization in limited areas—the broad outlines
of the business and occupational patterns. The first thing we
know we are talking about Mexico, Argentina, Brazil, or Colombia and have stopped using that misleading term "Latin
America."

Each one of these nations is an individual. They are no
more like each other than France is like England. A Mexican
is more like a Californian than he is like a Brazilian. An

Argentine is more like a Florentine than he is like a Colombian. There is a closer affinity in language, tradition, dress, and daily habit between Canada and the United States than between almost any two Southern republics whose borders meet. This is the result of the lack of modern transportation and communication in a rugged, isolated territory cut up for centuries into independent and mutually distrustful states.

There is (or was) an international groove down which North American tourists have been pushed by a multiplicity of travel bureaus. This groove is worn smooth by the efforts of many busy, earnest men and women engaged in the travel industry. When travel was a big business, from 1922 to 1932, there was developed a system whereby a banker, a bootlegger, a schoolteacher, or a grass widow could buy a ticket through alluring foreign lands shown in the gaudy travel folder. Things were so wonderfully managed that the traveler paid the bill in a lump sum ("Our Easy, Convenient Plan"), required no foreign language, and was assured of pleasant company—perhaps even from his own home town—during the trip. De luxe was the journey itself. Trained guides explained the Pyramids, the Inca ruins, the Boro-Budur, the Tower of London, so that no research of any kind was required of the tourist. He could just relax and watch the panorama of the world float past his eyes, which glazed a little more thickly each day until they registered the blank stare of travel-bureau hypnosis the last two weeks before reaching New York. This system was one of the greatest frauds ever perpetuated by the victims themselves. It is possible by that system to see the world expensively and get less out of it than from a series of intelligent lectures or even a course of short-subject motion pictures.

In connection with bureau traveling there grew up in every popular tourist center from Shanghai to Paris a cluster of hotels, souvenir stores, and night clubs where English was

spoken almost exclusively and where travelers could get the
same kind of personal service they were used to in Boston or
San Diego. At the height of this outrage it was almost impossible for a bureau tourist to get more than a quick glimpse
of the strange countryside from the window of a charabanc.

Any travel undertaken without an intense personal preparation in language, geography, biography, history, and sociol-
ogy is a waste of time. Any travel which puts the responsibility of asking directions, ordering food and lodging, and
devising itineraries on someone else is an education only for
someone else.

When the sheer boredom and later the growing difficulties
of European travel made the Latin republics popular with
North American tourists, they began to pour into Mexico
City, into Havana, into Rio de Janeiro, Santiago, and Buenos
Aires—along the new tourist grooves prepared for them. In
Buenos Aires they were ushered from the ship to the hotel,
from the *portería* to their rooms, from their rooms to the
"principal points of interest" (whatever they were), then
back to their rooms, to a night club where the manager had
been expecting them and had cleaned up the show a little,
to their rooms, to "a typical Argentine Criollo restaurant,"
back to the rooms, and shortly back to the ship. These people
were exhausted. They had been through the same routine at
each port. They were so tired that each inconvenience seemed
to them an international insult. They missed the good chocolate malts they used to get at Bender's drugstore. They
missed all the other comforts. They arrived with nothing to
give Buenos Aires but a few dollars in cash. They took nothing away but some perfume or lingerie they could have
bought in New York.

While this mass movement of vacationists and honeymoon-
ing couples flooded the tourist hotels, there was a very thin
stream of earnest students getting down by cattle boat or

overland, learning the language, living with native families, reading hungrily, and absorbing every color and pattern they could understand. While some of them had scholarships, most of them made it the hard way. Had these been encouraged and helped until they swelled by thousands through Central and South America, the United States might have gained a decade in good-neighborliness, a vital decade that might have knit the continent together for the hour of trial. Unfortunately most of the students and the honestly inquiring tourists of modest means find so much local color in Mexico, Central America, and Peru that they neglect Brazil and Argentina, the two most important South American nations in world affairs. Few of them get to Buenos Aires, despite the rich reward it offers North Americans with intellectual curiosity and a flair for languages. The consequence of this neglect is misunderstanding that increases with the distance south of the United States.

The kind of understanding that brings mutual respect is the basis of international co-operation. We can buy Argentine beef, Argentine mutton, Argentine hides and tallows, tannin extracts, linseed oil, and cheese. We can bolster the Argentine economy with loans. We can close up all the immediate gaps and congratulate ourselves that we have made a friend and collaborator of Argentina. But we will be mistaken. Economic domination is one thing; wholehearted co-operation is another. Articles have been written, books published, about the economic barriers between Argentina the exporter of food and North America the exporter of food. Most of these argue that the two nations must always be trade rivals, therefore political enemies. Many articles and books have appeared showing that the United States as a manufacturing nation will replace England and Germany as provider of Argentine finished goods and purchaser of Argentine raw materials. While all these factors are subject to continual change as

trade necessities and manufacturing processes and farm production indexes change, there is one solid, unchanging factor
that in the long run must govern our relations with Argentina: understanding.

Understanding between two peoples of widely divergent
cultural backgrounds can come only after effort. A Parisian
understands a *porteño* by instinct that follows a common
Latin heritage. It is no effort to the Spanish, the Italians, or
any other Mediterranean race to understand Buenos Aires.
But the Germans have learned to understand the city by the
long, difficult process of study and observation. The academic
interest of the German in things South American is proverbial. If you want to know the ethnic make-up of the Argentine
capital you must go to German scholars. If you want to know
the flora of the eastern slope of the Andes, you must go to a
German. From Humboldt to the present day Germans have
studied and written authoritatively about these things. There
are little German shops scattered all through Argentina. German commercial travelers have pioneered sales routes through
the most remote corners of this world, forging into control
of this business through personal interest and unflagging
energy. It is the German theory that initiative and energy
will conquer everything everywhere.

The people of the United States have not made a serious
effort to understand South America. They like to read superficial articles written by bright journalists after a three weeks'
flight over this tremendous continent. They like to see pretty
displays in department stores whipped up by window-dressers
who have never been south of Galveston. They like to get a
shot of Latin culture now and then in the form of a lecture
or a concert. Because they have learned to expect education
in pleasant pellets like vitamin capsules, they approach an
understanding of South America with the air of a dilettante—
if they approach it at all. Since there is no emigration prob-

lem, no overflow of crowded population from New York to Argentina, as there is from London, Paris, Berlin, and Vienna to Argentina, there isn't the same incentive to make an intensive study of the climate, economy, and anthropology of this New World nation.

There has been no serious effort to translate vital Argentine literature into English, no effort to screen Argentine motion pictures or to distribute by newspaper or magazine the rich humor that lives in Argentine caricature. There is no way the North American sitting by his fireside after a day at the office or in the plant can visit a Buenos Aires home. We can read and attend and listen to everything offered us from Spanish America without absorbing the facts about living people along the Calle San Martín or the Avenida de Mayo.

There is no way we can know about Buenos Aires until we can stand on the street corner ourselves or see the crowding, roaring thoroughfare through other sympathetic eyes: the hurrying doctor in his fedora hat, his tightly knotted, narrow tie, his starched collar, his closely buttoned, narrow-hipped suit, his pointed-toe shoes, carrying black bag and umbrella, looking quickly into the window of the caramel shop, then away guiltily; the schoolgirls arm in arm like noisy angels of mercy in their white smocks, their budding young breasts innocent beneath the cotton, their dark hair curling thickly down their straight backs, their soft, quick, liquid Spanish speech in eager counterpoint; the fat matron in black reboso, gypsy skirt, and shoes with tremendous, worn-off heels carrying an unwrapped loaf of bread under one arm and a huge grocery package by string and handle in the other hand; the overgrown boy in knickerbockers, speaking in a husky voice from a hard face in need of shaving, his eyes moving nervously between the candy shop and the figures of the girls in white; the tonneau taxi moving slowly like a spreading dowager in lusterless black, its driving proprietor a Latin W. C. Fields behind the planes of windshield glass etched in flower patterns; the flow and clot and flow of faces dark with mustaches or ruby-red with lipstick; the quick-stepping suits with pressed pants legs like the snipping blades of shears; the slowly swinging skirts nipping silk-clad legs at the plump knees. There is no way we can know about Buenos Aires until we can watch a *porteño* family of eight working and studying and dining and quarreling and reading the daily paper and listening to the radio in its tile-bright apartment off a shaded patio; or crowded into the family car of a Sunday to visit Uncle Carlitos and the cousins where their chalet is tucked away in the tree-green and stone-gray suburb of Juan B. Justo.

These are real people interested in the security of employment, in the talents and temperaments of their children, in the weather, in the progress of the war, in the scandal about the Bardinis next door, in the race results, the lottery numbers, the novena going on at the Church of St. Gabriel over on the avenue. They go to work and to school by subway or bus, visit the zoo out at the end of the carline on Saturday afternoons, and take a picnic basket out into the country two or three fine Sundays every summer.

The things that distinguish them from some of us are nothing compared to the things we have in common. If we can learn to forget our caricature notions of them, we can make a beginning at understanding and a beginning at finding common ground. When we have made this beginning, there is some possibility that the policies of government will follow the best thought and the best aspirations of both peoples. If we do not make this beginning, if we insist on our long-cherished unwillingness or inability to look at other people as anything but "funny foreigners," all the fancy speeches of earnest Pan-American promoters will echo hollowly through the sterile halls of state.

The things that distinguish these Americans from some of us are the things that make them for the most part Latin. As Latins they are slightly darker in coloring than the average Anglo-Saxon, but no darker than a cross section of New York. As Latins they are musical, artistic, critical, materialistic, dramatic, passionate, and selfish, but no more so than a cross section of Hollywood. As Latins they have a reverence for statute law, for scholarship, for individual heroism, for the art of conversation, and for the established forms of society. (These hardly represent a point of divergence from our formative way of life—only a different intensity in certain directions.) As Latins they are more delicately formed than most of us, except where North Italian, Slavic, or Teutonic blood dominates the Latin characteristics. As Latins they are more particular about their dress than most of us, and more formal in their social intercourse. But the Latin in Argentine life, like the Anglo-Saxon in North American life, is being filtered so thoroughly through so many new immigrant races that in time his blood will be mellowed and sublimated. Already the Argentine caricature that bewitches our critical faculties has disappeared together with the chin-whiskered prototype of Uncle Sam, and has left in its place a citizen of the world alert and flexible to the world's mental and spiritual currents.

If it is important to the future of the Americas that this intelligent citizen should be essentially a democrat, then the democratic propaganda that endeavors to keep him persuaded must be based on an intelligent understanding of his characteristics. The keen advertising executive who lays out an appeal to potential buyers of a new shaving cream first makes an effort to understand the men to whom he will address his advertisement. He learns their habits and the background that formed those habits. The Nazi propaganda served up to the Argentine citizen to persuade him to absorb the totalitarian drug is based on a thorough understanding of the Argentine market—the human market. If democracy fails to study this market with the same searching thoroughness, then its competitor will get the business. If democracy refuses to understand these people and to propagandize them—perhaps on the argument that propaganda is beneath its dignity— then it might as well refuse to meet the Nazi forces on the field of battle. The consequences will be the same.

There should be no doubts in the minds of any of us about the potency and the objectives of the Nazi propaganda spearhead into Buenos Aires. Since in modern ideological warfare the advantage is with the attacker, the forces of democracy in Argentina have been losing ground. Had they—had any of us—been alert to the attack when it was organized and set on the move, that advantage might have been short-lived. The same state of mind that told farm folks in Minnesota it was none of their business when Japan got into Manchuria and Italy got into Ethiopia and Germany got into Czechoslovakia persuaded us to ignore the appearance of Nazi blocks and cells in the suburbs of Buenos Aires.

Now that counterattack is being made, the advance of democracy again into its own must be won by bitter sacrifice —the price of relaxed vigilance. Despite every exhortation of democracy's patriots since the first awakening of individual liberty, we fell fast asleep at our job. Pearl Harbor was not an isolated disaster; it was an accurate symbol of the state of mind of the people on whose shoulders rests most of the responsibility for making freedom possible. There can be no rest in a world that harbors both forces, the totalitarian and the democratic. That fact should have been obvious the moment the total state was first conceived in the warped minds of disappointed men and preached to others.

You can stand on the corner of Corrientes and San Martín
in downtown Buenos Aires and take your choice of five cable
offices that will send your written word to any accessible place
on the face of the globe in five minutes. You can walk a block
and pass the offices of three world-wide news services whose
teletype machines are bringing in hundreds of words a min-
ute on every important event occurring in Burma, Alaska,
the Caucasus, the South Pacific, Murmansk, Washington,
Berlin. You can get in a cab and in a few minutes reach a
plane that will take you to Rome or New York in four days.
At the airport you can look up and see Boeings and Focke-
Wulfs flying together, each less than a week from the factory. The toilet bowl in your hotel room was made in Holland, the electric-light globe in Belgium. The locks on the
door were made in Germany. The radio is from North
America, the taxi waiting for you below was made in Italy.
The soap on your washstand is English.

These things aren't erratic, coincidental facts. They mean
that as the city-state merged into the principality and the
principality into the kingdom and the kingdom into the nation, the nation is becoming the world. Since democracy
neglected to take the initiative in assuring itself of perpetu-
ation as the dominant political force in that world, something
else has. That something else is ruthless, efficient, and all-
ambitious. It has the courage of its convictions. It has taken
the trouble to understand the people it must conquer and to
perfect a technique of conquest based on that understanding.
It has counted on the lethargy of its foe as accurately as it
has counted on the confusion of its victim. It has taken into
consideration the long sleep of democracy and the plump
citizen drowsily in bed of a Sunday morning who looks at
the papers, hears somebody talking on the radio, and turns
over muttering something that sounds like: "I wish these
guys would let up talking about what's the world going to

be like a hundred years from now. These things are getting too complex. Sometimes I wish it was like when I was a kid on the farm: just do the chores and eat and go fishing and not worry about things." This is the attitude of the adolescent who wants to use the family car, listen to the family radio, eat from the family refrigerator and the electric stove, warm himself by the furnace, go to the movies, play phonograph records, and buy his girl friend orchids flown up from the tropics, but wants none of the responsibility of fitting into the technical structure that makes all these things possible to him—to him as an individual—for the first time in the long history of mankind.

It is important that we understand what we are doing if we are to survive against a tide of disciplined robots in Japanese and German uniforms directed by Bushido or by the hard philosophy of Nietzsche and the cold system of Spengler.

It is important that we understand how well-planned, how enthusiastically executed, and how successful is the Nazi penetration into South America through Buenos Aires, as it is important to get the plain facts about the successes of the Axis on every front.

For a long time it has been the practice of North America's popular sources of information, newspapers and radio, to present only the pleasant side of life. There is some suspicion that this habit is largely responsible for the surprise registered in the minds of ordinary readers and listeners when the harsh truth seeps in upon them through other channels. It is hard to place the blame in this case. Newspapers, magazines, and radio stations in the United States must sell commercial products. In the course of time—affluent, money-making time —the sales effort has come uppermost in importance and the job of passing on information has merged into the job of creating a pleasant atmosphere conducive to larger sales for the products advertised. It is obvious that newspaper-readers will not respond to an advertisement for investment if the front page carries a story about the approach of inflation. If the readers don't respond to the advertisement, the advertising agency removes the ad from the paper and tries another paper, or tries another medium entirely. This would cause the newspaper to lose revenue, perhaps go out of business. In order to keep its advertising and its revenue and stay in business, the newspaper deliberately or unconsciously persuades its writers to sugar-coat the facts if possible, so as not to cause panic among its readers. The result is confusion.

In this remarkably subtle and fluid circle of errors and misunderstandings it is difficult to place the blame squarely on the management of newspapers. The advertiser is to blame; he has been shortsighted. The public is to blame; it has not taken the trouble to insist on the truth. This process has been going on so long that it has become second nature to news editors. Now out of sheer instinct they headline the civic reception for the town's returning hero and play down the disastrous crop damage wrought by last night's frost. They play up an isolated commando raid on a small French port and play down the loss of the Caucasian oil fields. They play up the bombing of a Japanese destroyer and play down the loss of a vital island system. And so it goes, with a badly deceived people trying to orient themselves in the greatest life-and-death struggle since the creation of the world. Until they orient themselves they will continue to lose.

The people of our country have intact the machinery for public enlightenment, a machinery available to few other peoples. It is possible that our salvation lies in the better operation of the machinery.

In the process of playing Pollyanna Across-the-Ocean through the totalitarian conquest of Europe we have at the same time missed the facts about the totalitarian designs on the rest of the world, including our own continent. With that North American optimism which makes us happy but out of touch with reality, we have taken it for granted that all the American nations are democratic, that democratic people are satisfied everywhere with their lot and ready to resist any kind of aggression, that a nation to be conquered must be assaulted by armies and navies, that the oceans are too wide to permit an attack on America.

While we have been taking all these things for granted the enemy has taken nothing for granted. He has carefully organized for conquest; he has spent no idle day since first his plans took shape. Where faith in democracy has been an obstacle, he has systematically broken down that faith through political confusion and ceaseless attack by spoken and written words. Where patriotism has been an obstacle, he has carefully insinuated himself into the minds of people as the champion of renascent nationalism, the ultra-ultra of all patriotic attitudes. Where military strength has been an obsta-. cle, he has put his own technical advisers into the entire military structure until it is as much his as his victim's. Where international diplomacy has been an obstacle, he has pressured his way into the councils of the chiefs of state until through their own mouths he has blocked the cementing of a system of defense. Where trade has been an obstacle, he has worked day and night to divert it to channels that suit his purpose, and where this was impossible, he has destroyed the routes of transport upon which that trade must depend.

Again, the only antidote is understanding; a clear conception of the quality and the objectives of the enemy. When the people of the United States understand Argentina and understand the nature of the assault it is already sustaining and must yet sustain, there will be laid the first groundwork for an intelligent common defense.

CHAPTER XVIII

SAM IN WONDERLAND

THAT overshadowing, slow-moving, terrifying giant which is the United States of America—or the Colossus of the North, as he is called everywhere below the Line—doesn't know his own strength. He doesn't even know in what way exactly he is different from the other creatures of the earth. Even among the giants he is a tremendous spectacle. But unlike the brooding, mystic giant that is Russia and the wounded, suffering giant that is China, he is too busy and too noisy to stop and look at himself. When the growing, immature North American giant finds out who he is and what he is, it will be his day to rule the world. He will rule it in example and in spirit, if not by sheer force.

Le jazz hot took Paris before the panzer divisions were in the blueprint stage. Model T Fords were beating across the granite shoulders of Patagonia before anybody heard of Hitler. Laurel and Hardy were wowing the Javanese kids in the Surabaya Crystal Palace when people still thought the Mikado was a musical by Gilbert and Sullivan.

There has never been a propaganda to equal the propaganda of North America in extent or potential effectiveness. It missed its mission and let the world slip into self-destruction because it was a propaganda without aim or direction. In the history of strategy it may be pointed out for many centuries to come how the North American civilization held a world in the hollow of its hands for one brief unthinking moment before it lost hold.

When the interisland liner *Tjinegara* slipped into the harbor of Menado in the Celebes one June morning in 1939, she was surrounded in an instant by native outriggers with their names painted on the slim bows. There were twenty-four little boats manned by Malays who had been ruled by the Portuguese and the Dutch for more than three hundred years. There were fifteen Malay names, one Portuguese, three Dutch, and five English names painted in block letters. Shining out proudly among their fellows were the outriggers *Clark Gable*, *Mickey Mouse*, *Chicago*, *Highball*, and *Whoopee*. Between the United States and the port of Menado in the Netherlands East Indies there was but one fragile line of contact: the movies. In a half-dozen years Hollywood motion pictures had broken down the influence of the Portuguese and the Netherlands empires based on ten generations of assiduous labor by a succession of sweating administrators. The Malay loves his boat. He lives on it. When he names it he is telling something about himself.

Buenos Aires after dark is a suburb of Hollywood. From nine o'clock until one you can't drive a car anywhere in the theater district. The streets are jammed with men, women, and children on foot going into or coming out of the show houses. The afternoon performance, the vermouth, is over. Most theaters show three features, although a half-dozen snooty first-run houses show two features, short subjects, and newsreels. Dorothy Lamour and Hedy Lamarr stir an undertone of pleased exclamation through the male section. Ladies watch fascinated as Rhett Butler carries Scarlett upstairs to her boudoir; you could hear a pin drop. Wave after wave of screams sweep through the darkened house as de cops move in on de mob with tommy guns blazing.

In the next picture, when the sophisticate at the Park Avenue cocktail party mentions his trip to Buenos Aires (he says Bewnas Airs), there is a ripple of incredulity through the audience, and people turn to exclaim to each other. This great, appreciative motion-picture audience is gathered and held spellbound under the most adverse mechanical circumstances. All pictures are tracked for sound in the original spoken English. Flickering subtitles spattered across the bottom of the film try to explain the action and the conversation. All they can do is give a rough idea of what's happening. Nuances and subtle references are lost to the Spanish-speaking audience. High-school, Harlem, and Western slang are not to be translated. You can't say "zoot suit" or "umpchay" or "what's cookin'" in Spanish.

Priests can solemnly warn from the pulpit, newspapers can editorialize until the type fonts wear out, parents can admonish their children and grandparents admonish the parents, but as long as Hollywood motion pictures get into Buenos Aires people are going to see them. Wherever people see Hollywood movies, the propaganda of the United States has moved in, for better or for worse. This propaganda insinuates itself slowly and thoroughly into its audience, impregnating entire sections of the receptive brain as colored water seeps through crushed ice in the soft-drink jars at the carnival.

There doesn't seem to be anybody else aware of it, but this propaganda is a weapon Hitler, Mussolini, and Hirohito would give their shirts to possess. They are more afraid of it than they are of our entire staff of diplomats in top hats and coattails. They have tried to fight it with doctored newsreels, with ideological motion pictures made in their own studios. They have tried encouraging and bribing Argentine film companies to produce something better than the North American product. They have tried to persuade the Government to embargo Hollywood films. They have thrown stench bombs into theaters. Nothing works. Wherever they live, whatever the language they speak, whatever it costs them, people go to the movies.

No doubt there have been smart bureaucrats in Washington itching to get their hands on the film industry and make it produce what the propaganda strategists know will persuade this almost numberless audience to militant democracy. (If they don't know its failures and its possibilities, they are blind.) If that should happen, the entire influence of pictures abroad and at home would in the course of time die as everything has died that depended on official inspiration. The problem is to produce pictures richly alive with the genius of individual men and women—but men and women aware of the power and the danger of the thing they are making.

Only a handful of sophisticates understands that motion pictures have nothing to do with real life, as the Victorian novel had nothing to do with real life. Most of the millions of people who sit spellbound through them are naïve people. Somehow in the back of their minds they identify themselves with Spencer Tracy or Lana Turner. They live through an hour and forty minutes of distilled life, a life carefully concocted by technicians devoted to the trade of carrying people's imaginations away into the ether.

Entire crime waves follow gangster pictures. Schoolgirls go into years of dreamy half-world romance following a series of Jimmy Stewart releases. This instrument is so explosive that the slightest touch may change hundreds of thousands of lives. Two or three smashing Air Corps pictures sent aviation enlistments skyrocketing. Motion pictures aren't entertainment; they are a passion, an existence. Motion-picture stars with no more intelligence or spiritual flame than your grocery clerk are worshiped as devoutly as the purest neophyte worships Our Lady of Mysteries. Some stars have their clothes torn off them when they step out into the street, their followers clutching at bits of shirt and trousers in a paroxysm of delight. The impression made by these living, speaking gods and the ideas they are coached to express through their words and actions go immeasurably deeper into the souls of their simple followers than any kind of ideological argument put forth on paper or from the lecture platform.

Because they are sophisticated themselves, motion-picture producers are unable to understand the exact quality of audience reaction. They know how to read box-office figures, but there is something else that changes with the varying mentalities and cultural backgrounds of the various "customers." It is this conflict between the conception of pictures as a business enterprise and the conception of pictures as a way of expressing life that confuses the strongest propaganda the United States ships to the rest of the world.

Often I have sat in the "Pullman" section of the Ideal or the Normandie in Buenos Aires and listened to the excited whispers around me: "You see, it's like I said. In the United States the secretary sits on her employer's lap while taking dictation." Or: "Now this is a new one. I didn't know that in the United States it is the custom for the butler to sit down and dine with the family." Or: "Look! The lady is pushing all her guests into the fishpond. What a civilization!" I have squirmed through Betty Grable's getting up from her table in a night club and kicking her lingerie to swing music. I have blushed while Senators got drunk, while soldiers eloped with a jeep and the colonel's daughter, while women enticed their husband's friends into their bedrooms, while hamburger-stand waiters sang love songs to their girl customers, while newspaper reporters stood around and chewed gum while the widow wept over the corpse.

I have blushed because I knew that every pair of eyes in the audience was glued on what it took to be a faithful reproduction of everyday life in Yankeeland. I have wished for a simple announcement at the beginning of each picture, something like: "Warning! The following fantasy has nothing to do with real life. Nobody since the beginning of time ever talked the way these characters will talk nor acted the way they are going to act. This does not represent the North American civilization. It is presented to you as an animated comic strip for entertainment purposes."

After a thorough course of motion pictures, it's pretty hard to convince anybody in Buenos Aires that the United States isn't full of dance-mad kids careening drunkenly in open roadsters, Oakies and Arkies driving vacant-faced up and down four-lane concrete highways, cowboys chasing Indians with quartets of yodelers in the background, rich men's sons with Charles Boyer eyes haunting the basement stores looking for shopgirls to marry, tap dancers in Army and Navy uniforms, Dead End youngsters stealing the pennies out of the church collection box, cigar-smoking business executives talking on three telephones at once and pushing buttons with their feet, truck-drivers working their way through college by playing halfback on the football team. There is nobody to tell them they have been treated to a glimpse of the lunatic fringe, and that the majority of North Americans are middle-class people interested in their families, in books, in good music; farm and factory and small business people with simple virtues and simple vices. They have no way to become acquainted with an average North American family in an average home, with the richness of life in that home.

Because North American propaganda has made no effort to acquaint the people of Argentina with the fundamentals of our culture, it is easy for those people to assume that Nazi, Fascist, Falangist, and nationalist propagandists are right when they describe us as it suits their purpose to describe us. *El Pampero* and the other papers simply set up a typical motion-picture North American and ask: "Do you want that for a Good Neighbor?" Or they thumb through the pages of the news-picture magazines showing bare-thighed girls sitting on college steps, strip-tease queens entertaining stag parties, bandits lying beside their bullet-ridden automobiles, midgets getting married on the mayor's desk in City Hall, society girls sterilized by relatives who want the family cash. Then they ask again: "Is this a civilization on which to build Pan-Americanism?"

The intelligent, objective *porteño* has nobody to tell him that these picture magazines are exotic, nervous by-products of our life, but in no way representative. But he has plenty of determined people to tell him otherwise, and to write books about us proving otherwise. Because if our propaganda is confused and at cross-purposes, the same can't be said for Axis propaganda in Buenos Aires.

There seems to be no common purpose, no basic philosophy, guiding the propaganda that goes to Buenos Aires from the United States. While the Government is sending down booklets showing the Army, Navy, and Marines ready to jump on the Axis, news magazines are being shipped south full of debate over bottlenecks, slackers, unobtainable vital materials, shipyard and factory strikes, and all the other time-wasting alarums and excursions Nazi propaganda has taught the Argentine people to expect of North America. These articles are reprinted with great glee in every Argentine periodical subsidized from Rome or Berlin, reprinted in Spanish where they reach into the homes of the humble and shake their faith in democracy as a workable method of government. Every North American businessman, every politician, understands the purpose and effectiveness of propaganda in his own private life and that of his neighbors. The garageman knows he can't sell his brand of tires if his boy is going around telling families in the block that the tires are no good. It is astonishing to see that the United States as a community of intelligent people can't properly co-ordinate such a vital activity as our collective propaganda effort.

It is no remedy, only an excuse, to say that the unofficial

propaganda such as motion pictures, news services, and magazines is provided by private enterprise and therefore is distinct from official propaganda, which is government enterprise. And it is a very thin excuse, since we are trying to convince the still neutral people of the world that we are as efficient as the Axis with weapons of war. Everybody knows by now that propaganda, no matter who or what produces it, is the most vital weapon of war short of the attack itself. Until we show the same efficiency with international propaganda we have shown in commercial propaganda at home we are going to have a hard time convincing others we are going to win this war. And Argentina wants to know we are going to win the war before it will make a wholehearted move toward joining us, or even resisting our enemy.

The most effective, conscious propaganda effort we make is made now through newsreels—after a bad start. When the great warships go off the ways and the tanks roll off the assembly lines and the fighter and bomber planes roar into the air, newsreel-conscious Buenos Aires feels the hackles stand up on the neck. Domination of the distribution of films gives us a tremendous advantage in this field. The showing of Axis newsreels, although worked out ingeniously so as to cut as deeply as possible into the normal audience for North American films, is by necessity limited. But Axis newsreels flaunting the growth of tremendous German military power have been showing many years in Buenos Aires, building up a long tradition of invincibility; North American newsreels were still in the silly stage up to a year ago. As a result of this handicap it will be a long time before we can convince the *porteños* that we are warriors. Only deep students of modern warfare understand the basic partnership of industrial potential and military victory. Others still look at war as a masculine game played by men in cavalry boots or wearing wings.

For years Germany and Italy have been bombarding Buenos Aires with newsreels showing picked shock troops at the assault. All the soldiers in the finished picture are handsome, determined, healthy, confident men in fine uniforms; the others have been edited out of the film. At the entry of the United States into the war a batch of newsreels came south showing volunteers and draftees getting their physical examinations. Some of them were pot-bellied, wore glasses, were slightly bald. Most of them looked disconsolate. They were candid shots for the most part, certainly not professionally posed.

Only a technical expert in the audience would understand that the German pictures were official propaganda and the North American pictures were a human record of ordinary folks going only half-willingly to war. The reaction of the theatergoer was immediate and definite. It hit him on the instant that the United States was a nation of tradesmen and industrial laborers forced into a conflict against a combination of natural fighting men. The conclusion was not quite accurate, but it was the only conclusion to be drawn from the evidence at hand. Such blunders are becoming less common, and there are indications that we will learn how to use the newsreel medium to give confidence to those Latin American nations which have thrown in their lot with us, give impetus to those still hesitating, and give pause to those making love to the enemy.

If you have nothing of high quality to sell, it is all right to make a lot of noise and confuse enough people so that some of them in the emotional excitement will buy your product. But if you have something good to sell, it is a lot smarter to give out samples, to describe or demonstrate the product, to show pride in it and an understanding of its worth.

The United States has something to sell all the nations of

SAM IN WONDERLAND

271

the world: the attitude toward life that has resulted in our
representative government and our individual happiness. It
is true that we haven't produced in music a Tschaikovsky,
a Brahms, or a Sibelius—not even a Johann Strauss. But we
can play that music and record it for other generations as no
others can do it. It is true that we haven't produced a Rem-
brandt, a Velásquez, or a Praxiteles. But we have gathered
and preserved a lot of their works that otherwise might have
perished and been forgotten. It is true we have produced no
Shakespeare, Cervantes, or Goethe. But we have become the
world's greatest reading market, absorbing those classics and
understanding them as no great mass of people has before.
We will some day produce men as great as all these. And in
the meantime we have shown the way toward technical perfection, toward democratic technique, toward efficient distribution, toward the mass manufacture of luxuries.

The men and women who produce the magazines, the
radio programs, the motion pictures, and all the other propaganda mediums with which we are consciously or unconsciously influencing the minds of our neighbors need to stand
back a moment and look at the thing they are selling. They
need to study their own civilization and the part their national culture plays in it. A serious lack of orientation shows
through almost everything we send south. A very few semiofficial agencies seem to have made any effort toward finding
out what we have to sell before trying to sell it.

It seems almost ludicrous that radio programs originating
in the United States for short-wave consumption in Buenos
Aires should be top-heavy with Latin American music. Yet
that happens. It proves nothing to a *porteño* that we have
imported Cuban orchestras that can play zambas, congas, and
rumbas. Nor does the tango interest him. He can hear that
all day on his local station. He listens to a North American
radio broadcast out of intellectual curiosity, the same curios-

ity that sends him to see Hollywood pictures. If the program he hears from Pittsburgh or Chicago or Schenectady tells him something about that curious phenomenon, North American life, then he is intensely interested. He wants to hear a little swing—the best. He doesn't understand it, but his interest is genuine. He would like to hear other folk music, perhaps the best of Stephen Foster, or perhaps Marian Anderson singing a good spiritual. If there is going to be talking, he wants as little stuffed-shirt good-relations declamation as possible and as much solid information as he can get. In other words, he wants to hear the same thing from North America that a North American would want to hear from Buenos Aires if he could name his own program: local color, local music, local information.

With all our technical excellence in radio, here is a project that could go a long way toward making a nation of admiring, sympathetic friends. The most spontaneous Latin neighbor we have is Mexico (despite our treatment of it in times past), simply because Mexico is near enough to us to get our local color and to understand that we are genuine and well-meaning. The only actually unfriendly Latin neighbor we have is Argentina, because we are so far away that the nation has had no intimate experience to counteract the bad impression we make from a distance, the bad impression of our haphazard, unthinking propaganda through the years. With our boasted domination of the air we can bring the country as near to us as it is to mother Europe, both physically and spiritually. Radio, properly understood and properly handled as a propaganda outlet, can bring Argentina winging.

We have perfected the technique of propaganda at home. We have control of more propaganda mediums than any other nation on earth. We have access to more open-minded people than has the Axis. By radio, motion picture, news agency, and magazine we still blanket a large area of the globe. But we are not using this machinery. A small part of it is grinding out a lot of dull stuff in lackadaisical fashion. The flow is not strong at the source.

The trouble is that we have been jockeyed into a defense position again, and we have no heart in defense. The moment the United States is content with the defensive it ceases to be the kind of country its great visionaries dreamed it would become. It can never capture the imaginations of its own people on the defensive, let alone the imaginations of the Argentine people, and all the other peoples. The defensive condition, a condition of the mind, embraces not merely military strategy but the fountainhead, the inspiration of national life.

There was a time we were not afraid of idealism, of real, positive idealism. There is frank idealism in aggressive action that has as its objective the triumph of justice. Scratch a good soldier and you find an idealist. The weakness of our propaganda is that it is hesitant; it fails to express the militant idealism inherent, for instance, in the Atlantic Charter. We have failed to make all of Latin America (perhaps all of ourselves) understand that we are the aggressors. *We* are fighting for a New Order, not Hitler. We are attacking the long-outmoded notion that men, women, and children can be driven like slaves to factories, farms, and offices and told to go to work for the state, which is the all-embracing master.

We are attacking to impose upon the world the Four Freedoms of Roosevelt and Churchill: freedom of religion and expression and freedom from the fear of military and economic slavery. Yet our hesitant propaganda would lead one to believe we were fighting a rear-guard action in an effort to preserve the livery stable, the corner drugstore, and the volunteer fire department. It would lead one to believe we are out to avenge Pearl Harbor and the razing of Coventry, and that we won't rest until we have taught the enemy they

can't threaten the good old way of life. When the truth of
the matter is that the good old way of life was none too good
and most of us don't ever want to hear of it again. The
people of the world will never fight their hearts out to defend the Old Order. They want a New Order—ours, not
Hitler's.

We have been guilty of letting the other side attack on
the propaganda front, of letting the other side capture the
imagination of people, of letting the other side play the part
of liberator and reorganizer. And we were born an imaginative, pioneering, liberating people. All this frustration shows
through our news stories, our magazine articles, our public
speeches, our motion pictures, our radio programs, the entire
paraphernalia of expression which as they fly south become
our propaganda. Where they are heavy enough to smother
the natural enthusiasm of our words and pictures they make
our propaganda our own worst enemy in the homes of our
neighbors the Latins.

It is not much good to impose now a censorship on written
and spoken material and on pictures going into Buenos Aires,
on the ground that the Government must take over our entire
propaganda effort to make sure that it is effectively co-ordi-
nated. Besides that, government control of every expression
comes near enough to fascism to make a lot of people wonder
for what they are fighting. There is no doubt that had we
chosen to propagandize officially the Southern republics with
the same thoroughness and in the same spirit with which
Nazi Germany has propagandized them for five years, continental solidarity would be an official fact. But unless we had
spent a like amount of time getting acquainted with these republics so that we might back up our official propaganda with
a thorough understanding of these peoples and their problems, with a thorough appreciation of their culture and their

ideals, then we would still be without that which we must have: mutual respect.

It is not an easy thing to fight totalitarianism, because totalitarianism is essentially a fighting machine. When it has no more battlefields on which to deploy, it must perish. Yet we must fight it lest it deploy across our free institutions and across our bodies. The Chinese, the Russians, and the British have learned how to match stupid, blind, disciplined soldiers with men ready to die for freedom. We are learning to do the same. The neutral people of the world will fall into the totalitarian propaganda trap—an extremely well-baited trap with a plausible look—by the hundreds of thousands until such time as we learn to match that propaganda with the honest expression of free people completely aware and completely serene.

The technique of Nazi propaganda follows a simple formula. Hitler and Goebbels have said over and over again that it consists only in the constant repetition of plainly worded lies which in the course of time come to sound like the truth. The propaganda chiefs despise the simple people they deceive, and fear those they don't. The moment the propaganda of a free people resorts to the same technique, it limits its audience. The best it can hope for is to divide the field with the Nazis. Those of a reflective turn of mind will reject both. But if the free people of the United States, convinced in their own minds of the righteousness of their cause and its ultimate triumph, pour spontaneously through all the private and official propaganda mediums at their disposal all the enthusiasm inherent in their optimism, then they can forge an alliance of all the free peoples. But there can be nothing spontaneous or convincing about propaganda (movies, magazines, news stories) directed as a commercial afterthought toward a people of whose very characteristics we are in complete ignorance.

All this is adding up to the conclusion that most of our propaganda in Buenos Aires is pointless, despite its tremendous volume and the excellence of its technical presentation. It is pointless and will be so for many years—or until the people of North America begin to show a solid, understanding interest in the people of Argentina. When in the course of time the Latins to our south begin to see shining through our propaganda a genuine interest not based on expedience or fad or official stimulus, we will have gained their everlasting friendship and respect. The official German propaganda is the most effective in Buenos Aires, but it is recognized by all intelligent people as official. It is the most effective only because nobody else has made an intelligent effort based on an understanding of the field of reception. A woman likes flattery even though she knows the flatterer wants something of her. She will absorb a surprising amount of insincere, professional flattery and if necessary convince herself in the course of time that it is honestly meant. But let some man notice her real attractive qualities and whisper just one sweet word of sincerely meant praise, and she will recognize it immediately and follow the whisperer to the ends of the earth.

Argentina is like that pretty little lady. She has been absorbing a tremendous amount of flattery from Berlin. She knows it is phony, because she has peeked into the textbooks, eavesdropped on lectures about mixed races. She has heard the Berlin radio shoot the same guff to Brazil, the same honeyed words, the same cheap, insincere flattery about "common destiny" and "warrior nations." Then when Brazil declared war the tone resumed its natural harshness, the wolf came out of grandma's nightie and snapped at Little Red Riding Hood. The dulcet flattery beamed to Rio de Janeiro suddenly switched off, and Berlin informed the world that another pipsqueak, upstart, mestizo nation had declared war. "So what?" It is impossible for intelligent Argentine people

to overlook these things. So the pretty little lady that is
Argentina is still listening to the canned Berlin flattery because that's about all she gets. Let some sincere young man
come along and whisper to her that he recognizes just one
of her many attractive virtues, and she will be his.

But he must be sincere, with a sincerity based on long and
close acquaintance. The lady is used to the other thing, and
isn't satisfied with it.

In diplomacy one learns to keep his mouth shut if he
doesn't have something pleasant to say. With modern communication all the warring world is a theater of intense diplomacy. When some red-faced Congressman from a handful of
Southwest cow counties gets up on his feet and starts spout-
ing about Argentine meat, he must know that in addition to
his alert constituents all Argentina is listening. If he has the
most rudimentary idea of Latin pride and the necessity for
respecting it in these troubled times, he refrains from saying
the thing that will bring him the most votes next election—
in favor of the courteous thing that will help his country
reach that understanding with Argentina which may be such
a vital factor in the survival of all of us.

But the chances are he can't resist the call of the ballot box.
He darkens the air of the House chamber with the most
folksy epithets that come to his mind in describing the rav-
ages of *afthosa* in the cattle of the pampa. Although he
knows about his subject only by hearsay, he frightens the
nation's housewives, brings a glow of happiness to the cheeks
of the cattlemen of the Red River Valley, and sets up a
tempest of indignant protest in the Argentine press. The
diplomatic representatives of the United States of America
are called out of bed for an emergency vigil in the halls of
the Foreign Office in Buenos Aires in order if possible to
straighten the matter out in the minds of government officials, but the people themselves can never forget it. If the

Congressman ever learns about the trouble he has caused, he is likely to rationalize with himself that, after all, the truth must be told, bitter though it may be.

This kind of stupid performance is repeated many times in the course of a year, undoing the patient labor of scores of goodwill missions. If it isn't somebody trying to embargo Argentine beef, perhaps with reason but undiplomatically, then it's someone else who shouts across the floor of the Senate that we should take off our kid gloves and "just go down and take over these dinky Spanish American countries." Of course he isn't simply shouting across the floor of the Senate; he's shouting across all Latin America, where millions of people are in the process of making up their minds whether or not they want to string along with us. Also he is shouting loudly through the Nazi propaganda mechanism, which like a bugler's megaphone picks up the sound and echoes and re-echoes it until it has done the damage. Then the Nazi propaganda chiefs go home and pray all night for more Senators.

CHAPTER XIX

NEGLECTED EMPIRE

THREE businessmen sat on the awning-shaded veranda of the American Club where it overlooks the Calle Bartolomé Mitre and the conservative gray-stone buildings of the financial district. Cubes of ice clinked pleasantly in their tall glasses. It was Saturday afternoon; in the mellow haze of the expiring day the war headlines of the *New York Times* and the *Chicago Tribune* looked as unreal as they were stale. One of the portly men was complaining about a recent talk made to the club by Frank Gervasi, a war correspondent who visited Buenos Aires on a flying trip from New York. It seems Gervasi in his hot-headed enthusiasm for the battle he knew at first hand had reached the point of exasperation, and called his hosts, mostly North American businessmen, "the real fifth column in Argentina."

This first portly man said he thought Gervasi had gone too far; that sort of irresponsible talk does no good. He was grumbling, too, about the war. It had cut into his business. He didn't stand to make over $14,000 this year, less than half of his accustomed take. The next man was talking about the number of Boeing bombers he thought he had seen when flying south through strategic Recife last month. The German waiter, Victor, was fumbling at the glasses on the table. Victor left for the taproom. He was slow in bringing the next drinks. The third man turned and yelled toward the taproom: "Come on, quit chewing the fat with those other lugs! We got some drinks ordered, haven't we?" He looked at his

partners: "These German waiters in this place. Always arguing. Time we were getting better service around here."

This intimate veranda scene was staged nearly two months
after Pearl Harbor. German waiters were still serving talka-
tive North American businessmen, although it was common
knowledge that the Gestapo operated in the city. How many
Caribbean sinkings, how many ferrying losses, how many
black-list evasions, can be charged to this one piece of carelessness we will never know. But German waiters are the
best.

Scattered over the reading tables of the club were late editions of a popular news magazine which sends a weekly air-
mail edition winging to Buenos Aires. Included in this edition
destined for Latin America were detailed reports on North
American arms production; industrial, transportation, and
mining strikes; developments in the military aviation industry; administrative accomplishments and difficulties. These
editions were for sale on the street.

Until the time the Condor-Lati air system was suspended
all these magazines were flown to Berlin and Rome for the
careful perusal of the Axis General Staff. After the airline
quit, the vital information contained in the magazines was
digested by Axis agents in Buenos Aires and Rio de Janeiro
and radioed promptly across the Atlantic. This made it un-
necessary for the Axis to maintain a large industrial espionage establishment in the United States. The zeal of North
American news magazine and news services involved in dol-
lar competition with each other blinded most of them to the
invaluable services they performed for our enemies. One
news service "covered" the Rio de Janeiro conference for the
German daily in Buenos Aires, the *Deutsche La Plata Zeitung*. Another took pictures of ships entering a Latin American harbor for its files in New York long after it was forbidden to make pictures of the same ships in New York

Harbor. Evidence of all this unthinking activity spread itself across the reading room of the American Club. It aroused no comment whatsoever.

More important than sheer carelessness in the North American community in Buenos Aires was the slogan "Business as Usual." At a time every German had given up his profits, had volunteered his spare time, had scuttled decades of careful building and promotion to do his part for the Reich, willingly or unwillingly, the Boston and New York importers and exporters, sales executives and manufacturers, doing business in Buenos Aires were mumbling about the sacrifices ahead and arguing about accessories on the new car to be delivered next week. The drone of voices from the deep leather chairs of the club merged into one continuous complaint. These were men never to be called to sacrifice their lives on the battlefield. They could get all the sugar, all the coffee, they wanted. They could have all the tailored cashmere suits with cuffs and vests they might afford. There was no question of hunger or hardship for them. They were in a peaceful land of plenty. But they grumbled almost as one voice over short shipping facilities and subnormal profits. It was the same tone they used when a quick summer shower spoiled a good day on the Hurlingham golf course.

"Business as Usual." Each one of them felt self-righteous about his patriotism, yet each was looking out for himself first. "That deal with Ybarguren y Compañia, for instance. True, there was some reason to believe that the chemicals were going to Schultz eventually, and it may be assumed they are being bought up to be flown to Germany. But Ybarguren is a good customer and it is good business to see that he gets what he wants. And that last shipment of newsprint paper. From Delfino it goes to the warehouse that supplies *El Pampero*. Of course, *El Pampero* is a Nazi newspaper, but if we don't supply them somebody else will. They always manage to get paper and we might as well do the business."

All this rationalizing was going on inside hard business heads, heads too hard to see the harm in what they were doing. This is the attitude of mind the Nazis have counted on; it is the attitude of mind they counted on among all the "soft, democratic nations" attacked or marked for attack. It is an attitude of mind that springs from a failure to grasp the meaning of total war and the results of total war. Business, profits, turnover, markups, warehouse stocks, invoices—all of them weapons of war in the hands of the Nazis but in the hands of these uncomprehending little men only markers in a private mah-jongg game. It wasn't so much that with the triumph of the Nazi idea their coveted profits could no longer mean individual security; the amazing thing was that they were able to insulate themselves against an entire world's changing concepts of money and its mission.

As I watched and listened, almost incredulous, I closed my eyes and saw the riot of individual selfishness that was Paris before the Nazis came. I saw the sons of the rich champagning chorus girls; the politicians clipping coupons and collecting graft; the industrial magnates hiking the price of living essentials and presenting their mistresses with Pekes and ermine wraps; the great, proud Army of France riddled with contract scandals and bought commissions; the whole structure of the ancient Gallic nation tottering while little people with greedy eyes and lecherous appetites rolled in money and swill through their few remaining hours of free life. I saw the broken bodies and drawn faces of the women and children of the poor where they stood uncomprehending in their winter fallow fields and their stinking barnyards while the planes of the Reich roared in never-ending waves overhead toward the city. All this was too fresh in my memory for me to listen patiently to these new pressing troubles

as they rose through the clear Havana smoke of the American
Club in Buenos Aires.

When a subcommittee of the House Committee on Ap-
propriations left Washington late in 1941 and toured the
South American nations, they found out some things about
North American business methods. In their official report to
the House they made a great deal of the unwillingness of the
businessman from the United States to forgo quick profits
in favor of a long-range market. Quick money is a siren;
men lose their heads over it. North Americans are lured
south by the prospect of big returns in a market not yet sat-
urated, or by raw materials or manufacturing enterprises that
offer scope to soaring dreams. They leave the United States
as on a holiday. They return home as often as possible, bringing back outlandish tales of Argentine customs only partly
understood. The first two or three years in Buenos Aires they
expect to make a killing and then go back with the cash. If
profits keep coming in, they can't resist the temptation to stay
and take more.

Some of them have been there twenty years or longer, still
strangers in the land, still counting incredulously their incomes, still investing the bulk of their profits back in the
States. They are impatient of any domestic or international
disturbance that threatens the steady increase of their take.
They want to maintain every factor favorable to their individual enterprise, regardless of the broader implications.
They refrain sensibly from politics unless their own private
business seems to be involved. They have no real sympathy
with the aspirations of the Argentine people. They have lost
contact with the social and intellectural currents of their
homeland, so that they can only dimly sense the aspirations
of their own people. If they did business in the States in the
lush '20's, they were afraid of the implications of New Deal
politics in the '30's and have grown progressively more irri-

tated with bureaucratic hindrances to unrestrained expansion and unrestrained profits. This has brought them down to the war out of sympathy at home and unoriented in the land of their commercial adoption. They have let the German and the Englishman spread through the hinterland to suffer the lean years before the harvest away from the centers of population. They wouldn't ask their wives and children to make the sacrifice made by the families of their German and English competitors. They wouldn't ask themselves to make a sacrifice. They came down for quick profits, and when the quick profits are finished they're going to get out, they keep telling themselves.

Sir Christopher Gibson is typical of the British businessman is Argentina. He and his brothers go far afield to find land and resources ripe for development. He is spare, gray at the temples, quiet, keen. He is equally at home in the solemn, elegant dining room of the Alvear Palace Hotel and riding through the jungles of Paraguay. One of his enterprises is a 600,000-acre cattle ranch in Brazil's Matto Grosso, high in the upper reaches of the Paraguay River. The first time he came to Porto Esperança on his way up the river to the ranch, the town was under nine feet of water. Only the second floor of the general store and tavern was dry. He was rowed from the river boat to the one dry spot, where he spent the night sleeping on a billiard table with a gaff at his side. There were thirty Brazilian Negroes in town celebrating payday. They found the same dry haven, drinking and intermittently shooting at each other across the billiard table. Into this green hell Gibson brought Tex Rickard and twenty-five Texas cowboys a few years back. A few of the Texans are still roaming the country doing odd jobs and a little de-luxe rustling. Perhaps the Gibson method isn't the best thing for an unexploited country. It is frankly foreign ownership, almost absentee ownership. But it is enterprise, and it has paid well as a reward for energy and privation. The British risk their lives and their money in South America. They live for years in hot interior towns if it's necessary to keep the business operating soundly. You can find good-looking, well-tailored young English clerks in the London Bank in Tucumán, clerks who haven't been home in many years and who haven't much chance of getting home for many more. As far as English social life goes they might be living on Mars.

The diligence of the German "drummer" through these forbidding regions is proverbial. There is no mountain village too remote for him, no cluster of mud huts too small, no rocky trail too steep. What the Briton accomplishes by imagination and daring Fritz accomplishes by methodical thoroughness. Behind his careful progress there is vision of the kind that sees the barren land transformed by dams and canals into flowering orchards and furrowed fields in time to come.

It is a strange thing to contemplate this good, patient man sitting on the porch of his clean home against the foothills of the Andes, sitting bemused by a stack of Nazi pamphlets calling him to the service of the frenzied little maniac in Berlin, calling on him to throw away all the long years of labor in this new land and plunge into the reckless adventure of blood that is rocking the faraway world. It is a pathetic thing to see him harried and driven by cruel-faced Nazi party men come up from Buenos Aires to force him into espionage, to force out of him his savings, and to harden him against the people he has grown to love. It is worse to see him change under the driving force of the party, to see him become cold and suspicious, efficient in collecting information, quick to click his heels and respond to "Heil Hitler," loud with boasts about the destiny of his race and the terrible vengeance visited on the weak by the irresistible army of the

Reich. But party man or simple country "drummer," the German has come into the wilderness, and in the wilderness he will stay until he has built a small business on a solid foundation, a business ample for his own simple comforts and for the expanding ambitions of his children and his children's children.

While the Briton and the German are working across the country putting their small returns back into the enterprise, taking out a little as they go along, the North American is cleaning up a quick market in the city and flying back to New York for a round of the night clubs or back to Cincinnati to see the folks.

The result is that North American business in Argentina is in a bad way except where the United States Government and a few giant corporations have poured unlimited dollars southward to keep the structure alive. Argentina doesn't care much for North American businessmen, although it is mighty glad to get North American automobiles, radios, and assorted gadgets. Despite the learned articles of economists of both nations, who point out that two producers of raw materials can never trade happily with each other, despite the lack of vision and industry which makes the North American businessman obnoxious and ineffective, despite the shrewd competition offered by European businessmen, Argentina wants some North American manufactured goods. It wanted them even before the war cut off its European sources. It will want them as long as motion pictures and newspaper and magazine articles make the country conscious of them. It doesn't take a House subcommittee to see that we have sent the wrong kind of people south to sell these articles.

Long study of these misfits dozing in the comfortable chairs of the American Club has persuaded me that the root of the evil lies deeper than the individual. These men are typical of their generation; they are away from home un-

happily, and only by accident. They might be sitting around
a businessmen's club in Detroit or San Antonio, where their
fathers denuded God's own forests for quick cash or over-
grazed God's prairies for immediate profit. They are the
product of a type of thinking that begins with the pocketbook
and ends with the bank balance. They are the people who
sold scrap to Japan and ignored the agony of the Chinese—
until they got a dose of it themselves. They are of the breed
that bribed legislators to let them ravage a nation's natural
resources and bribed governments to let them have a crack at
Mexico and Nicaragua. Their reaction in the American Club
to Gervasi's speech on the war convinced me they are beyond
redemption and will die out unregenerate, to make way for
more intelligent successors.

They make it difficult for the understanding, well-meaning
businessman who goes to Buenos Aires and finds he is under
suspicion and deep mistrust because he is a *Yanqui.* They
make it difficult for the State Department, alert at long last
to the situation.

It has become the fashion for critics to jump all over Uncle
Sam's State Department because things have been handled
awkwardly in Argentina and elsewhere in South America.
We must have a goat—an individual, tangible goat—so that
we can make speeches and write articles about him. It is very
difficult to blame ourselves. Yet the State Department, like
the North American business colony in any foreign country,
is a cross section of the population of the forty-eight states.
Whatever have been our diplomatic errors, they have in each
case stemmed from our own loose conception of international
ethics, from our collective failure to appreciate the people
with whom we dealt, from our own shortsightedness. As a
democratic people we insist on selecting our own representatives; then we must shoulder full responsibility for their
works. This is not an entirely pleasant thought as we look

back over our diplomatic record in the lands of the Latins. It is a waste of time to moon over that record, as it is a waste of time to worry now about the domestic political and economic shortcomings of which we have been guilty these many long years. But it is not a waste of time to examine our present policies in the light of past mistakes.

The personnel of the State Department is selected either by career examination or as a result of political pressure. In these troubled times it has become the custom to place more and more responsibility on capable career men and less responsibility on the cousin of the Congressman from Iowa or Vermont who has demonstrated only a certain extrovert charm and a penchant for cocktails. This has brought about a sifting process that is putting our representation in Latin America in surer hands. Latin America is duly grateful, having suffered for so long as a sort of political boneyard for North America.

It is inevitable, given the inertia and the lag of government, that there remain in service and in places of some responsibility dozens of incompetents as unimaginative and as unaware of the ebb and flow of life as the North American businessmen with whom they talk and think. There are a great many vice-consuls, Embassy secretaries, and commercial attachés in South America who have only a vague notion of what has happened at home in the last ten years. They are still representing Herbert Hoover's Administration. They are talking in terms of stocks and bonds, in terms of the investing public and the laboring class and the exploitation of resources, as if the world were a static paradise full of contented people managed largely by old Princeton graduates. Of the changed status of labor they are largely unaware. To them the managerial revolution is only a rumor spread by bright college boys who read too many books. They go ahead year after year making out the forms required by the State

Department, attending the necessary official functions, partying with a few friends.

They are not only untouched by events at home, but they
are in no way in contact with the real life of the countries in
which they find themselves. They don't go out and talk to
taxi-drivers, to janitors, to peons, to shopkeepers, to stenog-
raphers, to farmers. They know only what they read in the
papers and in the official bulletins, or what is told them by
their "contacts" in the Foreign Office. They report back to
the State Department the most encouraging nonsense just on
the eve of the revolution they had no idea, really *no idea*,
was coming. They ignore what disturbs them. Their lives
are safe and comfortable, and there is no reason why they
should look for trouble. The result, of course, is a serious
lack of information in Washington, a lack that results in mistaken policy only too often. With intelligence and planning
creeping into the State Department, this condition is being
abated. It seems a tragic thing that it should have gone on
so long as to jeopardize our relations with our neighbors to
the south.

Because it has gone on so long, the Monroe Doctrine,
meant to be an intelligent and farsighted declaration of policy, has been pretty well discredited in South America. Monroe's doctrine has come to be a symbol of North American
ego; our spokesmen have failed to represent it in its true
light as a determination to protect ourselves, and an honest
offer to help our neighbors protect themselves, from European aggression. With an inspired, sympathetic, and democratic Foreign Service at work for a generation or two in Latin
America we might by now have assumed our proper role in
hemisphere affairs—a role we are trying to play unprepared
—and not entirely welcome—at the last critical hour. The
present Administration has had a decade in which to clean
out the service and divest itself in Latin America of those

unaware of or out of sympathy with the social evolution of the United States and the Good Neighbor principle which was designed to be its best expression abroad. Had this been diligently accomplished, our affairs would be running with less friction and better results. The retention in key positions of men with a "Send for the Marines!" complex, men with one eye on Wall Street, and men catering to the local aristocracy has been almost disastrous. It has led us far away from the path toward mutual understanding. Perhaps it is too much to ask that the Foreign Service should conform completely to ideals and aspirations only half-formed in the minds of all of us at home. In a sense our diplomatic failures have been an expression of our failure at home.

The representatives of our Foreign Service have been guilty of the same shortsightedness that has characterized the representatives of our business. They have acted for quick results, ignoring the fact that we must build solidly if we are to enjoy the best political and commercial relations in the decades and centuries of intercourse ahead. We have fallen far behind our German and British competitors in both fields. The accidents of war, not our own effort, have brought us trade supremacy. At any time the accidents of war may take them away. Diplomatically, we are not where we should be, despite the real desire of the majority of thinking people in all the Latin American nations to make common cause with us against the Nazi terror. The failure of the Rio de Janeiro conference (a real failure at the time, although future events have taken away the sting) was inevitable given our long record of unsatisfactory relations with the Southern republics and given the record of smooth, smart operation on the part of the German diplomatic corps. It was inevitable despite the fact that our present Ambassador in Buenos Aires, Norman Armour, is the best in the business. Years of failure to understand the people of Argentina or help them to un-derstand us have borne their inevitable fruit.

It is very late, but perhaps not too late, to re-examine our approach to these people. At the moment we are engaged in an emotional spree which includes Cultural Relations, Good Neighborhood, Goodwill Tours, Pan-Americanism, Impres-sions of My Visit to the Land of the Latins, Want to Borrow Some of Our Money? and many other demonstrations of sympathy and kindness. We act like the long-aloof young man who has just discovered that the freckled-faced waitress who has been giving him the eye is in fact heiress to the Brewster millions. We are tripping over our own bonbons and orchids every time we ring the doorbell. This act fur-nishes the polished Argentine with his most satisfying laugh in many years. He goes into hysterics over it in the privacy of his own home. To think that the Colossus of the North suddenly wants his friendship, and just because a war is on!

There is a haunting similarity here to the rudderless Peace Ship that sailed to suffering Europe bearing the best wishes of North America for a long and happy life—followed by the official United States refusal to have anything to do with the League of Nations or anything else that didn't get votes in Idaho and California. There is another haunting similarity, this time to the metropolitan newspaper that sends its ace reporter to Glenn's Corners to bring the daughter of the town grocer to New York to live in the royal suite at the best hotel, dine at the best restaurants, step out in a movie wardrobe to the night clubs escorted by a Broadway star, write a piece for the paper titled "Cinderella for a Day"— then ships her back to Glenn's Corners, where she will be forever restless and forever unsatisfied by her home-town husband-to-be.

Our quick, possessive interest in Latin America, which seems so natural to us and so funny to the Latin Americans, who don't know us very well, can't get us much in the long run; it is built on nothing but expedience. We will really have a grip on the hemisphere when our trade relations and our diplomacy flow strongly and convincingly out of understanding and appreciation. That will require time, since understanding requires time. We must build for the time long after Cugat's rumbas have been forgotten, long after the grab-it-quick businessmen have drifted out of Buenos Aires, long after the Foreign Service fossils have succumbed to their last cocktail, long after the fad for Inca hats has faded from the short memories of Park Avenue's blondes.

We must build for a time when mature men and women of the United States can talk quietly and appreciatively of the real culture of their Southern neighbors. We will have learned to our great surprise that all the soldiers in the Mexican Army are not generals, and that there is not a revolution in El Salvador every other week. We will have learned that the gauchesque literature of Argentina is as rich and entertaining as James Fenimore Cooper, that the Government of Costa Rica is one of the most progressive in an unprogressive world, that Nicaragua has produced some of the best poetry in all the Americas, that the greatest ballet corps and orchestra directors make a point of playing the Colón Theater in Buenos Aires, that the Palacio de Bellas Artes in Mexico City is equal in taste and elegance to anything in the United States, that the passion for liberty burned like a flame through the souls of millions of Latin Americans while we were torpid and indifferent with material luxuries after the last war.

Until that time, we may as well be humble and ingenuous, approaching our Latin neighbors only with honest, mutually advantageous business propositions, unembroidered. They will respect us more for it.

EPILOGUE

ACROSS THE ANDES

TALL, handsome, nervous Raúl Damonte Taborda stood in shirt sleeves, a great cavalry saber in his hands. His feet were planted wide apart on the hard-packed soil. Behind him, close to the whitewashed farm buildings of the Don Torcuato place, there clung on anxious knot of men: Lieutenant Colonel Atilio Cattaneo and Ernesto Boatti, Dr. Ricardo Finochietto. They were his seconds and his physician. Facing the young duelist stood hard-faced Colonel Enrique Rottjer, a cold smile holding the corners of his mouth. Behind Colonel Rottjer stood his party of seconds. Aniceto Rodríguez, master of the field, spoke then a crisp word, and the clang, clang, clang of steel rang into the morning air. Colonel Rottjer's right arm was pinked, then Damonte Taborda's shoulder. The doctors examined their men, the seconds conferred, the two panting, sweating antagonists lifted their sabers and swung at each other again. When they dropped their arms, the Colonel had been nicked again and a third time. Damonte Taborda's wrist was cut.

The seconds conferred again a little apart from the sound of whistling breath and the low questioning of the doctors' voices. The seconds approached the men with the sabers. They took the weapons and announced in strained voices that honor had been satisfied. They asked Colonel Rottjer if he wanted to shake hands and part friends. He had been the offended party. He had sent his seconds to call on the young national Deputy after a political mass meeting in which he had been singled out for harsh words. His honor as an officer of the Argentine Army seemed to have been impugned. It was the second public challenge in a year in acrimonious debate over Nazi influence in Argentine official life. When the seconds approached him now, tired and scratched on the field of honor, he remembered his injured pride. In a loud voice he said: "I have no intention of shaking hands or of forgetting the insult." Without further words the two parties climbed into the waiting limousines and sped their separate ways back to the city.

That evening I stood on the deck of the river packet *City of Asunción*, as she loaded passengers at the South Dock. I picked up a copy of *El Pampero* and read its lurid account of the duel. Next to the news story was an advertisement: Japanese couple wanted for cooking, caretaking, and general housework on a Rio Negro estate. In the same column was a notice of a general election signed by Acting President Castillo and Minister of the Interior Culaciati. It announced Chamber of Deputies vacancies to be filled, including the seats of Raúl Damonte Taborda and his fellow committeeman, Bill O'Reilly. On the next page was an advertisement for the Falangist film playing at the San Martín Theater, *All Quiet in the Alcazar*.

The *City of Asunción* whistled twice. There were shrill farewells from the crowded dock, watered lavishly with tears and thrown kisses. An old woman in black left her chair on the after deck and walked quietly down the gangplank. She came aboard each of the river boats before it sailed, but she had never the money for a ticket. Hawsers were cast off, and we swung into the laggard current of the Riachuelo past the spaghetti joints of the Boca. A gray Chilean tanker, turning with difficulty in the narrow basin, missed our stern by inches; the air was blue with Spanish expletives. We slid into the rolling brown waters of the estuary, and our engines now throbbed eagerly for the current. There was a modest salute from the tug *Hercules* as she gave us our head.

Against the Indian summer sky the outline of the great city of the Plata faded like a tremendous theatrical backdrop while the house lights came by degrees down to dim and to black. At the port rail a cluster of tall, suave, deliberately indifferent Argentines discussed in low tones the duel, the beef market, the day's races at San Ysidro. They were in black, blue, and gray suits, solid colors and pin stripes. From breast pockets peeked demure kerchiefs. Their shoes were highly polished. As they talked they stared insolently at each other and at all the other passengers that walked past. Their backs were stiff. When they spoke in animation, they bent slightly at the waist and moved their hands in fluid motion from the wrists. As I passed them in sport slacks, open shirt, and scarf they stared longer than usual, then turned their backs. They were *porteños*, from the city where no man, however humble, dares appear on the open street without a coat to his suit, where a citizen sits out on his balcony all day Sunday in his pyjamas but never leaves his front door without complete business attire. For the four-day river journey to Paraguay they were dressed in their best.

The Italian refugee (Trieste to Paris to Lisbon to Buenos Aires in four years) turned to me with a hundred silent questions in his eyes, then stared again toward the new, expectant land that was to swallow him and his life at last.

I looked out beyond Paraguay, beyond the humid Chaco, the brick dust of Bolivia's plateau, the snow-tipped Andean peaks, the green rivers of Central America, and across the Mexican desert—toward home. There were forty days ahead across the last quarter of the globe yet unscarred by war.

We trooped down to the dining salon for polenta, fried *pejerrey*, and French bread. The smell of coming winter was already in the air, and we spiced it further with an aromatic wake of steaming coffee and burning cigarettes. The fresh rain of the Paraná delta closed in on us from the north.

"It is peace," the Italian said. He couldn't keep his eyes from the gloom beyond which lurked somewhere ashore.

In the morning the world was water. The still gallant top pennants of sunken trees marked a channel through the flood. Rain descended and lifted, now hiding, now revealing, the distant reaches of green and silver. Tree trunks and the bloated bodies of horses and cattle came down the current. There was a moving world of swamp and savanna and sky along the limitless waters. Toward evening, a distinct bank appeared on the left, where the Argentine province of Santa Fé laid its mud toward the horizon.

Next day we had the sun, turning the water to brilliants in the dawn, lighting the green carpets along the river, opening up a classic land like an Arnold Böcklin painting.

"There are dryads and nymphs," said the Italian.

There was another dawn and we awoke in the tropics. The river had narrowed to a mile. We forged close to the bank. Banana trees grew in emerald clusters. Stacks of red quebracho wood stood along the shore, waiting to render tannic acid for a distant world clamoring for leather. A chic Buenos Aires girl minced down the gangplank at Corrientes on the edge of the Chaco. She was fumblingly kissed by an awed peon father. The winter sun was kind to Asunción where the city lay across the bluffs above the river Paraguay, its gardens heavy with orange and jasmine, lemon and guava, lime, papaya, and mango. Barefooted women carried baskets of manioc root, entrails of beef, chirimoyas, along the rough flagstones of the streets. Or they rode sideways on pint-size mules while they puffed away at black cigars. They disputed the right of way with two-wheeled water carts and ragged detachments of fourteen-year-old policemen marching to the day's stations. Along these bullet-pitted walls ran a hundred years ago the first, terror-stricken rumors of the death of Dr. José Gaspar Rodríguez Francia, El Supremo, who cut this jungle nation from all intercourse with the world and set a policy of hostile isolation that has been interrupted since only by bloody border conflicts.

Streetcar 116, Line 5, careened down from the suburban hills into the traffic of the streets, its crew of two boys dressed like grenadiers and hard-faced before their time. They plunged their Toonerville relic downhill with the dash of a light-horse charge, clanging the bell with a spliced strand of manila rope. Not a flicker of fear crossed the faces of crew or passengers, and somehow miraculously the wild vehicle crossed the intersection without collision.

I stood three hours in the central police station answering questions. I had photographed the plaza.

"Was your purpose in taking clandestine pictures in Asunción purely in the pursuit of tourist activities?

"Have you not been informed of the law forbidding foreigners to photograph the Paraguayan people?

"If you are released, will you refrain from making more pictures without official sanction?"

I made the proper replies, then finished with a short laudatory address on the weather in Asunción, comparing it with Southern California and the Vale of Kashmir. In the course of time I was set free, to the great disappointment of assorted bug life lurking hungrily in the near-by walls.

Outside at the bulletin board of the telegraph company news of the battle of the Coral Sea drew a small crowd. Dr. Schmidt of Wichita, Kansas, stopped long enough in the lobby of the hotel to tell me he was flying home after six weeks operating in the Mennonite hospital up in the jungle at Filadelfia. There live and work 25,000 Hollanders who went to Russia to work for Catherine the Great, fled across

Siberia and the Amur River to China in the Bolshevik Revolution, then settled in the lost heart of South America to live out their time away from trouble and the rumors of trouble. Dr. Schmidt explained that the Paraguayan soldiers and cops were youngsters because the men had been killed off in the Bolivian war. Back in the 1850's no male between twelve and sixty survived the Paraguayan attack on Brazil, Argentina, and Uruguay. In parts of Paraguay the women still outnumber the men seven to one.

The side-wheeler *General Artigas* rumbled me downstream to Resistencia, unloading me on Argentine soil again along with a green-gold treasure of yerba maté from Brazil and the upper Paraguay. Sweating boatmen in shorts and wide hats brewed the stuff in little teapots as they worked. At Resistencia I had an evening to kill, so bought *By Velocipede to the South Pole* by Emilio Salgani, a hair-raising book bearing on the paper cover a 1916 lithograph revealing three determined explorers with Russian beards cycling across the polar ice, rifles across their backs and the light of high discovery in their eyes. I shopped the windows, elbowing Ukrainian, German, and Italian countrymen for a chance to gaze on the cheap clothes, toys, candies, and cosmetics retired because of age from the other markets of the world.

The opéra-bouffe Presidente Sáenz Peña express stood in the station at Resistencia: all three coaches, sleeping car, diner, and baggage car. With a toot of the whistle, the clang of the station bell, and the wailing of children from the hard second-class benches, we were off across the Chaco.

Within an hour cotton fields, gins, and sheds gave way to alternate marshes and wooded lands, the domain of the vulture, the falcon, and the great crane. We passed the lonely camps of woodcutters. The huts here were made of sticks and mud, topped with rushes. There were no windows, no chimneys, no floors but the hard-packed earth. In the hot weather the home folks lie in hammocks under the great sunshade covering the hut and an area as large again, making an outdoor room. In cool weather they sit around the fire in the center of the hut, sucking maté and breathing smoke. Each house was provided with its baked clay oven outdoors, where is made the hard bread that varies the meat-and-maté diet of the Chaqueño. The Chaco ostrich sometimes stalks in and out of his master's house, as one did at Machagay station among the venders of tangerines and roast sweet potatoes.

Here at Machagay, Grandma climbed aboard with one of her married daughters and two grandchildren. Unhappily, they spied an old friend across the aisle. Grandma was equipped with one of those high-pitched voices that make the Spanish language unpleasant, metallic, penetrating. Into every corner of the coach vibrated the story of the ills of her close relations, ills which confounded medical science.

Presidente Roque Sáenz Peña is deep in the wilderness. Its stiff, dirty, one-story brick buildings were plastered with political posters sternly demanding the end of speculation in primary goods and a revision of the high cost of living. Along the clay walks street venders opened their suitcases full of haberdashery, toilet goods, and trinkets, competing with the Bulgarian and Ukrainian shops. Here there were wonderful variations of the gaucho costume, yellow-and-black striped *bombachas*, great-roweled spurs on bare feet, blouses and innovations of all kinds from Central Europe.

In the dusty morning the foothills of the Andes stood blue against the bright sky. At the first tank stop a brakeman got off, sized up a herd of goats, grabbed a kid by the hind legs, and carried it bawling and nannying to the baggage car, to the cheers of the passengers. We had it later for dinner.

At the Metan movie palace: Tonight—Spencer Tracy in *Dr. Jekyll and Mr. Hyde*. Metan's clean tiled patios were Moorish. Horsemen wore the short Andalusian jacket with elaborate stitching, and a carved leather saddle had replaced the sheepskin pad of the gaucho's mount.

If you can pronounce offhand the name of the Argentine city Jujuy you don't have trouble with foreign languages. It's Hoo-hwee. At Jujuy I heard for the first time in Argentina the Castilian language with all its archaic grace. Jujueños greeted each other with "Adiós," a word used elsewhere in Spanish America only in formal farewell. The Jujueños were clean, alert, serene, devoutly religious. Most of them had heard only vaguely of the war.

The International Express puffed to the 14,000-foot Bolivian *planalto* and most of its passengers lay gasping with the mountain sickness, *puna*. As morning broke we were on the face of a land of monstrous and indecent detail, harsh, high, incandescent; changing from red to brown to yellow, transforming and hiding 20,000-foot peaks; bringing pinpoints of life out to gigantic size, then swallowing the whole landscape into Dante's Inferno. The brown-derbied Indian women and the white-hatted Cholas of mixed blood sat in the dirt at the railroad stations selling colored water, fruit, silver, and woven ponchos. In their tall, hard hats, their dozens of voluminous petticoats, shawls, cotton stockings, flat slippers, they looked like Mother Goose with a deep tan.

At Oruro we detrained Frank Redfield, Oregon mining engineer going back for another stint of three years in the mines of Patiño the Tin King. After a six-weeks fling in the outside world Mrs. Redfield was in for another session of burro-riding in the barren mountains at the roof of the world. She was worried because her housemaid had developed the habit of being "*robada*." When a Bolivian Indian girl disappears for a few days and reports back that she was "*robada*" it means she was carried away captive by "some man." This is a periodic Sabine abduction which seems to be part of social life and thoroughly enjoyed by both parties to the misfortune.

Late of an evening we dropped down off the *planalto* toward 12,500-foot La Paz, lying below us in the darkness like a handful of diamonds on a velvet counter. Above, the sun was sinking into a sea of saffron revealing a delicate crescent moon hanging just where the pale-blue sky met the lighted west. As we came slowly down into the gorge a shepherd's fire winked in the night as the shepherds' fires must have winked above Bethlehem.

It was Sunday morning. La Paz clung to the Andean walls, its cobbled streets, its bright houses and walled gardens, its great-domed churches, and its fountained plazas mocking the harshness of the plain above. Fantastic women in red, yellow, and orange spread their market through the streets of the city, choking sidewalks and passageways with trays and baskets, filling the brisk air with argument and laughter. Along the alameda strolled the families of the *correctos* while the Bolivian Army band clarineted through its repertoire of overtures and marches. This could have been Madrid or Seville. Aristocratic young Spanish beauties dressed in their finest watched the stag line out of the corners of their eyes, swinging their skirts and swelling their bosom fronts, playing the eager-eyed men as a matador plays the cape-crazy bull. The music and finery faded with the noonday; siesta claimed the city. Through the streets trotted barefoot Indians chewing coca leaves, bearing on their backs mountainous burdens. Cocaine defeats fatigue, altitude, and cold. In the evening I climbed the steep slopes into a flea-ridden mud metropolis where the sewer runs down the "street" and ghostly people dressed in rags sit in the open doorways selling frozen button potatoes and warm beer.

Back in the Sucre Palace Hotel the dining room was loud with the welcome voices of more North American mining engineers come down to step up production of strategic ores. After a drink or two they were bowing to each other with exaggerated Latin politeness, kissing each other's hands, and generally frightening the native waiters. One held up a local newspaper bearing the headline "John Gunther, Modern Tartarin, Forced to Revise His Book on South America." The second headline heralded the failure of the German spring offensive. The bar boy quietly polished his mahogany and brass.

This was still a Spanish world, but in the long days out of Buenos Aires the coldly objective *porteño* had given way to the jungleman, the hillman, and now the mountainman of easy sympathies and friendly speech. Here in the Bolivian capital the names of contending Buenos Aires *futbol* teams were scrawled across the faces of mud walls as one might find "New York Yankees" in chalk along the fences of St. Joseph, Missouri. The influence of Argentina was strong, but there were other influences at work from the north.

Wednesday afternoon the British-owned train for Peru climbed out of La Paz onto the *planalto* again and made straight for Lake Titicaca through a dull-red land broken by mud-walled villages like the kampongs of Bali. We boarded the night boat in an unbelievable sunset, crossing the lake in a night brilliant with stars. The Southern Cross still held the sky. In the dawn we slipped shoreward among the reed boats and entrained northward for Cuzco, the capital of the Inca Empire.

From Puno to Juliaca to Cuzco was a winding way among Alpine valleys painted into a patchwork of plowed fields, ripening grain, cropped stubble, shocked corn, with dizzily terraced squares and triangles lifting high into the heavens toward the snow. In the snout of a glacier was born the milk-white stream that becomes the river Vilcanota, grows into the Urubamba below Cuzco, joins the Apurímac at Atalaya to

become the Alto Ucayali, then the Bajo Ucayali, marrying
the Marañon and the Napo to become the mighty Solimões
that spreads its liquid weight through the upper jungles of
Brazil, flows thousands of miles into the Negro, and thus becomes the Amazon, the greatest river in the world, sweeten-
ing with its fabulous waters the Atlantic exactly at the
equator.

El Cuzco, the Navel of the World, slept in the high valleys as it did when Pizarro sacked it of its tons of wrought
gold. At Cuzco my room was over the railroad station,
whence I took a noisy vehicle half jitney bus and half railroad
car down the valley of the Urubamba toward Machupicchu,
scattering llamas, natives, and burros in all directions. By
muleback I reached the Inca stronghold set like a southern
Shangri-La across the granite backbone of the Andes.

Gladiolus, wax begonia, and wild strawberry grew across
the face of Machupicchu where it hung its delicate stone ter-
races among the clouds. I sat in the early twilight where the
imperial baths once dropped their miniature vaulted cataracts
through pipes of gold and silver among the chambers of living rock. A pair of condors soared listlessly overhead. The
peaks lifted themselves rank on rank into a wilderness of
white. Far below, the Amazon-bound river raced and sang
toward the monkeys and parrots and rubber trees deep in the
green lowlands. Where once a honey-skinned, bright-clad
people toiled and fought and loved among the hanging gardens and the galleries with their thousand-stepped staircases,
now the geometric confusion of roofless walls reared a lonely
profile against the moving curtains of mist. Out of Machupicchu came the first Inca. Back to Machupicchu fled the last
Virgins of the Sun when the Spaniards raped Cuzco. Then
Machupicchu was lost under jungle growth for four centuries, uncovered by a North American expedition only thirty
years ago.

Fanwise out from Cuzco lie the stone skeletons of Sacsawa-mac, Allantaytambo, and a dozen more Inca fortresses whose intricately massive works defy the analysis of modern engineers. Outlying, too, are the Indian villages where time has brought domed and towered churches to replace the flat roof and the square arch that housed the Inca governor. The village curate is now the law. At Pisacc I watched a hundred Indians leap to their feet and disappear in the mountains at the approach of the Guardia Civil. A guard blocked each exit from the plaza before the church, but only a handful of stragglers could be rounded up for the Army. This was the Peruvian draft board in action. Around Pisacc imported eucalyptus trees lined the lanes and the watercourses. Men were winnowing wheat with Biblical flails, the golden chaff riding like a sun-shot shower down the wind. Oxen trampled out the sheaves. Shocks of corn moved ghostlike toward the shucking circle, their Indian bearers lost under the stalks and leaves. In the market place the women were trading, some of them reeling away with a skinful of chicha. Occasionally a baby was dropped from a sling by a drunken mother.

Flores, the guide, had an invariable answer for all questions: "Could be. Could not be." Flores had his own version of the murder of the last Inca:

"The Espaniels was teaching the last Inca to play chest and because he learned right away and could play chest better than the Espaniels and beat them all the time, that was why Pizarro kills the last Inca."

The night train climbed back toward Juliaca, then cut across the 14,500-foot pass westward into the desert. In the morning we came through the stinging, choking, salt-laden dust into Arequipa, a Pan-American airways stop. Next evening I was put down on the airfield at Lima, back to the seacoast after four weeks. Lima, once Spanish capital of all South America, lives like a dowager, hovering over the bones

of Pizarro and the great priests and captains of Charles V
and Philip II. In Arequipa and Lima again, as at Buenos
Aires, the magazine and book racks reflected a Latin preoccu-
pation with sex.

For the first time in more than a year I felt a bond with
fellow diners, with the policemen of whom I asked directions,
with hotel clerks and shopkeepers. There was talk of the war
now, interested, friendly talk. There was evidence of an
intelligent understanding of common problems. There was
abroad a subtle, warming sense of mutual responsibility. It
was as if the word "American" meant something real here.

Here, as in La Paz, the barbershops and the bazaars were
Japanese, but their proprietors were little in evidence. Quiet,
too, was the great stone Banco Germánico branch.

When our great northward-winging transport plane
crossed the equator there was a festive dipping of the wings,
but the second and third times we crossed it the same day,
driven in a great circle by a tropical storm, there was no rejoicing. We finally came down on an emergency field between
the jungle and the beach, refueling from gasoline drums
wheeled across the sand by near-naked Negroes. Through a
sky that seemed to have burst apart we sped back to Guaya-
quil again for the night. Across the street from the hotel a
party of Ecuadorian jitterbugs were hitting it up to Andrews
Sisters recordings. For the first time in a year I felt a wave
of homesickness.

We made our way then in two days of flying to Mexico
City, after one more forced night in the Panama jungle. As
we forged northward we found the little Central American
airports full of uniforms and the rumble of war. Across the
aisle of the skyliner, Manuel Vargas of Texas, one of six
brothers serving with the United States Army from Australia
to Iceland, talked of his coming visit home. "When this is
over, I got me a little ranch picked out just outside San

Antone. But first, me and the kid brothers got some work to do."

Mexico roared into the war with an angry shout and a mighty pealing of cathedral bells while I was buying a train ticket to Los Angeles. The newspaper headline at the corner stand read "Jealous Woman Shoots Musician." I sat in Ed Morgan's United Press office and heard him telephone King Carol that the United States had decided to declare war on Rumania. At the Alameda Theater: TONIGHT—SHIRLEY TEMPLE IN "KATHLEEN." A phonograph down the block was grinding out "La Golondrina." At the Majestic Hotel the desk man leaned across at me and said in melodious Spanish: "We're going to lick the hell out of the Nazis and the Japs." Everybody was fighting-mad because Hitler had called Mexico a "dinky little country unworthy of notice."

Pullman car Zeno was hauled out of the Buena Vista station on the tail end of the Mexican National train to Guadalajara and I was on it. At Guadalajara, Zeno was hooked onto the Southern Pacific. Its generator quit, and with it the air-conditioning. The next three days we were in a Turkish bath crossing the barrancas and the mesquite flats of western Mexico. At Tepic a blind boy came out of the hills with his guitar singing "Ay, Jalisco" until he brought tears to the eyes of those who could see. In the gathering dusk campfires were confounded with the fireflies, and for the first time I noticed that the Southern Cross was gone. In the north now stood the Great Dipper. The night air was the air of home.

At San Blas a young Mexican was telling about his brother who married an American girl. "She was not speaking any Espanish and he was not speaking any Anglish. They was just for making signals. Now they have got a little dotter which of course does not yet speak anything."

Came now the land of white-face cattle, sorrel ponies, the red-flaming ocotillo. Two engines hauled us up the Sonora highlands toward Nogales, the mysterious blue Huachucas dreaming in the northeast. Lonely women looked out of box-cars on the sidings. They looked out over the window boxes of geraniums, the great-eyed women of northern Mexico.

As the long, tired train ground to a stop across the international line at Nogales there came up from the hot, bright streets a kind of music—the English language. A colored porter took over Zeno. "How long we got here?" I asked. "An hour." I was down the Pullman steps and at a drugstore counter in three minutes. "Gimme a chocolate malt," I gurgled, like a small boy who has come into money.